MARVEL
ENCYCLOPEDIA

Art by Alex Ross

CREDITS

WRITER
Syd Barney-Hawke

WRITER/RESEARCHER
Eric J. Moreels
Editor-in-Chief, X-Fan
(x-mencomics.com/xfan)

EDITORS
Mark D. Beazley
& Jeff Youngquist

ASSISTANT EDITOR
Jen Grünwald

COPY EDITOR
Sarah Fan

ART DIRECTOR
Matty Ryan

DESIGNERS
Patrick McGrath,
Victor Gonzalez &
Tim Smith III

RECOLORING
Jen Chan, Wing Lee
& Erik Ko of UDON

JACKET DESIGN
Tom Marvelli

COVER PAINTING
Gabriel Dell'Otto

EDITOR IN CHIEF
Joe Quesada

PRESIDENT
Bill Jemas

Special thanks: Chis Allo, Seth Biederman, Tom Brevoort, C.B. Cebulski, Michael Doran, Jerron Quality Color, Ralph Macchio, Mike Marts, Peter Mathews, Mike Raicht, Wilson Ramos Jr., Warren Simmons, John Miesegaes, Nova Ren Suma, Amy Rice, Sean Ryan, Cory Sedlmeier, Jeff Suter, Jeof Vita and Jonathan "The Boy" Watkins.

Eric J. Moreels would like to thank: Chuck Austen; Grant Morrison; Frank Tieri; Geoff Johns; Peter Milligan; Matt Nixon; Mike Marts; Mike Raicht; Andrew Lis; Axel Alonso; Brian E. Wilkinson; Al Harahap; Manolis Vamvounis; and, last but not least, my beautiful wife, Sarah Moreels, for her incredible patience, understanding and support!

Syd Barney-Hawke would like to thank: Jeff Youngquist, Mark Beazley and Bill Jemas... indeed, the better craftsmen.

MARVEL ENTERPRISES, INC.

CEO & GENERAL COUNSEL
Allen Lipson

CHIEF CREATIVE OFFICER
Avi Arad

PRESIDENT CEO, TOY BIZ
Alan Fine

CHIEF INFORMATION OFFICER
Gui Karyo

CHIEF FINANCIAL OFFICER
Ken West

EXECUTIVE SALES V.P.-TOY BIZ
Ralph Lancelotti

V.P.-HUMAN RESOURCES
Mary Sprowls

PUBLISHING GROUP

MANAGING EDITOR
David Bogart

PRODUCTION DIRECTOR
Dan Carr

DIRECTOR OF MANUFACTURING
Sangho Byun

MARKETING COMMUNICATIONS MANAGER
Michael Doran

PUBLISHING BUSINESS MANAGER
Chet Krayewski

SENIOR MANUFACTURING MANAGER
Fred Pagan

MANUFACTURING MANAGER
Christine Slusarz

MANUFACTURING REPRESENTATIVE
Stefano Perrone, Jr.

ADVERTISING—PROMOTION—RETAIL SALES

EXECUTIVE VICE PRESIDENT/ CONSUMER PRODUCTS, PROMOTIONS & MEDIA SALES
Russell A. Brown

DIRECTOR OF ADVERTISING
Jeff Dunetz

TRADE BOOK SALES MANAGER
Jennifer Beemish

ADVERTISING SALES
Sara Beth Schrager

MARVEL ENCYCLOPEDIA VOL. 2: X-MEN. First printing 2003. ISBN# 0-7851-1199-9. Published by MARVEL COMICS, a division of MARVEL ENTERTAINMENT GROUP, INC. OFFICE OF PUBLICATION: 10 East 40th Street, New York, NY 10016.

10 9 8 7 6 5 4 3 2 1

TABLE OF CONTENTS

SERENDIPITY-X

Serendipity is a truly amazing thing. One day in Liverpool, England, a kid named John bumps into another named Paul—and before you know it, they changed the world. In 1961, much the same was happening on the overcrowded, bustling Isle of Manhattan. While Americans were being taught to duck and cover, and children cowered under their school desks, a group of creative young artists led by a carnival barker named Stan were on the same road as John and Paul. They would change the way stories were told—influencing some of today's greatest directors, screenwriters and novelists—and the way we forever looked at the heroic ideal.

1961 was the year the Marvel Comics legacy was born. In the years that followed, the world was introduced to the likes of the Amazing Spider-Man, the Incredible Hulk and Daredevil, the Man Without Fear … heroes, warriors and gods whose adventures thrill men, women and children of all ages even more today than they did more than 40 years ago.

But for the mutant X-Men—a new breed of humans born with extraordinary powers and abilities, banded together to protect the world from fellow mutants who would use their genetic gifts for evil—1963 was just an average start.

A cult favorite among loyal fans in the book's early years, the X-Men were little more than also-rans when compared to the likes of Spider-Man, the Fantastic Four and the Hulk. The honest-to-God truth is that the title was considered one of Marvel's very few and incredibly rare failures. Hence, *X-Men*—with all of its beautifully subtle metaphors for puberty, tolerance, isolation and coming of age—was canceled in a way in 1970 even though rife with potential. From 1970 to 1974, the comic languished as nothing more than a reprint title, re-purposing material created as far back as 1963—but great ideas don't die, they just wait for the rest of the world to catch up with them. So in 1975, perhaps the world was finally ready, or perhaps the new wave of creators at Marvel had a uniquely recharged vision—it doesn't matter. It was serendipity, and the comic-book world was changed forever.

That year, a brand-new X-Men title was unleashed upon an unsuspecting public. Boasting on its cover, in a fashion that would make Stan the carnival barker proud, were the simple words, "All New, All Different"—and boy, was that a mouthful.

The plan was to create a team of characters that were not only diverse in their powers; their diversity would be compounded by their ethnicity, genders, political views and preferences within. A super-powered team that reflected the diversity of a world that was shrinking by the minute. A world whose future could be glorious if we all learned the lessons of tolerance and acceptance, or could end up as a black pit of despair if we let fear rule our lives. Needless to say, this struck a chord within all of us, and the X-Men were reborn.

The team's cultural and racial diversity broke radical new ground in the world of four-color adventure. Threatened by inner turmoil and social issues as often as superhuman villains, the X-Men raised the bar even further on the new storytelling standard Marvel had set a decade before. America's youth had their new heroes!

Oh, and did I forget to mention that there was also this little runt of a guy named Wolverine?

Just before the relaunch in '75, Wolverine was created to be one of the many new international characters to be introduced in the new X-Men. Marvel decided to give the little guy a guest appearance in an issue of *Hulk*—and wouldn't you know it, it was serendipity all over again. Not since the creation of Spider-Man had Marvel had such a cultural icon on their hands. The little Canadian scrapper named Logan touched a chord in almost every reader, and it wasn't long before the X-Men had their leading man!

In the almost 28 years since that landmark event, the X-Men have stood unchallenged atop the comic book world, becoming arguably comics' most popular title of all time. Their universe has grown into a world of myth and legend even more vast and fantastic than Tolkien's Middle Earth, and more magical and whimsical than Hogwart's Academy, yet as real as today's headlines or what lies beyond our kitchen windows.

This new encyclopedia volume serves as a guide for readers who have thrilled to the X-Men's adventures and understood their pain and triumphs for decades, and serves as a beautiful introduction to new fans who are just discovering this rich fictional tapestry for the first time. Some of the greatest creators in the history of comics have worked on the X-Men, from artists to writers, and this book is just a small sampling of what they've managed to create through the years and a tribute to their legacy. Enjoy the journey.

And if you're wondering what led you to this book and made you crack it open to this simple introduction, well it was just serendipitous.

See ya in the funnybooks,

**Joe Quesada
EEK!**

X-MEN

Art by Frank Quitely

X-MEN

Art by Frank Quitely

First Appearance:
X-Men #1 (1963)

THE FUTURE OF EVOLUTION HAS EMERGED.

Mutants. *Homo superior.* They now occupy the highest rung on the evolutionary ladder. And their predecessors are not taking the ascendance lightly.

Persecuted. Hated. Tortured. Mocked. Feared. By virtue of their genetic make-up alone, mutants—born every day in greater and greater numbers—suffer from humans' discrimination and prejudice. Forced to live among *Homo sapiens* who fear that mutants will steal their jobs and take human partners, their anger at their fate is understandable.

Angry at themselves, and angry at the powers they were born with, the mutants needed a leader—a man with a vision—to help them overcome their despair and see the blessing they have been given instead of the curse they thought it to be.

They found that leader in <u>Professor X</u>. Sensing the growing movement of anti-mutant sentiment, Professor X opened up his Westchester mansion and created living and learning spaces where special mutants could be trained to use their unique gifts for the betterment of all species—before it was too late.

Professor X foresaw a future consumed by genetic war, where man and mutant would battle in a bleak wasteland once known as Earth. He knows that maintaining the peace now will prevent endless warfare between man and mutant.

He knows that only a handful of mutants can help stave off this devastating future.

He calls them the X-Men.

They call themselves the future's only hope.

Art by Frank Quitely

Art by Adam Hughes

ARCHANGEL

Real Name:
Warren Kenneth
Worthington III

First Appearance:
X-Men #1 (1963)

Height:	6'
Weight:	176 lbs
Eye Color:	Blue
Hair Color:	Blond

Born into a family of privilege and power, Warren Worthington attended a prestigious boarding school on the East Coast. But while his preppy classmates sported boat shoes and khakis, Warren secretly sported wings. He kept them hidden, afraid that revealing them would cast him out of the only life he'd known.

While Warren's ability to fly terrified him, it was also exhilarating. He had to finally abandon his fear when a fire broke out in his dormitory. Desperately wanting to help—and desperate to conceal his identity in the process—Warren wore a blond wig and nightshirt as he gallantly saved the students. The onlookers had no idea it was Warren; they only saw what they believed to be an "angel."

This life-saving episode turned into a life-affirming mission for Warren. He soon after took to the New York City skies as the crime fighter called the Avenging Angel. His nighttime missions were quickly noticed by Professor X, who asked him to become one of the initial members of the X-Men.

Warren's good times, however, came to a grinding halt when the superhuman assassins the Marauders attacked the Morlocks, subterranean mutants in New York City. Warren helped battle back the assassins, but suffered devastating consequences: The Marauder Harpoon impaled his wings, which were amputated.

Deeply depressed by the loss, Archangel attempted to commit suicide by crashing his plane. Just before the explosion of his small aircraft, however, he was teleported to safety by Apocalypse. The mutant warlord offered to return Archangel's ability to fly, but for a steep price: Act as one of Apocalypse's Horsemen—Death. Desperate and confused, Archangel agreed and underwent the painful genetic re-engineering of his wings, now made of razor-sharp metal. Fortunately, his pact with Apocalypse was short-lived. Archangel has returned to the X-Men, where his wings have since molted and regenerated, once again regaining their feathery appearance.

POWERS/ WEAPONS

- Flight
- Accelerated healing factor, which also affects those who come in contact with his blood

Art by Kia Asamiya

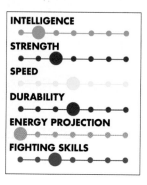

INTELLIGENCE

STRENGTH

SPEED

DURABILITY

ENERGY PROJECTION

FIGHTING SKILLS

BANSHEE

Keeping his mutant ability a secret, Banshee was making it through life with nothing but good fortune on his side. Born as the heir to the castle and estate of Cassidy Keep, Ireland, as well as a small fortune, Banshee graduated from Trinity College in Dublin with a Bachelor of Science degree and became a detective in the international law-enforcement organization known as Interpol. By the time he married Maeve Rourke (despite competition from his cousin, Black Tom Cassidy), Banshee had risen to the rank of Inspector. But things went horribly wrong when Banshee left on a lengthy secret mission for Interpol. His wife discovered she was pregnant and gave birth to their daughter, Theresa. As Maeve and the child were on a visit to Northern Ireland, a terrorist bomb exploded, killing Maeve. Black Tom secretly rescued Theresa (Siryn) and raised her as his own.

Returning from his mission only to find his wife dead and unaware of the birth of his only child, Banshee left Interpol in despair and became a detective with the New York City police department. But peace of mind eluded him, and he drifted into a life of crime. Saved from that fate by Professor X, a grateful Banshee joined up with the X-Men. Through them he found love again with Moira MacTaggert and, along the way, was reunited with his daughter Theresa.

Banshee later took on the role of mentor and tutor to a younger team of mutants called Generation X. But whatever happiness a new love, a reunion with his daughter, and mentoring a new generation brought did not last long. After the death of Moira at the hands of Mystique, Banshee attempted to drown his grief in alcohol. Distraught by the tragic turns in his life, Banshee abandoned the X-Men to build a new organization called the X-Corps that would maintain order among the mutant population. Enlisting the aid of Mastermind II to help brainwash former mutant villains into joining the X-Corps, Banshee couldn't anticipate how deadly his alliance would become. Secretly working with Mastermind, Mystique infiltrated X-Corps to try and take control of the organization from within. After discovering her plot, Banshee battled Mystique, who slit his throat, leaving him to convalesce in a hospital while he recovered from his injuries.

Real Name:
Sean Cassidy
First Appearance:
X-Men #28 (1967)

Height: 6'
Weight: 180 lbs
Eye Color: Blue-green
Hair Color: Reddish-blond

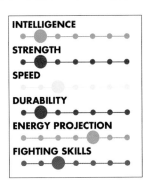

INTELLIGENCE
STRENGTH
SPEED
DURABILITY
ENERGY PROJECTION
FIGHTING SKILLS

POWERS/ WEAPONS

- Superhuman vocal cords, throat, and lungs that allow him to create powerful sonic waves with his voice
- Flight

Art by Ron Garney

BEAST

Real Name:
Dr. Henry McCoy
First Appearance:
X-Men #1 (1963)

Height: 5'11"
Weight: 402 lbs
Eye Color: Blue
Hair Color: Originally brown, bluish-black in furry form

Henry McCoy began his life with a few very distinctive traits: excessively large hands and feet. These outward manifestations of his mutant abilities at first served him well. During high school, Henry, able to mask his mutation, showcased his athletic prowess and superhuman agility on the football field. His awed teammates nicknamed him "Beast" for his ferocious tenacity on game days.

But as a *Homo superior* living in the *Homo sapiens'* world, Hank would shortly learn that even his prodigious athletic ability could not save him from fear and prejudice. When his talent on the field was exposed as mutant ability, the school asked Henry to leave. <u>Professor X</u>, however, stepped in and invited Henry to attend his School for Gifted Youngsters—a safe haven where Henry could hone not only his mutant skills but satisfy his insatiable thirst for knowledge. His training at the school served him well: He used both brain and brawn to aid the <u>X-Men</u> in the field, and helped them to prevent <u>Magneto</u> from exterminating humanity.

After his graduation, Henry stumbled upon a chemical compound that triggered mutation. Ignoring all good scientific testing measures, Henry opted to ingest the compound himself. In so doing, he altered the course of his life forever. While the chemical formula did exaggerate his incredible athletic prowess, several unintended side effects occurred: Henry's skin developed blue fur and his canine teeth grew significantly larger. Scared, Hank at first attempted to conceal his new persona—but he grew to accept the change.

Even with his own acceptance of his appearance, Beast continues to struggle for the acceptance of others. As a man of arts and letters and the sciences, Beast is very much the Renaissance man, and while his peers in the international intellectual community know this, they still consider him very much a mutant. His greatest achievement—building upon the work of <u>Moira MacTaggert</u> to find a cure for the mutant plague known as the Legacy Virus—was followed closely by his most heartbreaking rejection. His great love <u>Trish Tilby</u> left him because she chose to see only the Beast outside over the gentle man within.

Despite his ongoing battle with loneliness, Beast focuses on the X-Men's goal of building better relationships between man and mutant. In immersing himself in this campaign, Beast holds out hope that in the world he and the other X-Men dream of, he'll finally be known more for the genius within than for the creature outside.

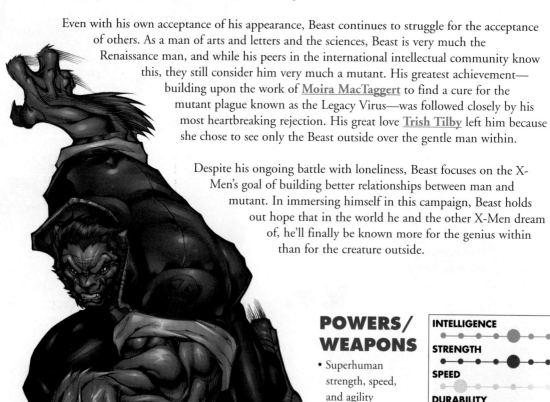

Art by Kevin Sharpe

POWERS/ WEAPONS

• Superhuman strength, speed, and agility

| INTELLIGENCE |
| STRENGTH |
| SPEED |
| DURABILITY |
| ENERGY PROJECTION |
| FIGHTING SKILLS |

BISHOP

Lucas Bishop came back from the future to join his heroes of the past.

This homicide cop, born 70 years after the time of the <u>X-Men</u>, grew up idolizing the X-Men and their dream for peaceful coexistence between man and mutant. But there was nothing peaceful about the world Bishop knew as his own.

Living in a world ravaged by an ongoing war being waged between man and mutant, Bishop learned at a very early age how to use his mutant ability to put an end to the violence around him. Xavier's Security Enforcers, the future security force founded on the principles created by <u>Professor X</u>, recruited Bishop as a teenager. He advanced quickly and eventually made a name for himself as an XSE homicide cop. As a member of the XSE, Bishop patrolled the mean streets of a planet shattered by war, with one whole continent rendered uninhabitable by radiation.

In pursuit of madman <u>Trevor Fitzroy</u>, a dangerous mutant criminal known for his ability to open portals through time, Bishop and other XSE agents traveled through one of Fitzroy's time tunnels and found themselves right in the middle of the X-Men's time. In the ensuing battle with Fitzroy and his minions, Bishop's XSE partners were killed and Bishop was seriously wounded. In an amazing turn, Bishop not only met his heroes the X-Men—they also saved his life.

Upon his recovery, Professor X invited Bishop to join the team, an invitation he accepted with great honor.

Today Bishop stands side-by-side with the heroes of his former past. Even though he's now an X-Man, he holds his lawman's ideals close and remains committed to upholding the basic tenets of justice while fulfilling his mission to protect and serve the very people who hate all that he is.

Real Name:
  Lucas Bishop
First Appearance:
  Uncanny X-Men #282
  (1991)

Height: 6'6"
Weight: 223 lbs
Eye Color: Brown
Hair Color: Black

INTELLIGENCE
STRENGTH
SPEED
DURABILITY
ENERGY PROJECTION
FIGHTING SKILLS

POWERS/ WEAPONS

- Energy absorption/ emission
- Variety of energy-projecting firearms

Art by Salvador Larroca

CANNONBALL

Real Name:
Samuel Zachary Guthrie
First Appearance:
Marvel Graphic Novel #4
(1982)

Height:	6'
Weight:	181 lbs
Eye Color:	Blue-gray
Hair Color:	Blond

Growing up in West Virginia, Sam Guthrie was never able to imagine what his future held. He knew he wanted to take off to find a better life—but he never dreamed he'd do it in such a dramatic way.

Forced by circumstance to work in the dirty, dangerous coal mines to help support his family, including his sister Paige (**Husk**), Sam Guthrie did what he could to help make ends meet. But Sam was no ordinary coal miner—it took only one day to change forever who he thought he was and what he was capable of becoming.

One day, the mine collapsed, leaving Sam and his partner trapped. With an impending cave-in and knowing that his time was running out, Sam experienced such stress trying to save himself and his partner that he triggered his latent mutant ability. Using his enormous propulsive power, Sam blasted them out of the cave to safety.

Donald Pierce, a renegade member of the **Hellfire Club**, learned of Sam's burgeoning powers and located the young man. Using his cunning powers of manipulation, Pierce coerced the naïve teenager into leaving the farm and serving as one of his operatives.

Pierce almost immediately sent Sam into battle against **Professor X** and the **New Mutants**. However, Sam refused to obey his handler's order to murder the young mutants, and in retaliation Pierce tried to kill him. Professor X defeated Pierce and thus saved Sam's life. Professor X realized Sam had been misled and invited him to join the New Mutants. Fighting alongside the New Mutants, the wide-eyed boy from a small West Virginia town blossomed into both a man and a hero. Under the tutelage of the team's one-time leader, **Nathan Summers**, Cannonball also developed sharp leadership abilities.

As he realized his leadership potential and more carefully honed his pronounced mutant powers, Cannonball received the ultimate accolade from Professor X: an invitation to join the **X-Men**. Cannonball, thrilled at the opportunity to graduate to the finest team of mutant fighters assembled, seized upon the chance.

POWERS/ WEAPONS

- Ability to generate thermochemical energy and release it from his skin
- Flight
- Protective blasting field

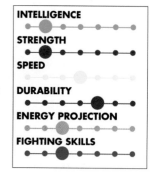

INTELLIGENCE	
STRENGTH	
SPEED	
DURABILITY	
ENERGY PROJECTION	
FIGHTING SKILLS	

Art by Salvador Larroca

CHAMBER

Things seemed to be going great for British teen Jonothon Starsmore and his girlfriend, Lady Gayle Edgerton. But their good times were ruined when Jonothon's mutant abilities unexpectedly erupted: An explosion of pure psionic energy blasted from his torso, tearing a hole in his body and shattering Lady Edgerton's legs. The blast also destroyed the young man's mouth and voice box, so he can only speak telepathically.

The teenaged Chamber took comfort in Professor X's invitation to attend his Xavier's School for Gifted Youngsters at the school's branch in the newly re-opened Massachusetts Academy. As a member of Generation X, Jonothon could learn to control his abilities among other young mutants facing similar fates.

Chamber eagerly accepted, and met with a dubious welcome at the airport when Emplate was the first to greet him. Generation X stepped in to prevent Chamber's certain doom. Narrowly escaping Emplate's deadly grips, Chamber returned with Generation X to the Academy, joined the team, and learned to control his burgeoning powers. Unfortunately, he suffered something of a setback after accidentally destroying the girls' dormitory in a panic after being kissed by Husk.

In time, Generation X was disbanded, but not before Chamber received the highest honor: Professor X asking him to serve with the X-Men. It was an honor, however, he only reluctantly accepted.

On a recent assignment for the X-Men, Chamber enrolled in Empire State University's pro-mutant program to investigate the deaths of mutant students on campus in a suspected bomb attack on a co-species organization called Students for Tolerance. While on campus, Chamber discovered the sad truth about the blast: The mutant boyfriend of Students for Tolerance's human leader, Gigi Martin, accidentally caused the explosion and Gigi hoped to use the accident as a means to martyr her dead friends, thus furthering her organization's cause.

Though the mission was successful, its aftermath left an indelible imprint on Chamber. When Cyclops chose him to lead the next X-Men mission, Chamber turned him down, opting instead for a life in the classroom. Chamber chose to become a teaching assistant at Professor X's school and hoped he could learn more about himself from the students under his tutelage.

Real Name:
Jonothon Evan Starsmore
First Appearance:
Generation X #1 (1994)

Height: 5'9"
Weight: 140 lbs
Eye Color: Brown
Hair Color: Reddish-brown

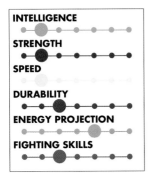

INTELLIGENCE

STRENGTH

SPEED

DURABILITY

ENERGY PROJECTION

FIGHTING SKILLS

POWERS/WEAPONS

• Projection of bio-blasts from his torso
• Limited telepathy

Art by Chris Bachalo

COLOSSUS

Real Name:
Piotr "Peter" Nikolaievitch Rasputin

First Appearance:
Giant-Size X-Men #1 (1975)

Height: 6'6" (normally), 7'5" (transformed)
Weight: 250 lbs (normally), 500 lbs (transformed)
Eye Color: Blue (normally), silver (transformed)
Hair Color: Black

A man of both enormous size and heart, he was the mutant that men feared and other mutants revered. At once a farmer, an artist, and a gentleman, he was also a brute force in battle. His name was Colossus. Never again will there be another.

Born Piotr "Peter" Rasputin in Lake Baikal, Siberia, Peter first manifested his tremendous mutant ability in his adolescence. Though he was content to help his fellow farmers with his incredible strength and durability, another man needed him too: Professor X. Reaching out to Peter after his X-Men had been captured by Krakoa, Professor X asked him to use his mutant strength and muscle to help other mutants in need. While he preferred to stay on his collective farm with his parents and little sister, Illyana (Magik), Peter reluctantly agreed to help Professor X and left for the United States at once.

Having liberated the X-Men from their captivity, Peter decided to stay in America with the team. Young and idealistic, he believed he could make a difference and help others like him live in peace with mankind. But Peter, a gentle man, would have to face great adversity after his decision: His parents were slaughtered by vicious mutants, his brother Mikhail Rasputin became his enemy, and in perhaps the worst blow of all, his beloved sister Illyana succumbed to the deadly Legacy Virus, a disease that affects only mutants.

To Peter, all this was too much. He split from the X-Men and despair drove him to the Acolytes, disciples of the mutant terrorist Magneto. But his stint there did not last long; a change of heart sent him back to the X-Men one last time.

The X-Men's resident scientist, Beast, developed a cure for the Legacy Virus. His cure, however, was a double-edged sword. In order for it to work, the serum would need to be administered to a mutant host, causing his powers to flare, thereby spreading the cure into Earth's atmosphere and protecting all mutants—but the host would perish in the process.

Nearly defeated by his lifetime of loss, and desperate to stop the disease, Peter, without revealing his intentions to anyone, strode into Beast's empty laboratory and injected himself with the formula. In that one act, Peter rid the world of the Legacy Virus, ensuring the disease would never take another mutant and leave others to grieve. For this honor, Peter paid with his life.

At one time, Peter might have only been remembered for his ability to transform his body tissue into an organic, steel-like substance. But after his final selfless act he was remembered as something even greater: a hero to all mutantkind.

POWERS/ WEAPONS

• Ability to transform flesh into organic steel

Art by Leinil Francis Yu

INTELLIGENCE						
STRENGTH						
SPEED						
DURABILITY						
ENERGY PROJECTION						
FIGHTING SKILLS						

CYCLOPS

He lives for the dream. And he is willing to die for it. Not one thing or person can stand in the way of Cyclops's steadfast belief in the one man who made all the difference in the world to him: <u>Professor X</u>.

Scott Summers holds the profound honor and privilege of being the first mutant recruited to participate in Professor X's dream for the future. As the first member of the <u>X-Men</u> as well as its de facto leader, Scott remains the most dedicated to the pursuit of peaceful coexistence between man and mutant.

Cyclops's mutant ability manifests in the continual emission of force beams from his eyes. Even the slightest glance without a ray-shielding device could vaporize an unsuspecting, innocent person. While closing his eyes prevents the emission of rays, he cannot choose to live his life as a blind man. In an effort to see while keeping innocent people out of harm's way, Cyclops dons his ever-present ruby quartz visor and glasses, which manage to keep the destructive rays in check.

Cyclops knows the devastating power of his ability all too well. In his youth, his power erupted in a sudden blast that destroyed a construction crane. As the crane's contents plunged toward a crowd of terrified onlookers, a quick-thinking Cyclops unleashed a second blast from his eyes that obliterated the deadly debris during its descent. While his actions were life-saving, the crowd interpreted the display with all the fear of *Homo sapiens* the world over: They formed an angry lynch mob and chased the scared mutant. Professor X rescued Cyclops from life on the run and invited him to be the first X-Man.

It was an invitation Cyclops was only too eager to accept. Having grown up as an orphan after losing his parents in an airplane accident and his brother Alex (<u>Havok</u>) to foster parents, Cyclops deeply wanted to belong to a real family. The relationship between Cyclops and Professor X evolved from one of teacher and student to one of father and son. In addition to helping Cyclops harness his optic powers, Professor X led by his own sterling example

Art by Frank Quitely

Real Name:
Scott Summers
First Appearance:
X-Men #1 (1963)

Height: 6'1"
Weight: 181 lbs
Eye Color: Red
Hair Color: Brown

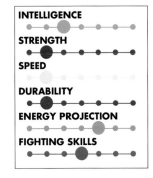

INTELLIGENCE
STRENGTH
SPEED
DURABILITY
ENERGY PROJECTION
FIGHTING SKILLS

POWERS/ WEAPONS

• Optic force blasts

CYCLOPS

and helped Scott become the exemplary man he is today. Cyclops's devotion and dedication to his father figure and mentor is unwavering.

As the years passed, more X-Men were recruited and trained, including one who, aside from Professor X, would become the most important person in Cyclops's life: Jean Grey. At first, he believed his powers made it impossible to be close to her. But with time, Cyclops's tentative demeanor gave way to the amazing power of love—but things did not go exactly as planned.

A cosmic entity known as the Phoenix Force assumed Jean's identity and took her place on the team. When the Phoenix Force committed suicide to save the world, Cyclops believed the love of his life had died along with it. Grief-stricken, he met and married Madelyne Pryor (Goblin Queen)—unaware she was a clone of Jean created by Mr. Sinister and designed to dupe him. This union produced their son, Nathan Summers.

But Jean was not dead, merely in suspended animation. When she emerged, Cyclops left his wife and eagerly went back to his true love. After Madelyne died, Scott married Jean. And while the marriage sometimes suffers from Scott's distant and distracted manner, it has so far withstood the test of time.

Art by John Byrne

Putting his personal life aside for the greater good of the team's goals, Cyclops's detachment often serves him and the other X-Men well. When Professor X steps away from his duties or is in some way incapacitated, it is Scott's cool head and stoic nature that help him serve as a valuable interim leader of the team.

Today, Cyclops lives and works with the people he knows as his family and friends: the X-Men. His desire to see Professor X's dream realized is his primary focus, above the wishes of all others—including his wife Jean. It is because Cyclops knows that when the time comes, it is he who will succeed Professor X. A time that Cyclops hopes will not arrive too soon.

DAZZLER

In the world of celebrity, the right kind of disclosure can enhance a career just as much as the wrong kind can kill it. Alison Blaire took her chances—and her disclosure led to more than she had ever imagined. Even though she was keenly aware of her ability to transform sound into light, the last thing on Alison's mind as a teenager was using her mutant ability to become a super hero. But no one thinks about one's own destiny—it just shows up and happens.

What she did consider was her singing career. Blessed with a wonderful voice, a strong-willed Alison pursued her dream of being in show business. To promote herself and create her unique stage persona, she summoned her mutant powers to create specialized lighting effects for her shows. Depending on the song or the mood, she would conjure the corresponding effect—anything from disconcerting cascades of color to hypnotic strobe effects and even soothing gentle glows. Alison adopted the stage name the Dazzler.

Her audience never had any inkling that the light shows were anything more than special effects generated by a combination of electricity and technological ingenuity. But Alison knew they were so much more and eventually chose to reveal herself as a mutant instead of hide behind the lie. But her candid revelation of her mutant abilities backfired, and Alison was blacklisted out of the business. Her only recourse was to embrace her amazing abilities and join forces with the **X-Men**.

Leaving behind her failed career in show business allowed her to flourish in the mutant realm. Her association with the X-Men not only let her capitalize on her already-powerful skills but also led her to the love of her life, **Longshot**.

Side-by-side with Longshot, Dazzler and the X-Men returned to Longshot's home planet of Mojoworld to rid it of its merciless and tyrannical ruler, **Mojo**. Once Mojo had been defeated, Longshot opted to stay and rebuild the planet. Eventually Dazzler and Longshot married.

Though content with who she is and what she has become, Dazzler rejoined the X-Men temporarily to help them rescue **Professor X**, who was being held captive by **Magneto**. She is now in the process of rebuilding the singing career she dreamed of so long ago.

Real Name:
Alison Blaire
First Appearance:
X-Men #130 (1980)

Height: 5'8"
Weight: 135 lbs
Eye Color: Blue
Hair Color: Blonde

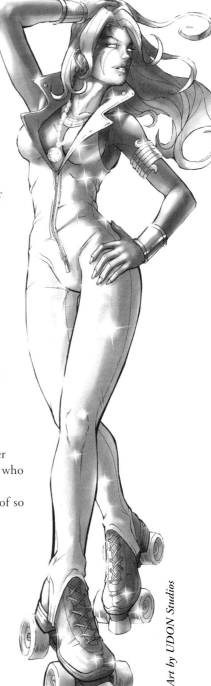

Art by UDON Studios

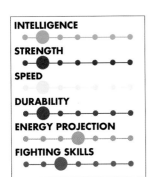

INTELLIGENCE

STRENGTH

SPEED

DURABILITY

ENERGY PROJECTION

FIGHTING SKILLS

POWERS/WEAPONS

- Ability to generate light from sound
- Ability to manufacture holographic images
- Creation of protective force fields to deflect or vaporize oncoming objects

FORGE

Real Name:
Unrevealed
First Appearance:
Uncanny X-Men #184
(1984)

Height:	6'
Weight:	180 lbs
Eye Color:	Brown
Hair Color:	Black

INTELLIGENCE

STRENGTH

SPEED

DURABILITY

ENERGY PROJECTION

FIGHTING SKILLS

POWERS/ WEAPONS

• Intuitive genius at inventing
• Mystical abilities

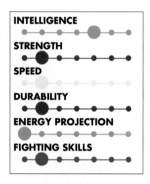

Known by no other name but Forge, this intuitive mutant inventor started out as a Cheyenne Indian and a dutiful pupil of Naze, his tribe's shaman. As a result of his training, Forge developed considerable mystical powers along with his unusual talent for inventing mechanical devices.

Called by his country to serve in Southeast Asia, Forge lost his right hand and right leg during a B-52 bombing. Sinking into a suicidal depression, he tried unsuccessfully to kill himself. During his recovery, he used his mutant skills to help him design an artificial hand and leg to replace those he lost. He did not—and could not—summon his mystical skills for assistance. Somewhere back in the jungles he fought in, he had sworn to give them up.

Back home, Forge became an inventor, and he picked up a Defense Department contract to create advanced weaponry. Among his many inventions was a neutralizer weapon that could eliminate the superhuman abilities of any powerful being. Forge became enraged when his untested neutralizer fell into the hands of government operative Henry Gyrich. Using the device, the agent inadvertently struck Storm, stripping her of all her powers. Guilty and dismayed, Forge took the stricken Storm to his home in Dallas, Texas, where he nursed her back to health; the pair fell deeply in love. When Storm found out that it was Forge's neutralizer that had taken away her powers, she felt angry and betrayed and left him.

Desperate to give Storm her powers back and to regain her love and trust, Forge destroyed all known versions of his original neutralizer and invented another device that restored her powers. Forge joined the X-Men and Storm to fight a critical battle. Back in his own hometown, Forge and the X-Men fought the Adversary. During the struggle, the X-Men learned why Forge had left his mystical powers behind: During a secret mission in Southeast Asia, Forge's entire battalion was killed. In a fit of rage and desperation, he used his shamanic magic power to call upon the spirits of the dead soldiers to open up a dimensional portal, allowing them to return to Earth and slaughter the enemies who had killed them.
Concerned about the consequences of his actions, Forge ordered the fateful B-52 bombing run to close up the portal in an attempt to destroy the spirits—a decision that cost him his hand and his leg.

Forge eventually signed on full time with the X-Men. Back at the Xavier Mansion, he helped redesign the Danger Room and completely revamped the Blackbird jet, outfitting it with stealth technology and a cloaking device.

Art by Aaron Lopresti

EMMA FROST

Heiress. Intellectual. Charmer. Seductress. Emma Frost is all of the above. But it's another word that haunts her: mutant.

As the middle child of an old-money Boston mercantile family, Emma became a majority stockholder of a multibillion-dollar electronics and transportation conglomerate. Despite her young age, her myriad personal charms, innate intellectualism, and the secret use of her psionic powers led to her early rise to power, and she was swiftly named chairwoman of the board and CEO of Frost International. In addition to her amazing business acumen, she pulled double duty as the chairwoman of the board of trustees of the Massachusetts Academy, a college preparatory school for grades seven through 12.

Emma's brains and beauty earned her acceptance into one of the planet's most elite organizations, the Hellfire Club. Members of this prestigious and ultra-exclusive club include some of the world's wealthiest and most powerful people. But even among these elite men and women, Emma felt like an intellectual superior. She decided to seize control of the club and became its new White Queen.

Emma even placed her mutant recruits at the Massachusetts Academy in peril, and her Hellions fought with the X-Men on numerous occasions. But after a catastrophic battle that killed all of her Hellions, nearly claimed Emma's life and rendered her psychically incapacitated, her school's reins were turned over to Professor X and he added the facility to his growing Xavier Institute. Not one to cede control quietly, Emma resumed her role at the Academy once she regained her powers and set out to train a new breed of young mutants called Generation X.

In a series of dramatic turns, she was forced to disband Generation X and close her Academy. After the vast genocide perpetrated in Genosha by Cassandra Nova and the Sentinels, Emma ultimately joined the X-Men, seeing the team as the only alternative to a world in which mutants are marginalized, persecuted, and exterminated. Now, as part of the X-Men and a teacher at the Xavier Institute, Emma is content to fight alongside her one-time adversaries to defend a world on the brink of genetic war.

Real Name:
Emma Frost
First Appearance:
Uncanny X-Men #129 (1979)

Height: 5'10"
Weight: 150 lbs
Eye Color: Blue
Hair Color: Blonde

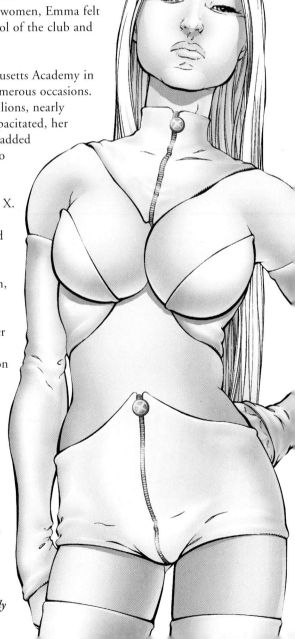

INTELLIGENCE
STRENGTH
SPEED
DURABILITY
ENERGY PROJECTION
FIGHTING SKILLS

POWERS/ WEAPONS

- Telepathy
- Diamond-hard, nearly indestructible skin (cannot access her telepathic abilities in this form)

Art by Frank Quitely

GAMBIT

Real Name:
Remy LeBeau
First Appearance:
Uncanny X-Men #266
(1990)

Height: 6'1"
Weight: 183 lbs
Eye Color: Red
Hair Color: Brown

Remy LeBeau's life had all the earmarks of a modern-day tragedy: Abandoned, orphaned, and forced into the streets, he led a life built on crime, shameful acts—and, finally, redemption. Orphaned in infancy, Remy was stolen off a New Orleans street by the members of the Thieves' Guild, whose leader Jean-Luc LeBeau eventually adopted the boy. As a member of the legendary Guild, Remy, with the help of his foster father, grew up to become a master thief himself. This tough-as-nails street kid also had one significant trademark: the mutant ability to charge objects with kinetic energy generated by his body.

As part of a peace agreement with their rivals, the Assassins' Guild, the Thieves' Guild arranged a marriage between Remy and his childhood sweetheart **Belladonna**. But Belladonna's brother Julien saw things differently. After the marriage, Julien challenged Remy to a duel and was severely wounded in the ensuing fight. In an effort to prevent a Guild war, Remy left town—and Belladonna—forever. He turned his back on the only world he knew and set out to ply his trade as a thief around the world.

Gambit came under the tutelage of **Mr. Sinister** and was duped into helping him organize a team of mutants called the **Marauders**, whom he then led into the **Morlocks**' tunnels. The Marauders systematically slaughtered the Morlocks—much to Gambit's horror. Abandoning Sinister, Gambit met up with **Storm**, and helped her do battle with the **Shadow King**. Impressed, Storm sponsored his membership into the **X-Men**. Gambit saw this as his chance to atone for the Morlocks' massacre—a secret sin he kept to himself until it was unwittingly revealed: During his one kiss with his great love **Rogue**, her ability to absorb memories drew out his deepest secret—and the X-Men learned of Gambit's hand in the terrible murders. Gambit was filled with shame, and the X-Men abandoned him to his fate. After much self-examination, Gambit realized he had found his calling among the X-Men. Consumed by remorse, Gambit returned and made his peace with the team.

POWERS/ WEAPONS

- Charges inanimate objects, most frequently playing cards, with explosively released biokinetic energy
- Master thief

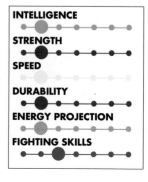

INTELLIGENCE
STRENGTH
SPEED
DURABILITY
ENERGY PROJECTION
FIGHTING SKILLS

Art by Georges Jeanty

JEAN GREY

Jean Grey came to know death—literally—at quite a young age. And that death would forever change her entire life.

When she was just ten years old, Jean saw her best friend Annie Richardson get struck and killed by an automobile. Touching her dying friend, Jean's emotions awakened her latent telepathic powers and she experienced Annie's dying thoughts as if they were her own.

Jean was unable to cope and became deeply depressed. Her parents sought out the help of **Professor X**, who treated the mutant for the next several years. Professor X erected psychic shields for Jean's mind so she wouldn't be able to fully use her telepathic abilities until she matured and had the ability to control them. Professor X counseled Jean's parents and asked them for permission to enroll Jean as his first student in his Xavier's School for Gifted Youngsters, a learning facility designed for talented mutants such as Jean. Professor X eventually inducted Jean into the newly formed **X-Men** and gave her the code name Marvel Girl.

As a teenager, Jean fell deeply in love with **Cyclops**. Years passed before either shy teen could admit their true feelings to one another. And there was one deadly, near fatal reason that almost kept them apart forever: the Phoenix Force.

After a mission in outer space, Jean and the other X-Men were forced to fly back to Earth during a powerful radiation storm. Because the pilot's cabin lacked sufficient shielding, Jean insisted on flying the craft, assuming that her powers would protect her. But her powers weren't enough of a shield.

POWERS/WEAPONS

- Telepathy
- Telekinesis

Real Name:
Jean Grey-Summers
First Appearance:
X-Men #1 (1963)

Height: 5'8"
Weight: 143 lbs
Eye Color: Green
Hair Color: Red

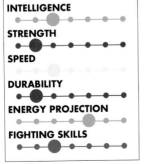

INTELLIGENCE

STRENGTH

SPEED

DURABILITY

ENERGY PROJECTION

FIGHTING SKILLS

Art by Frank Quitely

JEAN GREY

Succumbing to radiation poisoning, Jean was touched by a cosmic being known as the Phoenix Force. The entity duplicated Jean's body, her memories, her personality, and absorbed some of her consciousness. It then guided the plane to crash-land in Jamaica Bay, near New York City. The Phoenix Force placed the real Jean in a cocoon-like pod that came to rest at the bottom of the bay.

Now free to roam the world in the guise of Jean, the Phoenix Force eventually became corrupted by its limitless power—but Jean's persona ultimately regained dominance and her psyche caused the entity to sacrifice itself to save the universe. Scott watched in horror as the Phoenix Force committed suicide, thinking it was Jean herself who was dying. Months later, after her pod had been located, Jean broke free of the cocoon and released herself, running straight into the arms of Scott, the man she loved.

Jean returned to the X-Men, and, after she rebuilt her relationship with Cyclops, the two finally married.

While she remains true to her marriage, Jean must forever conceal her feelings towards another X-Men member, **Wolverine**. With Cyclops sometimes a distant partner, Jean sees in Wolverine great animal passion and killer instincts that merely serve to mask a gentle soul. When Cyclops is worlds away, either physically or emotionally, Wolverine stands by Jean in the here and now. He shares her feelings, but, like Jean, chooses not to act on them to preserve the best interests for everyone involved. To the other X-Men, the unspoken attraction between the two reads only as a deep and abiding friendship.

These days, Jean throws all her energy and devotion into her job as headmistress of the **Xavier Institute**, teaching and mentoring troubled mutant teens to survive in a world that hates and fears them.

Art by John Paul Leon

HAVOK

As a child, Alex Summers and his older brother Scott (Cyclops) lost their parents in an airplane accident; the children escaped in the plane's sole parachute. Hospitalized with injuries, Alex suffered traumatic amnesia after the accident. Thinking his parents dead, and with his brother in a coma, he left the hospital within two weeks and was placed in an orphanage. It would be years before he saw his brother again.

It wasn't until his college years that Alex learned of his mutant abilities. A professor of archeology named Ahmet Abdol (Living Monolith), a mutant himself, had discovered a psychic link between himself and the boy. Abducting Alex to Egypt, Adbol found a way to take the ambient cosmic radiation from Alex and allow his own body to attain its latent potential. When the X-Men, including his brother Cyclops, came to his rescue, Havok's powers manifested.

Working with the X-Men, Havok learned to keep his powers in check. During this time, Havok fell in love with teammate Polaris. But Havok, consumed by comparisons to his revered brother, longed to get out from under Scott's shadow. After serving for a time as team leader of a

government-funded mutant strike force, Havok was ripped from his own reality by an airplane explosion and deposited on a dark, twisted alternate Earth. There, he found himself allied with a team of mutants who were sinister, parallel incarnations of his friends and family. In a cataclysmic battle to preserve the fabric of all reality, Havok tapped into a well of raw power never again to be unleashed in all the dimensions and destroyed his adversary. But the price of victory appeared to be death, as Alex's soul was cast adrift in the void while his original, physical body lay in a coma on his own Earth.

Havok was a comatose "John Doe" patient at the Rosy Manor Convalescent Hospital in upstate New York when nurse Annie Ghazikanian recognized him from a newspaper article about the Xavier Institute. After she contacted the Institute, Cyclops came to collect his brother and returned him to the mansion—along with Annie, who had developed an unrequited love for Alex and sought to continue his rehabilitation. Havok was eventually brought out of his coma thanks to Annie's son Carter Ghazikanian, himself a mutant, who managed to reconnect Alex's consciousness to his body.

Real Name:
Alexander Summers
First Appearance:
X-Men #54 (1969)

Height: 6'
Weight: 180 lbs
Eye Color: Brown
Hair Color: Blond

INTELLIGENCE

STRENGTH

SPEED

DURABILITY

ENERGY PROJECTION

FIGHTING SKILLS

POWERS/ WEAPONS

• Solar-generated plazma blasts

Art by Phillip Tan

HUSK

Real Name:
Paige Elisabeth Guthrie
First Appearance:
X-Force #32 (1994)

Height: 5'7"
Weight: 128 lbs
Eye Color: Blue
Hair Color: Blonde

INTELLIGENCE

STRENGTH

SPEED

DURABILITY

ENERGY PROJECTION

FIGHTING SKILLS

POWERS/ WEAPONS

• Skin manipulation

Growing up poor on a West Virginia farm, Paige Guthrie longed for another life, one filled with excitement and adventure. Unlike so many others, she got exactly what she wished for. After the death of her father, Paige, like all of her siblings, was forced to take on the responsibilities of running the family farm. With her brother Sam (Cannonball) working in the coal mines to help the family's income, Husk spent day after day with her mother. Once Cannonball manifested his mutant powers, he left the farm and eventually became a member of the New Mutants. Husk was left behind and worked with her mother to run the farm. Husk lived vicariously through Cannonball; he would send home letters filled to the brim with all the exciting and dangerous adventures he was having at Xavier's school. Husk yearned to have the same kinds of experiences, too. Before long, she got her wish.

At age 13, her superpowers manifested, but she kept them to herself until her brother and his teammate Meltdown visited the farm. Shortly after they arrived, a group of reckless mutants captured Cannonball and Meltdown in an effort to win a diabolical game created by Gamesmaster. Using her new powers, Husk shed her outer skin and her body morphed into the temporary guise of an insect. In this new form, Husk challenged the Gamesmaster to a contest with heavy stakes: the very lives of her brother and his fellow mutants. Husk defeated the Gamesmaster in a contest of wits, and Cannonball and the others were freed.

Husk returned to the farm only to be kidnapped by the Phalanx, who wanted to experiment on mutants in order to learn how they could be assimilated into their own masses. Joining other similarly abducted young mutants, Husk and her fellow captives were rescued thanks to the combined efforts of Banshee, Jubilee, Emma Frost, and Sabretooth.

After the rescue, Husk did not return to the farm. Instead, she and the young mutants became the founding members of Generation X, a new team of mutants enrolled in Xavier's School for Gifted Youngsters at the institute's campus in the newly re-opened Massachusetts Academy.

After many adventures with Generation X, including a brief relationship with fellow teammate Chamber, Husk left when the Academy closed and ultimately went to work for X-Corporation, a global search-and-rescue unit for oppressed mutants. In time, the form-changing Husk finally "graduated" and joined the ranks of the X-Men.

The life Husk had always dreamed of while living on her family's farm is now the very life she lives. From a simple farm girl to a powerful mutant, Husk knows no dream is too big to come true—including Professor X's dream of peaceful coexistence between man and mutant.

Art by Kia Asamiya

ICEMAN

Normal. That's what Bobby Drake wanted. A normal life. A normal town. A normal routine. But despite his best efforts, he couldn't always get what he wanted.

Bobby was just an ordinary schoolboy growing up in Long Island, New York. But his hope for a similarly average adult life ended abruptly during his teen years when he discovered he possessed the mutant ability to control ice. His parents knew the world would come to hate and fear him if his superpowers became apparent, and they encouraged Bobby to keep his mutant skills hidden.

When Bobby was out with his girlfriend one day, a group of local bullies appeared and began to assault them. Without hesitation, Bobby summoned his lone line of defense against the main aggressor and temporarily encased the young thug in ice.

It didn't take long for the small community to get wind of what the mutant teen had done. Instead of rallying around the boy for his swift thinking, they formed a lynch mob and broke into the Drakes' home on a mission to stop the mutant. Bobby tried to contain the mob as best he could, but their sheer number overwhelmed him. Fortunately, the local sheriff took Bobby to the nearby jail—mostly for the boy's own protection.

Dismayed by Bobby's treatment, **Professor X** sent **Cyclops** to survey the situation. But Bobby resisted Cyclops's efforts to remove him from the town. Outside the jail, the mob had regrouped and prepared to hang the two mutants inside. In an effort to save both mutants, Professor X used his psionic powers to halt the mob and erase their memories of the entire event. Grateful for escaping with his life, Bobby accepted Professor X's invitation to join the **X-Men** and became their youngest member: Iceman.

Iceman also bore another distinction as the team prankster. Always quick to crack a clever joke, Iceman lends levity to the team during the times when they need all the good cheer they can get.

Despite his good sense of humor, Bobby suffers the same pains of all mutants brought on by a lifetime plagued by insecurity and discrimination. He works hard to surmount these problems by perfecting his mutant ability. Bobby has come to grips with both his destiny and his true, heartfelt belief in fulfilling the dream of peaceful coexistence between man and mutant.

Real Name:
Robert Drake
First Appearance:
X-Men #1 (1963)

Height: 5'8"
Weight: 145 lbs
Eye Color: Brown
Hair Color: Brown

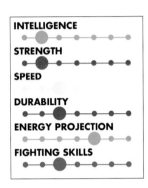

INTELLIGENCE
STRENGTH
SPEED
DURABILITY
ENERGY PROJECTION
FIGHTING SKILLS

POWERS/ WEAPONS

• Organic ice control

Art by Kia Asamiya

JUBILEE

Real Name:
Jubilation Lee
First Appearance:
Uncanny X-Men #244
(1988)

Height:	5'5"
Weight:	115 lbs
Eye Color:	Blue
Hair Color:	Black

Her life seemed extraordinarily good—until it turned extraordinarily bad.

Born to wealthy parents, Jubilation Lee was raised in the exclusive, elegant confines of Beverly Hills, California. Wanting for nothing, she received a first-class education and grew into a talented gymnast. But any hope of a peaceful life came to a devastating end when her parents were murdered.

Beset with unexpected poverty in addition to her orphan status, Jubilee became a ward of the state. Her tolerance for those in authority was not just limited—it was nonexistent. She fled her state-sponsored keepers and sought refuge in a Hollywood mall, where she learned to survive on the spoils of petty theft. When mall security caught her, Jubilee panicked. Her moment of crisis brought forth her mutant powers—powerful energy bursts—which startled the police and allowed her to escape.

Her lonely life ended when <u>Storm</u>, <u>Rogue</u>, <u>Psylocke</u>, and <u>Dazzler</u> rescued her from capture at the hands of a mutant hunter. Soon after, Jubilee joined forces with the <u>X-Men</u>. Although initially reluctant to trust them—as she was with any other authority figure—she learned how to be a team player and even signed on to join Generation X, a team of younger mutant counterparts to the X-Men.

For a time, Jubilee paired with <u>Wolverine</u>, who had sponsored her membership into the X-Men. While at first glimpse they appeared to be an unlikely duo, Jubilee found a father figure in Wolverine and Wolverine counted on Jubilee to prevent him from taking actions that he might one day regret.

Having gotten over her initial fears and suspicions, Jubilee now loves and trusts the X-Men as she did the family she once had. Her explosive energy bursts, sarcastic nature, spitfire personality, and constant ability to speak her mind help Jubilee cope with the task at hand: making the world a better place for peaceful coexistence between man and mutant.

POWERS/ WEAPONS

- Generation of explosive energy bursts similar to fireworks, varying in power and intensity

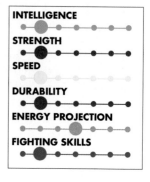

INTELLIGENCE	
STRENGTH	
SPEED	
DURABILITY	
ENERGY PROJECTION	
FIGHTING SKILLS	

Art by Art Adams

JUGGERNAUT

As a jealous and spiteful young boy, the thuggish Cain Marko took great pleasure in tormenting his stepbrother Charles (<u>Professor X</u>). Forced by his father's marriage to Charles's mother to cohabit with the unwanted sibling, Cain grew more enraged by the day as it became evident his father preferred Charles over him. The rage grew stronger with every blow Cain took from his father—beatings brought on as punishment for his own actions against Charles. When Charles unwittingly entered Cain's mind with his telepathic powers, Cain saw the invasion as a deliberate personal assault.

Cain was drafted into military service, and he wound up in the same unit as Charles. When Cain deserted, Charles trailed him in a bid to bring him back before court martial proceedings were ordered. Following his stepbrother into a cave, Charles saw Cain pick up a large ruby—a gem that would forever alter Cain's life. They had entered the long-hidden temple of Cyttorak. And the ruby Cain had discovered came with an ominous inscription: "Whosoever touches this gem shall possess the power of Cyttorak. Henceforth, you who read these words shall become forevermore a human juggernaut." Charles watched in horror as his stepbrother Cain became the monstrous Juggernaut, gaining supernatural poweres and invulnerabiliy. But just as the transformation completed, the cave collapsed around them. Charles escaped, but Cain did not.

With great efficiency, he dug his way out of the cave and made his way back to America. Year after year, Juggernaut battled viciously against the <u>X-Men</u>, fueled by his lifelong hatred of his stepbrother. Though Juggernaut brought only vengeance and chaos, Professor X always believed he could be saved. When the powers of his frequent partner, <u>Black Tom Cassidy</u>, went out of control, Juggernaut sought the X-Men's aid. Tom unsuccessfully attempted to kill Juggernaut, who later accepted Xavier's offer to recuperate at the <u>Xavier Institute</u>. Juggernaut fought alongside the X-Men in a battle against <u>Maximus Lobo</u>, and experienced perhaps for the first time in his life a sense of camaraderie and accomplishment. This experience so dramatically altered him that he sought out his stepbrother's approval and asked to join the team. Charles, who had always waited for this day, gladly gave his blessing.

Real Name:
Cain Marko
First Appearance:
X-Men #12 (1965)

Height:	6'10"
Weight:	900 lbs
Eye Color:	Blue
Hair Color:	Red

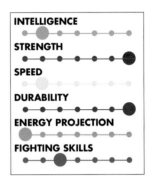

INTELLIGENCE
STRENGTH
SPEED
DURABILITY
ENERGY PROJECTION
FIGHTING SKILLS

POWERS/ WEAPONS

- Supernatural strength
- Invulnerability
- Telepathy-blocking helmet

Art by Ron Garney

LONGSHOT

Real Name:
Longshot
First Appearance:
Longshot #1 (1985)

Height:	6'2"
Weight:	80 lbs
Eye Color:	Blue
Hair Color:	Blond

When Longshot declared to his owner **Mojo** what every slave knows and nurtures in his heart, he had the means and the power to make good on his word.

With the exception of his three-fingered, single-thumbed hands, Longshot appears to be human. But he is not. He is actually an artificially manufactured humanoid, specifically assembled to serve as a slave to the ruling class known as the Spineless Ones. Because Longshot possesses a hollow bone structure, he weighs only 80 pounds. His litheness, along with his strengthened muscle tissue, grants him superhuman agility and reflexes.

Created by the genetic scientist Arize on Mojoworld, a planet in another dimension, Longshot bravely resisted his life as a slave and encouraged others sharing his "birthright" to do the same. Fortunately for Longshot, Arize gave him some help. Arize, torn between doing his job and doing the right thing, had endowed Longshot and other engineered humanoids with special abilities, hoping one day those abilities would aid them in an eventual slave revolt against their masters. Arize had given Longshot superhuman agility and the power to alter probability in order to gain good luck.

It took time and patience, but Longshot's good luck would serve him well in the end.

As Longshot's "owner," Mojo exploited the handsome humanoid's athletic prowess, forcing him to be a stuntman in Mojoworld's increasingly bizarre film productions. But Longshot broke free and fled to Earth, where he joined forces with the **X-Men** and convinced them to help him conquer Mojo and the other Spineless Ones.

Before returning to Mojoworld to exact his retribution, Longshot met and fell in love with the stunning X-Man **Dazzler**, a singer also known as Alison Blaire.

Returning to Mojoworld with the X-Men, Longshot rallied the other slaves into a rebellion against Mojo. The battle came to its brutal and inevitable conclusion when Longshot impaled Mojo on one of his razor-sharp knives.

To the victor go the spoils: After his time on Earth and brief affiliation with the X-Men, Longshot married Dazzler.

POWERS/ WEAPONS

- Superhuman agility
- Power to alter probability to give himself good luck

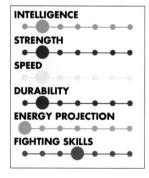

INTELLIGENCE							
STRENGTH							
SPEED							
DURABILITY							
ENERGY PROJECTION							
FIGHTING SKILLS							

Art by Art Adams

NIGHTCRAWLER

Save for his indigo fur, Kurt Wagner resembles every bit the Western world's idealized notion of the devil: a prehensile tail that ends in a point, pointed ears, fanged teeth, three-fingered hands, and two-toed feet. But looks are deceiving.

A deeply religious man, Nightcrawler had a rough start in life. When Bavarian villagers discovered his true mutant identity, they tried to kill both him and his mother, Mystique. As the villagers got dangerously close, Mystique made a ruthless decision: She chose to save her own life and tossed her infant over a waterfall. As luck would have it, Nightcrawler survived the fall, and a band led by a nearby gypsy queen, Margali Szardos, took him in and raised him in a traveling circus.

It was in Margali's traveling circus where Nightcrawler flourished. He became a gifted acrobat and high-wire performer. While audiences cheered his stunts, they believed his appearance was merely a costume covering a normal human form.

His daring feats eventually caught the eye of a Texas millionaire who wanted to purchase the circus with the hopes of making Nightcrawler a star in an American freak show. Choosing escape over exhibition, Nightcrawler fled the circus and ended up in Winzeldorf, Germany. Mistaken by its citizens as the perpetrator of a recent spate of murders, Nightcrawler faced imminent death when a mob approached him with upraised stakes. A quick-thinking Professor X interceded and psionically paralyzed the mob, allowing Nightcrawler to escape and join the X-Men.

These days, Nightcrawler's faith allows him to believe that the X-Men are fighting a winning battle for universal acceptance of their kind—no matter how high the odds are stacked against them.

Real Name: Kurt Wagner
First Appearance: *Giant-Size X-Men #1* (1975)

Height: 5'9"
Weight: 161 lbs
Eye Color: Yellow
Hair Color: Black

POWERS/WEAPONS

- Teleportation
- Accomplished circus acrobat and aerialist
- Prehensile tail
- Limited invisibility
- Master fencer

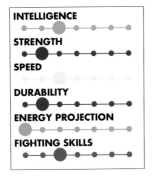

INTELLIGENCE
STRENGTH
SPEED
DURABILITY
ENERGY PROJECTION
FIGHTING SKILLS

Art by Matt Smith

NORTHSTAR

Real Name:
Jean-Paul Beaubier
First Appearance:
X-Men #120 (1979)

Height:	5'11"
Weight:	175 lbs
Eye Color:	Blue
Hair Color:	Black

By the age of six, Jean-Paul Beaubier had lost both his birth parents and his adoptive parents. Forced into a foster home, he struck out on his own and wound up in Quebec City, where he met Raymonde Belmonde. Belmonde would become his mentor and guardian, helping him cope not only with his emerging mutant powers but with his homosexuality as well.

In his late teens, Jean-Paul secretly used his powers to become a world-champion skier. He ultimately took home an Olympic gold medal for Canada. His achievements on the ski slopes also helped make him a wealthy young man. But Jean-Paul yearned for better; as he grew older, he sought to use his powers more openly and less selfishly.

After some time spent in a radical separatist group, Northstar came to join forces with the Canadian government's super hero program **Alpha Flight**. One of the other recruits stuck out—a woman named **Aurora** who bore an astonishing familial resemblance to Northstar. The pair learned they were in fact brother and sister, and had been separated by fateful choices made by Northstar's adoptive parents.

After Northstar told the press he lived his life as a gay man, the Canadian government dispatched an operative to pull him back from the media limelight—not just because Northstar had revealed his homosexuality, but also because they feared he was somehow involved in the murder of a journalist who had previously threatened to out him.

Northstar was exonerated and eventually returned to Alpha Flight, but he soon tired of living life in the spotlight. He left to write his autobiography, *Born Normal*. At a book signing in Philadelphia, Northstar was recruited by **Jean Grey** to join an ad-hoc team of **X-Men** to combat **Magneto** and his planned all-out attack against mankind. At **Professor X**'s behest, Northstar now teaches business and economics at the **Xavier Institute**.

Art by Kia Asamiya

POWERS/ WEAPONS

• Flight
• Super-speed
• Light projection

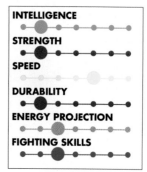

INTELLIGENCE
STRENGTH
SPEED
DURABILITY
ENERGY PROJECTION
FIGHTING SKILLS

POLARIS

Only through a sinister plot did Lorna Dane learn she was a mutant. Mesmero captured Lorna and placed her in a machine that activated her latent mutant power to control magnetic forces. In the nick of time, Iceman found the captive girl and freed her from her imprisonment.

Grateful for her release, Polaris teamed up with the X-Men and entertained an attraction to Iceman—but it was Havok who stole her heart. Using her skills to fight for peace between man and mutant with the X-Men, Polaris worked side-by-side with Havok. But the X-Men's enemies continued their efforts to seize her magnetic powers. Growing tired of these threats to her safety, she, along with Havok, eventually left the X-Men to pursue graduate studies in geophysics.

Only months after finishing her degree, Polaris was possessed by the psychic entity named Malice, who forced her to battle Havok and to join the Marauders in their quest to slaughter the Morlocks. Once out from under Malice's control, Polaris joined Havok on a government-funded mutant strike force. After an extended period of time with the team, Polaris ended her romantic relationship with Havok and her professional relationship with the team.

Thinking she was doing a good deed, Polaris traveled to Genosha with Magneto to supply him with power and help him keep order over the country he ruled. Her plan backfired when Magneto launched a full-scale assault on the last Genoshan town opposing his rule. Polaris attempted to stop him, but she was unsuccessful and left the island. Along with Quicksilver, Polaris returned to covertly intercede in Magneto's tyrannical rule. But she got caught up in catastrophe when mutant-hunting Sentinels, sent to the island by Cassandra Nova, appeared and murdered more than 16 million of its citizens. While Polaris survived, she carried millions of magnetic patterns within herself—including recordings of the last moments of Genosha, and the last words of Magneto himself. Professor X tried as best as he could to exorcise Polaris's mind of the magnetic demons. But she remains traumatized, slowly heading towards insanity.

Real Name:
Lorna Dane (legal name since adoption, given name unrevealed)
First Appearance:
X-Men #49 (1968)

Height: 5'7"
Weight: 138 lbs
Eye Color: Green
Hair Color: Green

INTELLIGENCE

STRENGTH

SPEED

DURABILITY

ENERGY PROJECTION

FIGHTING SKILLS

POWERS/ WEAPONS

• Magnetic manipulation

Art by Kia Asamiya

PROFESSOR X

Real Name:
Charles Xavier
First Appearance:
X-Men #1 (1963)

Height: 6'
Weight: 173 lbs
Eye Color: Blue
Hair Color: None

He is the man from whom the dream was born and the man who leads the others in pursuit of it. The dream is simple yet profound: that someday both man and mutant and all of humanity will live in peace together, setting aside fear and prejudice for understanding and acceptance.

It is a dream worth pursuing—and one not yet fulfilled.

The son of nuclear researcher Brian Xavier and his wife Sharon, Charles's superior telepathic abilities came to light after tragedy. After his father's accidental death, his mother married Dr. Kurt Marko, a former colleague of Brian's, and both Kurt and his son Cain (**Juggernaut**) moved into the family mansion. It didn't take long before Cain—a brutal, mean-spirited boy—began to bully Charles. To punish his son, Kurt beat the boy. But Charles had made a telepathic connection with Cain and, unable to control his burgeoning powers, felt every blow Cain received as if he were being hit himself.

A natural genius, Charles graduated high school at the age of 16. He completed college in only two years, and went on to do his graduate work at Oxford University.

It was at Oxford that fellow student **Moira MacTaggert** crossed his path. After spending

Art by Adam Kubert

many hours together passionately discussing genetic mutation, the two fell deeply in love and decided to marry. But when Moira's estranged husband, Joe MacTaggert, a lance corporal in the Royal Marines, showed up and started to bully Charles, something in Charles snapped. To prove that he wasn't the wimp MacTaggert accused him of being, Charles enlisted in the military after his Oxford graduation.

His efforts ultimately proved futile: Moira unexpectedly and without explanation called off their engagement. Charles, in turn, quit the military and set off to see the world. His first stop was Cairo, Egypt, where he met and battled the criminal mutant Amahl Farouk, the **Shadow King**. His great victory led to his greater epiphany. After this encounter Charles swore to devote his life to protecting humanity from misguided mutants hell-bent on using their powers to dominate the world—and to protecting innocent mutants from those in humanity who would oppress them.

Art by Frank Quitely

After Cairo, Charles headed to Israel, where he befriended a man named Magnus, later known as **Magneto**. Together, Charles and Magneto battled terrorists and came to learn of each other's mutual mutant abilities. But that was where their paths diverged: Charles vehemently believed in peaceful man and mutant coexistence and Magneto did not. Instead, Magneto saw mutants, *Homo superior*, as just another class of people primed for exploitation, harassment, and ultimately annihilation by *Homo sapiens*. He believed war with humanity was the only solution to the problem. The two mutants not only parted philosophies; they eventually parted ways.

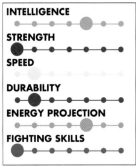

On his way back to the U.S., Charles was crippled in an accident—but a brilliant mind cannot be broken by withered limbs and Charles returned to his family's mansion in New York more resolved than ever to realize his dream of peaceful coexistence between man and mutant. He began by helping a traumatized 11-year-old girl named **Jean Grey**, a mutant with similar, though less heightened, telepathic abilities. After succeeding with Jean, Charles—with help from his former fiancée Moira—opened Xavier's School for Gifted Youngsters and Jean became the first in a long line of equally gifted yet misunderstood mutants he helped. In time, he altered and redesigned the mansion to accommodate all the mechanisms and methods that were needed to fulfill his dream. He also recruited five highly skilled mutants to form the **X-Men**, assembled to fight for all of humanity under a veil of secrecy.

POWERS/ WEAPONS

- Telepathy
- Astral projection

Through his tireless efforts to save and train young mutants, Professor X recruited dozens of them into his school in the ensuing years. In addition, he is constantly redefining and fine-tuning his X-Men to meet the changing needs of an increasingly hostile world. Charles had always received wide acclaim as an advocate for peaceful relations between man and mutant, and as an expert authority on genetic mutation. But he operated in silence, closely guarding his own mutant status and that of his X-Men. That all changed when the malevolent **Cassandra Nova**, inhabiting her brother's body, addressed a worldwide television audience and broke the news about who Charles and the X-Men really were. In hindsight, Charles realized she had done what he should have done. To this day, Charles Xavier is proud of who he is and what he stands for. He leads by example—a man guided by high principles and an unwavering focus upon peace for all.

PSYLOCKE

Real Name:
Elisabeth Braddock
First Appearance:
Captain Britain #8 (1976)

Height:	5'11"
Weight:	165 lbs
Eye Color:	Blue
Hair Color:	Black, dyed purple

While her twin brother Brian became Captain Britain, Betsy Braddock took a different route. By day, photographers shot her for the covers of the world's most popular fashion magazines, and she did runway shows from Milan to New York. By night, she used her psychic powers to live out her secret life of serving her homeland as a special agent.

When Brian stepped down as Captain Britain, Betsy was persuaded to take up the mantle. But Betsy's career as England's preeminent costumed champion came to an untimely end when one of her brother's foes savagely beat her until she was blind and near death. Realizing that her telepathic abilities compensated for her lack of sight, Betsy traveled to Switzerland to recuperate. But Mojo abducted her there and outfitted her with artificial, camera-like eyes in an attempt to beam what she saw into the homes of the citizens of Mojoworld. Ultimately, Professor X's New Mutants rescued her and short-circuited Mojo's programming while preserving her ability to see. Psylocke joined up with the X-Men but faced a new peril when the villainous Mandarin and Spiral captured her and transplanted her psyche into the body of the Ninja assassin Revanche. Likewise, Revanche's soul came to dwell in Psylocke's form. When the assassin succumbed to the Legacy Virus, Psylocke became trapped forever in her new form.

Ultimately, Psylocke left Xavier's mansion with a small strike force of fellow X-Men in search of Destiny's diaries, which contained the map of human history for the next thousand years. While in Spain, most of the team was captured and trapped within a maze. Psylocke, Beast and Rogue found themselves in the headquarters' control center. Separated from their teammates, they battled Vargas. Betsy engaged her opponent in a duel to the death; she lost, dying when Vargas speared his sword through her abdomen. Psylocke's sudden demise left her teammates to balance the scales and complete the quest for the missing diaries. Psylocke will forever be remembered as a fierce fighter and a powerful mutant who wanted nothing more than to strive for peace between man and mutant.

Art by Josh Middleton

POWERS/ WEAPONS

- Telepathy
- Mind bolts
- Psionic ability that allows for the creation of a "psychic knife"

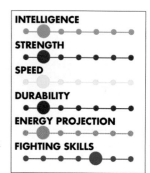

INTELLIGENCE

STRENGTH

SPEED

DURABILITY

ENERGY PROJECTION

FIGHTING SKILLS

ROGUE

A first kiss is long remembered for its sweetness, a fond reminder of a more innocent time. But for Rogue, her first kiss will forever be remembered as the first sign of her extraordinary gift—and curse.

Rogue recalls growing up along the banks of the Mississippi River in the Deep South, but remembers little else. In her adolescence, she and her boyfriend, Cody Robbins, snuck away to steal a kiss. As their lips touched, Rogue momentarily assumed Cody's memories and became him, with his thoughts and realities competing against her very own for dominance in her mind. With Cody in a coma from the experience, and her own mind unable to process what had just occurred, Rogue panicked and ran—a pattern she'd find herself repeating many times in her young life. Desperate to keep her real name a secret, she dubbed herself "Rogue" and vowed to live her life as a hermit. By doing so, she believed she could keep her mutant ability in check; by never touching anyone again, she could never risk injuring herself or another person again.

Shortly afterwards, Mystique, another mutant, found the young Rogue. Rogue agreed to leave with the shape-shifting mutant only after Mystique appealed to Rogue's outsider status by revealing her true bluish form. Mystique raised Rogue as her foster daughter and the two became very close.

But Mystique had other ideas for her adopted next of kin, including inducting the girl into her terrorist organization, the Brotherhood of Evil Mutants. In the Brotherhood, Rogue participated in jailbreaks, assassination attempts, and superhuman brawls. During a pivotal battle against the super hero Ms. Marvel, she permanently absorbed the woman's power of flight, superhuman strength, near-invulnerability, and—much to Rogue's dismay—Ms. Marvel's psyche. Her mind became a war zone of competing thoughts and memories as she struggled to maintain her own identity alongside that of Ms. Marvel.

Real Name:
Unrevealed
First Appearance:
Avengers Annual #10
(1981)

Height: 5'8"
Weight: 142 lbs
Eye Color: Green
Hair Color: Brown, with a white streak

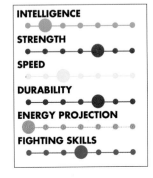

INTELLIGENCE
STRENGTH
SPEED
DURABILITY
ENERGY PROJECTION
FIGHTING SKILLS

POWERS/ WEAPONS

- Ability/memory absorption through physical contact
- Invulnerability
- Superhuman strength
- Flight

Art by Jim Lee

ROGUE

Rogue's powers grew increasingly out of control. Desperate, she had but one option: turn to Professor X for help. Breaking free of the Brotherhood meant betraying her foster mother for Mystique's adversary Professor X, but to Rogue, it was the only way she could make her life at all worth living.

Professor X decided the best way to help her manage her ability—and to use it for the greater benefit of humankind—was to let her join the X-Men. However, not all the X-Men thought the idea of fighting alongside a recent enemy held much merit. Professor X stepped into the fray and explained to the skeptical X-Men that only they could help her achieve her potential for using her abilities for good and not evil. Helping her own cause, Rogue displayed genuine sincerity in her commitment to turn her life around; eventually, the other X-Men came to embrace her as truly one of their own.

And one X-Man, Gambit, embraced something more: her heart.

Gambit and Rogue fell deeply in love. The only thing that stood between them were her powers. Forced to wear a costume that keeps nearly all of her skin covered to prevent unwanted skin-to-skin contact, Rogue can never even touch the one she loves out of fear her absorption powers will have devastating effects. She learned this lesson when, in a moment of weakness, she first kissed Gambit and absorbed a memory he had never wished to be known: his unwitting participation in the deaths of countless scores of Morlocks.

But their love is strong and deep, and Rogue continues to struggle with the physical and emotional conflicts surrounding her absorption powers. While she does use her abilities to perform critical tasks that benefit the cause, she still battles with adjusting her life around them.

Despite her own personal crises, Rogue always remains capable of profound compassion and deep commitment to Professor X's dream. Whatever she can contribute she will, knowing that no contribution is too small when the future of all her species is on the line.

Art by Rodolfo Migliari

SAGE

This beautiful fighter and spy often relies on something far more important than brawn: the power of her beautiful mind. From computing to healing, Sage's brain is the ultimate source of power in times of need.

Known only as Tessa, she came to the X-Mansion in secret when Professor X recruited the first team of X-Men. No one but Professor X knew of Tessa's presence; it was his intention to use her as a spy.

On her first mission, Tessa infiltrated the Hellfire Club to gain the trust of its leader, Sebastian Shaw. Shaw took a shine to the young woman, and for years, Tessa advised and counseled him in all aspects of his shady business—all the while gathering information to report back to Professor X. Shaw never once suspected her and gratefully relied on her for her uncanny ability to function as a living computer.

After years of seemingly loyal service to Shaw, Tessa left the employ of the Hellfire Club and worked for the X-Men, acting as a member of the team's support crew. Later, Tessa left Xavier's mansion with a small strike force of fellow X-Men in search of Destiny's diaries, which mapped out human history for the next thousand years. Dubbed "Sage" by Storm, Tessa proved instrumental in saving the life of Beast after he was injured in an encounter with Vargas. She revealed a previously unseen mutant ability, advancing Beast's evolution to its next stage, which healed him of his injuries and activated his latent secondary mutation.

But her former employer would come calling one more time. After uncovering Sage's deception, an enraged Shaw allied himself with Lady Mastermind to exact revenge on his former assistant. Lady Mastermind trapped Sage in a convincing illusion, making her believe that she was once again Shaw's assistant back in the Hellfire Club. Sage was freed by Lifeguard and returned the favor by catalyzing Lifeguard's brother Slipstream's latent mutant power.

What she sees, she remembers; what she remembers can be recalled in an instant, with perfect clarity. Yet she still remains an enigma. Her teammates know little of her, yet she seems to know everything about them.

Real Name:
Tessa (full name unrevealed)
First Appearance:
X-Men #132 (1980)

Height: 5'7"
Weight: 135 lbs
Eye Color: Blue
Hair Color: Black

Art by Salvador Larroca

| INTELLIGENCE |
| STRENGTH |
| SPEED |
| DURABILITY |
| ENERGY PROJECTION |
| FIGHTING SKILLS |

POWERS/WEAPONS

- Telepathy
- Ability to record and analyze vast amounts of data, and recall specific information with incredible speed and accuracy
- Projection of astral form
- Manipulation of mutagenic fields
- Ability to catalyze latent mutant abilities

SHADOWCAT

Real Name:
Katherine Pryde
First Appearance:
X-Men #129 (1980)

Height: 5'6"
Weight: 132 lbs
Eye Color: Hazel
Hair Color: Brown

For any normal 13-year-old, a headache could simply be the physical manifestation of the daily stresses of life. But for Kitty Pryde, a simple headache turned out to be so much more.

In her suburban bedroom in Deerfield, Illinois, Kitty closed her eyes briefly to find some respite from the troubling, intense headaches she'd been suffering. Upon opening her eyes, she found herself not in her bed, but on the living room floor directly below it. This was the first time Kitty Pryde passed through a solid object. It would not be her last.

The headaches Kitty had been having were no ordinary headaches—they were the first sign of her emerging mutant abilities. And very powerful people knew about them. Courted by both Professor X and Emma Frost to join their very different academies for mutants, Kitty took an immediate dislike for Emma and chose to go with Professor X.

Unused to rejection, Emma kidnapped Kitty's visitors and Kitty participated in a fight to rescue them. Her achievement did not go unnoticed, and she soon joined the ranks of the X-Men as Shadowcat.

Despite her young age, Shadowcat stayed on with the X-Men even though Professor X organized the New Mutants, who were closer to her own age. Through the X-Men, Shadowcat experienced a world vastly different than the one she had known: She traded suburban comfort for battles in outer space and experienced her first love not in the hallways of high school, but surrounded by the walls of the Danger Room.

While she is content to spend time with her loyal companion, the dragon Lockheed, Shadowcat has maintained tight relationships with other mutants as well, including Wolverine, who served for a time as her mentor, and her great love, Colossus, who wound up sacrificing himself for Professor X's dream. Numb and disillusioned after Colossus's death, Shadowcat left the X-Men to find new ways to live out Professor X's vision. Today, a student at the University of Chicago, she makes her own effort to fight for the dream in which she still believes: peace.

POWERS/ WEAPONS

- Ability to slide through solid objects
- Walk on air
- Disrupt inner workings of electrical devices

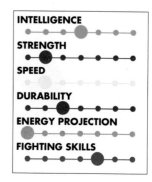

INTELLIGENCE
STRENGTH
SPEED
DURABILITY
ENERGY PROJECTION
FIGHTING SKILLS

Art by Leinil Francis Yu

STACY X

$\mathcal{S}$he is a woman with a past. She has made choices no woman should ever have to make—yet so many tragically must. But now she has one shot at redemption with the <u>X-Men</u>.

Alone and on the run from her past, Stacy X had nowhere to turn. With no job skills, a volatile personality, and no money to support herself, she had to take the route so many other girls in the same situation had taken to survive: prostitution. Using her mutant abilities to her benefit, Stacy walked the streets and earned her living. Eventually, Stacy was scouted by Madame Drache of the X-Ranch, a mutant brothel located in Nevada. If only to have a safe, stable place to live, Stacy agreed to go.

But Stacy's safe place to live didn't stay safe for long. The congregants and leaders of the mutant-hating Church of Humanity attacked the mutant brothel and burned it to the ground. The X-Men arrived and rescued Stacy, but no one else survived. Stacy, having no other options, reluctantly agreed to join the X-Men and use her mutant abilities in ways she had never entertained.

Stacy would have to confront the Church members who so eagerly sought her demise. During one of her first missions with the X-Men, Stacy was accidentally teleported by a member of the Church to the Church's cathedral headquarters. Stacy's interrogation by the <u>Supreme Pontiff</u>, however, was cut short by the X-Men who arrived and rescued her before any harm could be done.

While Stacy's brash personality often rubbed the team the wrong way, the X-Men couldn't deny her pivotal role in their defeat of <u>Vanisher</u>, the head of a drug cartel that peddled a drug granting short-term mutant abilities. Stacy used her powers to distract Vanisher for several days, allowing <u>Archangel</u> enough time to use his significant financial resources to shut down the cartel. Stacy's transformation from streetwalker to super hero came full circle when she played a key role in the X-Men's victory over <u>Black Tom Cassidy</u>. Using her mutant pheromones, Stacy stopped Cassidy from draining the X-Men's vital bodily fluids, which he was using to nourish himself.

Despite occasional infighting with her teammates, Stacy's affiliation with the X-Men has proven to be nothing short of life-affirming. Instead of using her mutant pheromones to ply an illicit trade, Stacy now makes practical use of them, allowing the X-Men to gain ground on those who would do harm. With the X-Men, Stacy walks the path to redemption after heading down a road leading straight to nowhere for so long.

Real Name:
Unrevealed
First Appearance:
Uncanny X-Men #399 (2001)

Height:	5'11"
Weight:	160 lbs
Eye Color:	Green
Hair Color:	Black

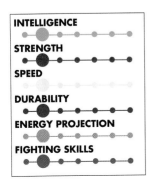

INTELLIGENCE

STRENGTH

SPEED

DURABILITY

ENERGY PROJECTION

FIGHTING SKILLS

POWERS/ WEAPONS

- Pheromone control
- Snakelike skin

Art by Tom Raney

STORM

Real Name:
Ororo Munroe
First Appearance:
Giant-Size X-Men #1
(1975)

Height: 5'11"
Weight: 159 lbs
Eye Color: Blue
Hair Color: White

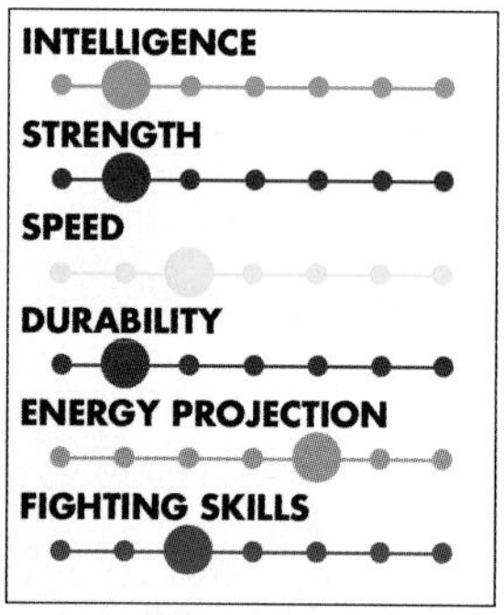

INTELLIGENCE

STRENGTH

SPEED

DURABILITY

ENERGY PROJECTION

FIGHTING SKILLS

POWERS/ WEAPONS

- Weather control
- Flight

She commands nature—but, by her very mutant nature, defies it at the same time.

Born to N'Dare, a princess of an African tribe, young Ororo bore all the physical trademarks of the long line of African priestesses before her: white hair and blue eyes. When she was only six months old, her mother and photojournalist father relocated from Manhattan to Cairo, Egypt.

Five years after the Munroes' arrival, Cairo transformed into a hotbed of conflict. A terrorist bomb exploded in their home, killing Ororo's mother and father. Terrified but still alive, Ororo was trapped under tons of rubble, right next to her mother's lifeless body. This traumatic experience scarred Ororo in many ways, and contributed to her lifelong battle with claustrophobia.

Ororo, now an orphan, wandered

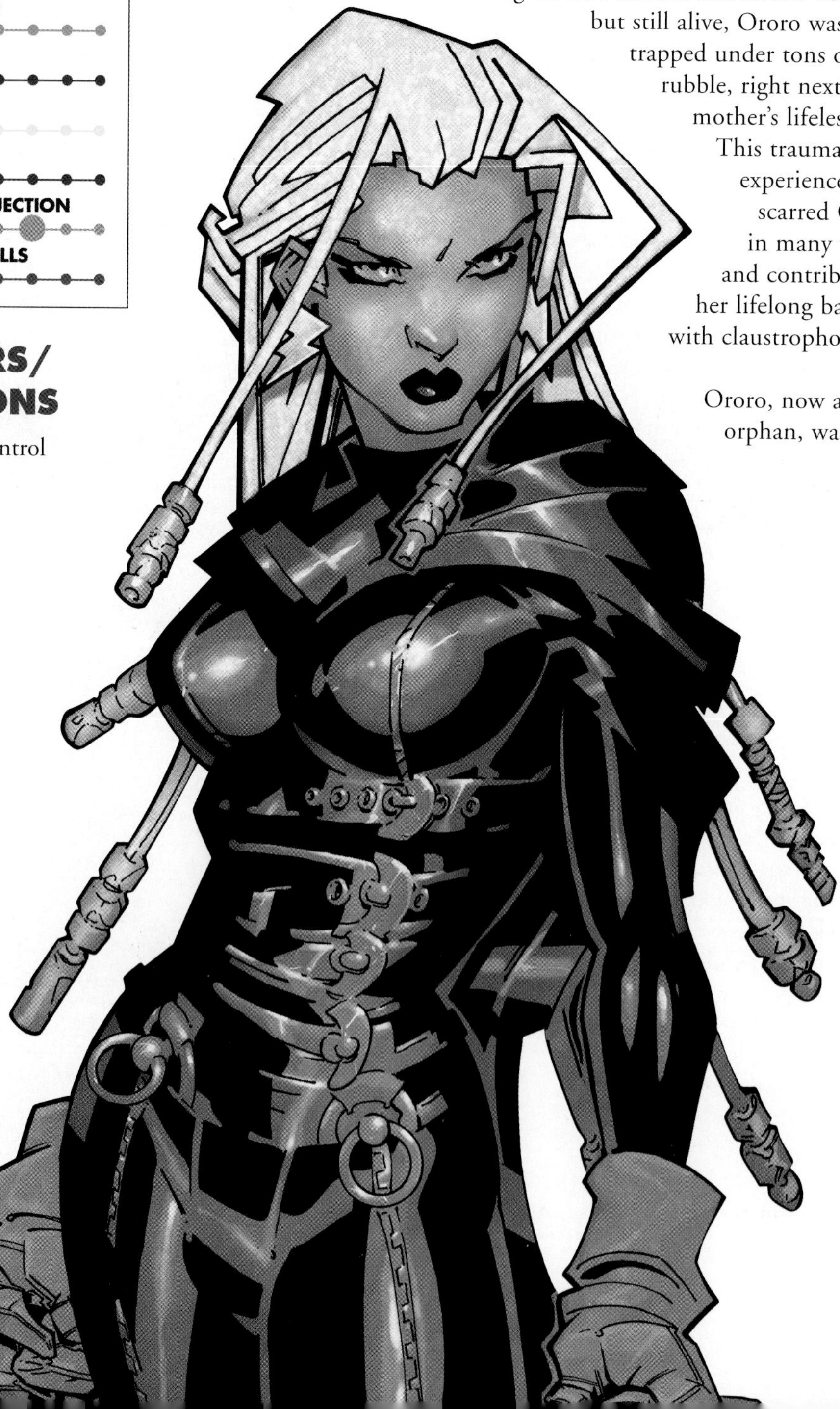

Art by Chris Bachalo

the streets and came under the care of a master thief, Achmed el-Gibar. El-Gibar offered the young girl more than a hot meal and safe place to stay—he offered her a trade, and Ororo quickly became the best pickpocket and thief in all of Cairo.

Yearning for her true homeland, Ororo ended her life of crime at age 12 and left the city. Traveling by foot, she crossed the Sahara Desert alone, bound for her ancestral home on the Serengeti Plain.

In the shadow of Mount Kilimanjaro, Ororo carefully honed her ability to manipulate the weather. So adept had she become that she aided the local tribes, ensuring they suffered neither drought nor floods. With harvests plentiful, the locals worshipped Ororo as the Storm Goddess.

Knowing of her weather-altering abilities with the peoples of the Plain, **Professor X** appealed to Ororo to help rescue the **X-Men**, who were trapped on the mutant island of **Krakoa**. She agreed and quite ably assisted the X-Men in their time of need.

Once her mission had been completed, Professor X asked her to join the second generation of the X-Men. Ororo, sensing she could use her powers on a much broader scale and reach many more people in need, accepted his kind offer.

Storm's power over the weather is dictated by her emotions. Annoyed, she causes storm clouds to gather; angry, she can summon winds that carry her high in the sky where she commands thunder to rumble and lightning bolts to crackle. But these episodes of fury belie her true nature—a peaceful woman content to surround herself with the beauty of nature.

Hated and feared for her strange and frightening abilities—rather than revered as she had been in Africa—Storm has stood fast with the X-Men in their attempts to promote peaceful coexistence between man and mutant. Except for brief periods away from the team, she has remained a member, and they have stuck by her, even during the temporary loss of her mutant abilities.

A powerful presence among the X-Men, Storm bears responsibility for the safety of those she leads and is deeply loyal to her friends and teammates. As one with the Earth, Storm truly understands the sanctity of life and feels a strong obligation to help preserve life in all its forms—man or mutant, plant or animal, good or evil.

Art by Rodolfo Migliari

NATHAN SUMMERS

Real Name:
Nathan Christopher Summers

First Appearance:
Uncanny X-Men #201 (1986)

Height: 6'8"
Weight: 350 lbs
Eye Color: Blue
Hair Color: White

When an incurable techno-organic virus threatened his young life, Nathan's father, <u>Cyclops</u>, made a difficult decision and sent his child 2,000 years into the future—a future ravaged by the ongoing genetic war between man and mutant. There, Nathan could learn to manage the virus with help from the Askani, a tribe of mutants who taught and lived by a practical belief system that focused on the psyche as a way to bring about inner peace. In the postapocalyptic landscape of the future, the Askani tutored Nathan in their spiritual and martial disciplines and taught him to use his telekinetic powers to fight the aggressive virus running rampant through his body. Nathan was a success in all of his Askani studies, save one: Despite controlling the virus, he could not entirely keep it from taking its toll, and when he reached his teens, half of his body took on a metallic, robotic appearance.

The Askani felt strongly that Nathan was predestined to save the world from the coming genetic war—and the reign of <u>Apocalypse</u>. Their philosophies compelled Nathan to come to terms with his destiny, no matter how daunting it seemed. Upon reaching maturity, Nathan returned to the present to fight for the future.

Nathan fought in mercenary and intelligence groups and learned to be a master soldier. Ultimately, he left that life behind and chose to fight for the same goals espoused by <u>Professor X</u> and the <u>X-Men</u>, which included his father Cyclops and stepmother, <u>Jean Grey</u>. Nathan soon formed a team comprised of Professor X's former students, a proactive strike force that exacted retribution on anyone who might threaten to persecute mutantkind. Such activity contradicted the X-Men's philosophy of responding to outbreaks of violence rather than prevention of hostility. Ultimately, Nathan and Professor X could not mend the chasm in their ideologies and so parted ways.

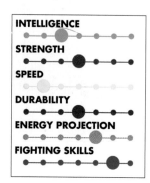

Although he has ended the threat of Apocalypse, Nathan firmly believes that the war between *Homo superior* and *Homo sapiens* is very much a thing of the present—and that only he has the wherewithal to stop it. All over the globe, Nathan intercedes in the gravest of struggles: terrorist attacks, ethnic cleansing, and the oppression enforced on minorities by tyrannical dictatorships. Not one to impose his will on others, the man now known as Soldier X sows the seeds of peace wherever he visits, hoping the Askani philosophy in which he so fervently believes will one day save the world from itself.

POWERS/ WEAPONS

- Telepathy
- Telekinesis
- Extremely proficient with any number of conventional weapons

INTELLIGENCE	●●●○●●●
STRENGTH	●●●●●●●
SPEED	●●○●●●●
DURABILITY	●●●●●●●
ENERGY PROJECTION	●●●●○●●
FIGHTING SKILLS	●●●●●●●

Art by Igor Kordey

SUNFIRE

America murdered his mother, he believed. And America would have to pay. But this fierce nationalist also came to believe something else: that differences must be set aside in order to avoid any war—including the one between man and mutant.

He was born Shiro Yoshida, the son of a woman severely and irrevocably affected by the devastation wrought when the United States dropped an atomic bomb on Hiroshima during World War II. After his mother died giving birth to him, Shiro was left in the care of his fiercely anti-American uncle Tomo in order for Shiro's father to continue his work as one of Japan's greatest statesmen. As Shiro's father worked to improve relations between Japan and America, his uncle Tomo diligently instructed Shiro in anti-Americanism. Shiro came to know Americans as his mother's murderers, and was willing to avenge her death at any cost.

At his uncle's urging, Sunfire traveled to the United States to destroy the Capitol Building in Washington, D.C. His father was present and attempted to persuade Sunfire out of completing his terrorist act—but as Sunfire listened to his father's reasoning, his uncle Tomo arrived and killed Shiro's father. Furious, Sunfire killed his uncle in retaliation and returned to Japan.

Proclaiming himself Japan's protector, Sunfire soon found some common ground with American super heroes; while his anti-Americanism considerably lessened over the years, his nationalist pride remained strong. Professor X took notice and invited Sunfire to join the X-Men—but after a single mission with the team, Sunfire resigned due to his unwillingness to leave Japan, his preference for operating solo, and his lack of ambition to act as a full-time costumed adventurer. Sunfire still remains a steadfast ally of the X-Men and aids them on numerous occasions. Sunfire also uses his powers on special missions for the Japanese government.

Sunfire recently accepted an offer from Professor X to join the global mutant search-and-rescue operation known as the X-Corporation, based in its Mumbai, India branch.

Working with Professor X, Sunfire now balances his allegiance to his beloved home country Japan with his allegiance to serve the best interests of man and mutant throughout the world.

Real Name:
Shiro Yoshida
First Appearance:
X-Men #64 (1970)

Height:	5'10"
Weight:	175 lbs
Eye Color:	Dark brown
Hair Color:	Black

Art by Alan Davis

INTELLIGENCE

STRENGTH

SPEED

DURABILITY

ENERGY PROJECTION

FIGHTING SKILLS

POWERS/ WEAPONS

- Ionization of matter into a fiery plasma state, capable of reaching 1,000,000 degrees Fahrenheit
- Flight

THUNDERBIRD II

Real Name:
Neal Sharra
First Appearance:
X-Men #100 (2000)

Height: 5'9"
Weight: 165 lbs
Eye Color: Brown
Hair Color: Black

Neal Sharra knows all about loss. He lost his brother. He lost his lovers. But he'll never lose sight of one thing: winning the war against mutant discrimination and prejudice at the hands of humankind.

Born into a wealthy family in Bangladesh, Neal led a carefree life until he returned home one day to find his brother Sanjit missing. While Neal's father dispatched a police detective named Karima to find his son, Neal struck out on his own search. Before long, trouble arose and Karima had to rescue Neal. Together, the pair pushed forward in hopes of finding Sanjit; after awhile, the two found something else: love.

But their love could not save them from capture at the hands of **Bastion**'s cyborg **Sentinels**— one of whom turned out to be Sanjit. As Bastion tried to turn Neal into another of his Sentinels, the stress manifested Neal's latent mutant abilities and he destroyed Bastion's base in short order. Sanjit overcame his Sentinel programming long enough to disable the other Sentinels, but was fatally wounded in the ensuing melee. Neal attempted to escape with Karima, but discovered she had already become a cyborg Sentinel. Neal fled alone.

Upon his return home, Neal's parents learned of his mutant abilities. Knowing of the discrimination he might suffer in Bangladesh, they suggested that he meet with their old friend, **Moira MacTaggert**. Through Dr. MacTaggert, Neal met **Professor X** and was asked to join the **X-Men**. He gratefully accepted.

As part of the X-Men, Thunderbird helped with the search for **Destiny**'s diaries, purported to map out the history of humans and mutants for the next thousand years. He also formed a romantic relationship with his teammate **Psylocke**. But the relationship was doomed: Psylocke died at the hands of **Vargas**, and Thunderbird took the loss hard.

After he allowed time to heal his pain, Neal began to take tentative steps towards a relationship with **Lifeguard**. Together, the pair decided to leave the X-Men, dedicating themselves to the search for her missing brother, **Slipstream**.

POWERS/ WEAPONS

- Ability to convert ambient heat energy into super-heated plasma
- Concussive force blasts from his hands
- Flight

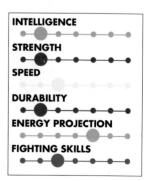

INTELLIGENCE					
STRENGTH					
SPEED					
DURABILITY					
ENERGY PROJECTION					
FIGHTING SKILLS					

Art by Kevin Sharpe

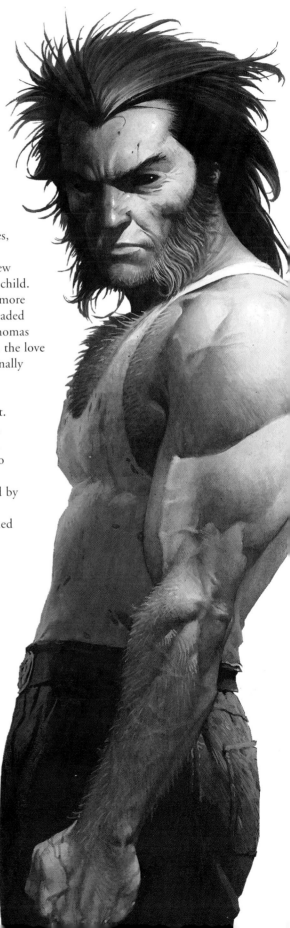

WOLVERINE

Real Name:
Born James Howlett, currently known as Logan

First Appearance:
Incredible Hulk #180 (1974)

Height: 5'3"
Weight: 195 lbs
Eye Color: Brown
Hair Color: Black

*S*mall in stature yet ferocious in battle, Wolverine's greatest enemy might just be himself. Having taken many years to tame his overwhelming impulses to kill, Wolverine knows that even the slightest lapse in control could easily allow him to slip into a berserk rage.

In the 19th century, John and Elizabeth Howlett welcomed their second son, James, into their privileged family. But having privilege never entitled young James to an easy life. His mother withdrew and became distant after the untimely death of her first child. And James—a sickly, asthmatic child—relied more and more on the companionship of his friend and tutor, the redheaded Rose, and "Dog," the son of the cruel groundskeeper Thomas Logan, to help him through his childhood and give him the love and attention he so desperately wanted from his emotionally absent mother.

But James's good times with his companions did not last. During a struggle at the Howlett home, Thomas Logan, with his son by his side, killed James's father. A terrified James witnessed the event and even before it had time to sink in, another trauma emerged: bony claws suddenly protruded from the back of each of his hands. Confused by what was happening to him, James lashed out; in the ensuing panic, he inadvertently killed Thomas and slashed Dog's face. Elizabeth, while unharmed by the violence surrounding her, could not cope with what she had witnessed and killed herself soon after.

Turned out of his home by a grandfather who feared what he had become, James suffered a complete breakdown. While his mutant abilities helped heal his mind, they also blocked all memories of the terrible events that had just occurred. Authorities blamed Rose and James for the murders, and Rose ran

INTELLIGENCE

STRENGTH

SPEED

DURABILITY

ENERGY PROJECTION

FIGHTING SKILLS

POWERS/ WEAPONS

- Animal-keen senses
- Accelerated healing factor
- Adamantium-laced skeleton
- Retractable adamantium claws

Art by Esad Ribic

WOLVERINE

away with James to a British Columbia mining colony. She renamed the boy "Logan" to disguise his true identity.

At the mining camp, Logan concealed more than just his identity—he also concealed his growing love for Rose. He began to spend time with the wolves in the wild, convinced in his heart he had more in common with them than with people. The locals nicknamed him "Wolverine" after his remarkable tenacity in refusing to back away from all of the bullying he took. Day by day, Wolverine worked on his strength and built up his ferocity—qualities which would later serve him well.

His time at the mining colony ended when Dog tracked him down. Finally remembering the night of his father's death, Wolverine viciously fought Dog. But during the battle, Wolverine accidentally impaled his beloved Rose on his claws, killing her. Haunted by the deed, he ran into the woods and disappeared for many years. After his disappearance, the legend of Wolverine was born.

For years he traveled the world, even stopping in Japan for a length of time, where he trained as a samurai. Along the way, his mind again healed itself, helping him forget his tragedies while combating the effects of the aging process. Today, though more than a century old, Wolverine resembles a man in the prime of his life.

In the late 20th century, the CIA, working through the Canadian government, forced Wolverine to participate in a diabolical experiment called **Weapon X** in which scientists grafted the indestructible metal adamantium to his skeleton and claws. Even worse, they implanted memory devices that shaped a new, convoluted past—one more suitable to their needs than his. Because of their experiments, Wolverine can no longer separate fact from fiction and knows little of his own true past other than it was filled with pain and loss.

While Wolverine worked as an operative for the government, **Professor X** asked him to join the **X-Men**. Wolverine agreed to join Professor X—partly because he truly believed in Professor X's vision, and partly because he was attracted to the beautiful, yet already attached redhead **Jean Grey**.

Serving with the X-Men has given Wolverine what he had been missing for so long: a cause worth fighting for. Still somewhat unpredictable in battle and prone to an occasional berserk rage, Wolverine has nevertheless proven to be a tremendous asset to the team, living up to the slogan, "He is the best there is at what he does."

At home in the **Xavier Mansion**, Wolverine continues to work on recovering his lost memories. And thanks to his affiliation with Professor X and the X-Men, Wolverine now feels he has the closest thing to his own family for the first time in his life.

Art by Frank Quitely

XORN

All he wants is peace. Peace for mutants. Peace among humans. Peace within himself. Born in China, Xorn lived an ordinary life until he reached his adolescence, when everything changed. Just two days after reaching puberty, a microscopic star exploded in Xorn's head, causing panic among Chinese authorities who imprisoned him and forced him to wear an iron mask to contain his powers. After years of imprisonment, a depressed Xorn came to see no other alternative to suicide. He decided to kill himself by creating a black hole that would not only envelop him but destroy the whole world. But the X-Men had been alerted to the Chinese mutant's plight and arrived to liberate him from the prison. Cyclops talked Xorn out of suicide and offered him a place with the X-Men. Xorn accepted, but chose not to stay in Westchester, but at a Tibetan monastery where he hoped he could find some peace.

Before long, Cyclops came calling on Xorn at the monastery in an effort to help rid himself of a nano-Sentinel infection brought on by Cassandra Nova. But members of the Shi'ar Imperial Guard, also under the control of Cassandra, captured them and took them aboard their spacecraft. After freeing themselves, Xorn and Cyclops teleported back to the Xavier Mansion, where Xorn successfully rid the team of the nano-Sentinel infection. He also performed another miraculous feat: He healed Professor X's body, allowing him to walk again.

In America, Xorn drew on his devout Zen Bhuddist beliefs to come to terms with the mutant-hating fervor of the masses, and continues to look for ways to spread beauty and peace. He thought he had discovered such a way in a boy named Sonny. Xorn found the young mutant with his mother, who had just overdosed them both in an effort to end their lives peacefully rather than suffer the violent deaths they knew they would soon meet at the hands of humans. Xorn was convinced that Sonny, now in a transitional giant-sized state, would evolve in a few short days into something much more beautiful. But neither Xorn nor Sonny would see that happen. Despite the course of drugs ravaging his body, Sonny somehow still rose to his feet—and went on a rampage through the streets. Xorn tried to stop him but failed, and the police shot and killed Sonny. And someone that was to have been so beautiful died because he entered an ugly world too soon.

Xorn was crushed by the senseless loss and could do nothing more than remind himself that life goes on. After taking up a teaching position at the Xavier Institute, Xorn can concentrate on helping himself—and the world at large—find peace and beauty among themselves, and among those whom they hate and fear.

Real Name: Unrevealed
First Appearance: *New X-Men Annual* (2001)

Height: 6'2"
Weight: 240 lbs
Eye Color: Inapplicable
Hair Color: Inapplicable

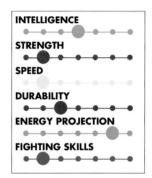

INTELLIGENCE
STRENGTH
SPEED
DURABILITY
ENERGY PROJECTION
FIGHTING SKILLS

POWERS/ WEAPONS

- Manipulation of gravitational wavelengths
- Extraordinary healing abilities

Art by Frank Quitely

CHANGELING

| Real Name: | Kevin Sidney | **Height:** | 5'11" |
| **First Appearance:** | *X-Men* #35 (1967) | **Weight:** | 180 lbs |

POWERS/WEAPONS
• Shapeshifting

Serving in the subversive mutant organization Factor Three, Changeling learned of the group's plot to wipe out both man- and mutantkind. Unwilling to go along with the plan, he freed <u>Professor X</u> and <u>Banshee</u>, captives of his organization, in the hope they could thwart Factor Three. The <u>X-Men</u> defeated the mastermind of the scheme. Soon afterwards, Changeling was diagnosed with terminal cancer. Hoping to redeem himself, he offered to impersonate Professor X so he could go into seclusion. Changeling died heroically staving off an attempt to destroy the Earth.

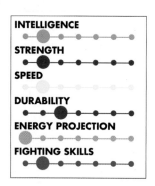

INTELLIGENCE
STRENGTH
SPEED
DURABILITY
ENERGY PROJECTION
FIGHTING SKILLS

DUST

| Real Name: | Sooraya (full name unrevealed) | **Height:** | Unrevealed |
| **First Appearance:** | *New X-Men* #133 (2002) | **Weight:** | Unrevealed |

POWERS/WEAPONS
• Ability to transform herself into a living dust cloud

A prisoner of an Afghan mutant slave trade, Sooraya unleashed a deadly attack when her captors tried to remove the burka from her head. The young girl activated her mutant power: Transforming herself into a living dust cloud, she stripped the flesh off her captor's bones. <u>Wolverine</u> arrived after the attack and took her to the Mumbai, India, branch of the global mutant search and rescue organization known as the <u>X-Corporation</u>, where she was befriended by <u>Jean Grey</u>.

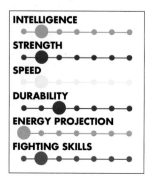

INTELLIGENCE
STRENGTH
SPEED
DURABILITY
ENERGY PROJECTION
FIGHTING SKILLS

GATEWAY

| Real Name: | Unrevealed | **Height:** | 4'6" |
| **First Appearance:** | *Uncanny X-Men* #229 (1988) | **Weight:** | 80 lbs |

POWERS/WEAPONS
• Creation of teleportational gateways
• Psionic speech

He is a mystery, a man who operates in silence, always in touch with the spiritual force of his people. Christened "Gateway" by the criminals who captured him and forced him into service, the aborigine spent most of his time at the <u>Reavers</u>' Australian headquarters silently sitting atop a rock. After defeating the Reavers, the <u>X-Men</u> took over their headquarters and freed Gateway. Soon after, Gateway began voluntarily using his teleportational powers to transport the X-Men from place to place. Gateway, though still an enigma, has become an unofficial member of the team.

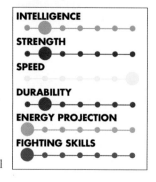

INTELLIGENCE
STRENGTH
SPEED
DURABILITY
ENERGY PROJECTION
FIGHTING SKILLS

POWERS/WEAPONS

- Master of magnetism

| **Real Name:** | Joseph | **Height:** | 6'2" |
| **First Appearance:** | *X-Men* #46 (1995) | **Weight:** | 190 lbs. |

INTELLIGENCE

STRENGTH

SPEED

DURABILITY

ENERGY PROJECTION

FIGHTING SKILLS

Unaware of his true origins and believing he could be Magneto, Joseph sought out the X-Men, thinking his powers of magnetism could be of some use to them. While he proved a valuable asset to the team, Joseph eventually left to find out who he really was. After discovering he was a clone of Magneto, Joseph sought to make up for all the troubles the original Master of Magnetism had wrought. Joseph finally sacrificed his life to repair the Earth's magnetosphere after Magneto damaged it.

JOSEPH

POWERS/WEAPONS

- Subconscious manifestation of whatever power or ability is necessary in a given situation

| **Real Name:** | Heather Cameron | **Height:** | 5'10" |
| **First Appearance:** | *X-Treme X-Men* #6 (2001) | **Weight:** | 156 lbs |

INTELLIGENCE

STRENGTH

SPEED

DURABILITY

ENERGY PROJECTION

FIGHTING SKILLS

Heather Cameron saved lives on the beaches of Australia, but she could not save herself from the form she would eventually assume. During her rescue by the X-Men from the murderous Chinese Triad, Cameron was forced to reveal herself as a mutant. After she and her brother Davis (Slipstream) joined the X-Men, Lifeguard began to become more alien- and avian-like, giving rise to the belief that her mother was a member of the Shi'ar race. Sliptream, panicked over the possibility of sharing the same fate, ran away and Lifeguard left the X-Men to search for him.

LIFEGUARD

POWERS/WEAPONS

- Flight
- Ability to breathe fire
- Resistance to telepathy

| **Real Name:** | Unrevealed | **Length:** | 2'6" |
| **First Appearance:** | *Uncanny X-Men* #166 (1983) | **Weight:** | 20 lbs |

INTELLIGENCE

STRENGTH

SPEED

DURABILITY

ENERGY PROJECTION

FIGHTING SKILLS

Belonging to an alien race called the Flock, Lockheed ran across the X-Men while fighting the Brood and saved Shadowcat's life. When the X-Men fled Broodworld shortly before it was destroyed, Lockheed managed to hitch a ride back with them and wound up at the Xavier Mansion. The little dragon soon won the affection of Shadowcat and became her near-constant companion. Shadowcat named him Lockheed after a character in a fairy tale she had created, which itself had been named after the X-Men's jet.

LOCKHEED

MAGGOT

Real Name: Japheth (full name unrevealed)
First Appearance: *Uncanny X-Men* #345 (1997)
Height: 6'8"
Weight: 350 lbs

Told by doctors his terrible stomach pains were caused by cancer, and not wanting to drain the family's finances with medical treatment, young Japheth left his small South African village to commit suicide. He wound up in the desert only to be found and saved by **Magneto**, who helped uncover the true cause of the boy's malady: two slug-like creatures that dwelled within Japheth's guts. Years later, Maggott joined the **X-Men**. Some time after leaving the team, Maggott was captured by **Weapon X** and executed at the Neverland mutant concentration camp.

POWERS/WEAPONS
• Two slug-like creatures dwelling in his digestive system that allow his body to absorb the energy from the matter they digest

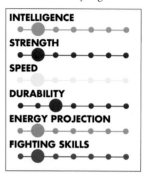

MIMIC

Real Name: Calvin Montgomery Rankin
First Appearance: *X-Men* #19 (1966)
Height: 6'2"
Weight: 225 lbs

Brazen, conceited, and arrogant, Calvin Rankin acquired his ability to "mimic" both human abilities and superhuman powers after an accident in his father's lab, and he exploited them for his own benefit. At college, he met many of the **X-Men**, whom he mimicked one after the other. Blackmailing them with the threat of exposing their true identities, Mimic pressured them to let him join the team. **Professor X** agreed, knowing that Mimic's abilities could be of some use. But his arrogance and combativeness got him thrown out of the X-Men.

POWERS/WEAPONS
• Able to mimic any human or superhuman abilities or powers

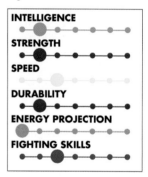

CECILIA REYES

Real Name: Cecilia Reyes
First Appearance: *X-Men* #65 (1997)
Height: 5'7"
Weight: 138 lbs

Once her mutant power awakened, Dr. Cecilia Reyes caught the attention of **Professor X**. He offered her the chance to join the **X-Men**, but she refused in order to continue her medical career. Fired after being blamed for the escape of one of her patients, **Pyro**, and with nowhere else to turn, Reyes reluctantly joined the X-Men. After an unintentional addiction to the illegal drug Rave jeopardized her life and career, Cecilia sought Professor X's help to overcome the dependence. Once she got clean, Cecilia left the X-Men and opened her own medical clinic.

POWERS/WEAPONS
• Subconscious generation of force-fields

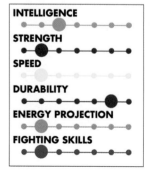

POWERS/WEAPONS

- Instantaneous transportation to another location via a tachyon stream

INTELLIGENCE

STRENGTH

SPEED

DURABILITY

ENERGY PROJECTION

FIGHTING SKILLS

Real Name: Davis Cameron
First Appearance: *X-Treme X-Men* #6 (2001)

Height: 6'1"
Weight: 170 lbs

Marked for death by the Chinese Triad because of his father's criminal ties, Australian surfer Davis Cameron and his sister Heather were rescued by the <u>X-Men</u>. After the Triad was defeated, Davis chose to travel with the team to stay close to Heather, who had joined their ranks as <u>Lifeguard</u>. Over time, Lifeguard began changing into a more alien- and avian-like form, giving rise to the belief that her mother was a member of the <u>Shi'ar</u> race. Slipstream panicked. Out of fear that the same transformation might befall him, he transported himself away from the team.

SLIPSTREAM

POWERS/WEAPONS

- Telepathy
- Telekinesis
- Generation and manipulation of fire
- Projection of force bolts

INTELLIGENCE

STRENGTH

SPEED

DURABILITY

ENERGY PROJECTION

FIGHTING SKILLS

Real Name: Rachel Summers
First Appearance: *X-Men* #141 (1981)

Height: 5'7"
Weight: 125 lbs

Rachel Summers, the daughter of <u>Cyclops</u> and <u>Jean Grey</u>, hails from an alternate future in which genocidal <u>Sentinels</u> rule. Hoping she could change history, Rachel traveled back in time and joined the <u>X-Men</u>. Rachel eventually managed to return to the future from which she had come; she and her teammates were able to change the directives of all the Sentinels of the era to preserve all life, thereby ending the genocide that had prevailed for years. Later shunted to yet another alternate future, Rachel became Mother Askani and helped raise <u>Nathan Summers</u>.

RACHEL SUMMERS

POWERS/WEAPONS

- Superhuman strength, speed, stamina, and durability

INTELLIGENCE

STRENGTH

SPEED

DURABILITY

ENERGY PROJECTION

FIGHTING SKILLS

Real Name: John Proudstar
First Appearance: *Giant-Size X-Men* #1 (1975)

Height: 6'10"
Weight: 225 lbs.

John Proudstar's mutant abilities manifested when he returned to his Apache reservation after military service, and <u>Professor X</u> discovered and recruited Thunderbird into the second generation of <u>X-Men</u>. Thunderbird aided in the rescue of the original X-Men from <u>Krakoa</u>. Later attempting to stop a fleeing extortionist, Thunderbird jumped onto the criminal's plane as it took off. He ripped open part of the plane and wreaked havoc on its internal systems. Thunderbird furiously pummeled the aircraft until it finally exploded, killing him instantly.

THUNDERBIRD

ACOLYTES

Art by Leinil Francis Yu

First Appearance:
X-Men #1 (1991)

The Acolytes started out as a group on the run from American soldiers, and were led to <u>Magneto</u> by their leader <u>Fabian Cortez</u>. When Magneto granted them refuge within his headquarters on Asteroid M, they left Fabian out in the cold and reformed as Acolytes under Magneto. But Fabian was incensed; before escaping Asteroid M, he helped bring about its destruction. When Asteroid M plummeted to Earth, the Acolytes perished and only Magneto survived.

Fabian Cortez was then free to lead a second incarnation of Acolytes whose first mission involved an attack on Our Mother of the Sacred Heart School to search for a child they hoped would become a powerful mutant in his adolescence. Once the <u>X-Men</u> stepped in, the Acolytes released the child— but only after finding out the boy had Down's syndrome, which made him untrainable in the eyes of the Acolytes. Following the brutal murders of dying hospitalized humans at Our Mother of the Sacred Heart School and an aborted attack on a military base, Magneto returned. Magneto, bitter about Cortez's betrayal, found and recruited the mutant known as <u>Exodus</u> to help reclaim the Acolytes. After ousting Cortez, Magneto returned to space and established Avalon, a new space station headquarters for the group created from alien <u>Shi'ar</u> technology.

When Exodus retreated to Avalon, he and the other Acolytes noticed a floating cocoon in outer space and brought the object onboard. But the cocoon housed the dimensionally displaced mutant called Holocaust who, after reawakening, killed several Acolytes. During Holocaust's battle with Exodus, Holocaust sent Avalon and its occupants hurtling towards Earth. Only those Acolytes who made it to an escape pod were saved.

By the time Avalon crash-landed, Magneto had been granted control over Genosha by the United Nations, and he attracted more Acolytes to help serve him on the island. But Magneto also faced the retribution of other Acolytes, who mounted the Carrion Cove rebellion against his rule of Genosha. But this uprising was nothing compared to the <u>Sentinel</u> attack initiated by <u>Cassandra Nova</u> that saw the destruction of the mutant homeland. Every Acolyte, as well as their leader Magneto, is now presumed dead.

FABIAN CORTEZ

Originally just a leader of a group of mutants on the run from American soldiers, Fabian Cortez's life and mission were forever changed when he led his group to seek sanctuary on Asteroid M, a space station base created by Magneto that orbited the Earth. The group turned away from Fabian and swore allegiance to Magneto; they called themselves Acolytes.

But Fabian, once safely ensconced on the craft, quickly dismissed safety as a concern after losing his followers. Intent on wresting control of the group back from Magneto, Fabian wanted nothing more than to once again bask in the homage heaped upon him by a legion of followers. Using his "healing" power to harm Magneto, Cortez then helped orchestrate the destruction of Asteroid M. Cortez escaped, leaving Magneto and his Acolytes trapped on Asteroid M.

Thinking Magneto dead, Fabian elevated the leader to martyr status, and claimed to be Magneto's chosen successor—a successful tactic that enabled him to attract new mutants into the ranks of the Acolytes. Once his legion was assembled, a determined Fabian sent his Acolytes on one diabolical mission after another—all with murderous results. After an attack on a hospital in which Acolytes killed humans who were already dying, coupled with an aborted attack on a military base, Magneto returned with Exodus, exposed Cortez's betrayal, and reclaimed control of the Acolytes.

Though furious over the loss, Fabian was a patient man. He knew another opportunity would eventually present itself, allowing him to once again ascend to his leadership role. He did not have to wait long.

When Magneto was rendered incapacitated, Fabian eagerly resurfaced and vowed to take control of the war-torn island of Genosha. But before Fabian had the chance to cause the mutant revolt he thought would once again allow him to rise to power, Exodus arrived and put a stop to his plans.

It seemed that Fabian would never get what he ultimately wanted, so when a recovered Magneto was given control over Genosha by the United Nations, he offered Fabian a chance to redeem himself. Fabian, having given up any hope of becoming the Acolytes' leader, had no choice but to accept, and reluctantly became one of Magneto's advisors.

But Magneto tired quickly of his former adversary, and when he used his extraordinary powers to propel Fabian 50 miles to Carrion Cove, the physical trauma killed Fabian instantly.

Real Name: Fabian Cortez
First Appearance: X-Men #1 (1991)

Height: 6'5"
Weight: 214 lbs
Eye Color: Blue
Hair Color: Brown

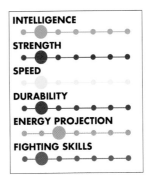

INTELLIGENCE
STRENGTH
SPEED
DURABILITY
ENERGY PROJECTION
FIGHTING SKILLS

POWERS/ WEAPONS

• Amplification of any super power or energy source

Art by Derec Aucoin

AMELIA VOGHT

Real Name: Amelia C. Voght
First Appearance: *Uncanny X-Men* #300 (1993)
Height: 6'1"
Weight: 156 lbs

POWERS/WEAPONS

- A form of teleportation called "transubstantiation" that allows her to transform the molecules of her body into an intangible mist that she can maneuver with her thoughts

Art by Leinil Francis Yu

After Professor X lost the use of his legs, Amelia Voght was the nurse who tended to him. Before long, the two fell in love, but Professor X's increasing talk of bringing together a team of mutants to help keep peace between man and mutant worried her. Believing his X-Men would only exacerbate already troubled human/mutant relations, Voght decided she loved Xavier too much to see him throw his life away on such folly and left him. If Voght could not make peace with Professor X's dream, perhaps she felt she needed to believe in someone else. Long after leaving Professor X, Voght found herself recruited by Fabian Cortez to join the Acolytes. Voght came to meet Joseph, an amnesiac who was certain he was the missing Magneto. Knowing he was not, Voght kept Joseph from claiming Magneto's terrible legacy. This act branded Voght a traitor in the Acolytes' eyes, and she was forced to sever all ties with them. When Magneto offered her a place in Genosha, Voght reluctantly accepted. She was present on Genosha when the deadly Sentinel attack was unleashed by Cassandra Nova. Voght is now missing and presumed dead.

INTELLIGENCE
STRENGTH
SPEED
DURABILITY
ENERGY PROJECTION
FIGHTING SKILLS

RUSTY COLLINS

Real Name: Russell Collins
First Appearance: *X-Factor* #1 (1986)
Height: 5'11"
Weight: 160 lbs

POWERS/WEAPONS

- Flame generation

Young Rusty Collins's powers manifested while he was in the Navy, and he accidentally burned a woman. Imprisoned for his act, Rusty burned a hole through his cell and, with the help of the original team of X-Men (including Cyclops and Jean Grey), he escaped. Cyclops and Jean took Rusty back to their headquarters, where they began training him in the use of his powers. Eventually, Rusty learned how to keep his power under control. There, Rusty also came to form a close relationship with another teammate, Skids. But the pair were kidnapped and brainwashed by mutant criminals, who then forced them to serve in the terrorist group the Mutant Liberation Front. After a particularly brutal battle, Rusty and Skids were transported to Avalon, where Magneto helped release them from their altered states. A grateful Rusty and Skids accepted Magneto's offer to join his Acolytes. On a mission with his team, Rusty and the other Acolytes discovered a frozen Holocaust drifting in space and brought him aboard their craft. But once the villain thawed, he needed energy to regenerate. As Holocaust drained Rusty's life force to restore himself, he killed the young man in the process.

INTELLIGENCE
STRENGTH
SPEED
DURABILITY
ENERGY PROJECTION
FIGHTING SKILLS

Art by Terry Shoemaker

POWERS/WEAPONS

- Enhanced strength and durability
- Steel-hard skin

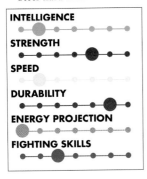

INTELLIGENCE	
STRENGTH	
SPEED	
DURABILITY	
ENERGY PROJECTION	
FIGHTING SKILLS	

Real Name: Joanna Cargill

First Appearance: *X-Factor* #4 (1986)

Height: 6'11"
Weight: 230 lbs

Originally allied with the Alliance of Evil, a group that battled the <u>X-Men</u>, Cargill was persuaded to join the <u>Acolytes</u>. When the Acolytes' orbital base Avalon was destroyed, Cargill helped <u>Cyclops</u> escape and find the X-Men's former base in the Australian outback. She was arrested, but escaped custody and returned to the Acolytes, eventually enlisting in the Genoshan Unified Military Patrol. Brainwashed by <u>Jean Grey</u>, Cargill helped rescue <u>Professor X</u>, who was being held prisoner by <u>Magneto</u> on Genosha.

JOANNA CARGILL

POWERS/WEAPONS

- Generation of quantum energy

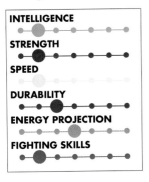

INTELLIGENCE	
STRENGTH	
SPEED	
DURABILITY	
ENERGY PROJECTION	
FIGHTING SKILLS	

Real Name: Unrevealed

First Appearance: *X-Men* #1 (1991)

Height: 6'4"
Weight: 190 lbs

As one of the founding members of the <u>Acolytes</u>, Chrome was aboard Asteroid M as it plummeted towards Earth. In an effort to shield <u>Magneto</u> from harm, Chrome used his powerful abilities to encase his leader in a protective shell. This act protected Magneto when the asteroid crashed. Chrome, however, could not act in time to save himself or the others—they all perished. Chrome was the very definition of an Acolyte, devoting all of his time and dedication to the cause and even offering the ultimate sacrifice to ensure the works of his leader would go on.

CHROME

POWERS/WEAPONS

- Hyper-empathetic awareness
- Limited psionic abilities

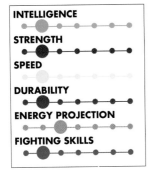

INTELLIGENCE	
STRENGTH	
SPEED	
DURABILITY	
ENERGY PROJECTION	
FIGHTING SKILLS	

Real Name: Anne-Marie Cortez

First Appearance: *X-Men* #1 (1991)

Height: 6'1"
Weight: 158 lbs

She was one of the first <u>Acolytes</u> to serve <u>Magneto</u>. But her service would not last long. Wounded when she and other Acolytes were fleeing agents of the law-enforcement agency S.H.I.E.L.D., Anne-Marie was healed by her brother <u>Fabian Cortez</u>. After the S.H.I.E.L.D. attack, Magneto took control of the Acolytes and ensconced his team on Asteroid M. But Fabian, consumed by his ambition to once again take charge of the group, struck out against Asteroid M. Anne-Marie was onboard the stricken asteroid as it hurtled towards Earth. She did not survive the crash.

ANNE-MARIE CORTEZ

DECAY

Real Name: Unrevealed
First Appearance: *Quicksilver* #9 (1998)

Height: 5'8"
Weight: 139 lbs

POWERS/WEAPONS
• Absorption of bio-energy

Thanks to a life force that constantly depleted itself, Decay aged rapidly. To survive, he absorbed the bio-energy from organic matter, which caused him to revert to a stable younger state. But Decay made a significant—and ultimately deadly—miscalculation when he siphoned off the energy from a source far too powerful for him. On the <u>Acolytes</u>' mission to Wundagore Mountain, Decay attempted to absorb the <u>High Evolutionary</u>'s energy. But the power proved too great for him to handle and caused him to explode. This energy ended his life instead of extending it.

INTELLIGENCE	
STRENGTH	
SPEED	
DURABILITY	
ENERGY PROJECTION	
FIGHTING SKILLS	

HARRY DELGADO

Real Name: Harry Delgado
First Appearance: *X-Men* #1 (1991)

Height: 6'8"
Weight: 240 lbs

POWERS/WEAPONS
• Ability to increase strength and size

A major in the international law-enforcement agency S.H.I.E.L.D., Harry Delgado led a team of agents chasing a shuttle stolen by <u>Acolytes</u> seeking refuge at <u>Magneto</u>'s orbital base on Asteroid M. Magneto took in the Acolytes, and Delgado snuck aboard, but was coerced into Magneto's service by the mental manipulations of <u>Anne-Marie Cortez</u>. Delgado was also a latent mutant, and those Acolytes who were able to manipulate the abilities of their brethren used his superhuman talents for their own ends. Delgado died in the destruction of Asteroid M, engineered by the treacherous <u>Fabian Cortez</u>.

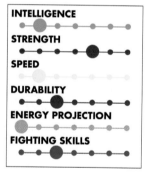

EXODUS

Real Name: Bennet du Paris
First Appearance: *X-Factor* #92 (1993)

Height: 6'
Weight: 195 lbs

POWERS/WEAPONS
• Vast psionic abilities
• Teleportation

Lying dormant in a rejuvenation chamber within a stronghold in the Alps since the 12th century A.D., Exodus's latent mutant powers slowly developed over time until <u>Magneto</u> liberated him in the 20th century. After ascending to become Magneto's trusted lieutenant, Exodus tried to exert his power over Genosha in his own quest for dominance. In Magneto's absence, Exodus disguised himself as the <u>Acolytes</u>' beloved leader. After the <u>X-Men</u> exposed his act as a charade, he left Genosha an island with no leader, and it soon erupted into civil war.

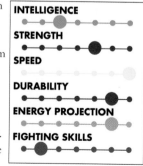

POWERS/WEAPONS

- Absorption of kinetic energy, which he then projects as explosive force
- Conduit for atmospheric wavelengths

Real Name:	Katu
First Appearance:	*Uncanny X-Men* #300 (1993)
Height:	5'11"
Weight:	171 lbs

INTELLIGENCE

STRENGTH

SPEED

DURABILITY

ENERGY PROJECTION

FIGHTING SKILLS

During a clash with powerful Soviet superagent <u>Omega Red</u>, Katu lost both of his arms. Swearing revenge, Katu equipped himself with bionic arms and joined the <u>Acolytes</u>. He seized upon an opportunity for vengeance, and he and other Acolytes briefly aligned themselves with <u>Nathan Summers</u> to stop Omega Red. In the ensuing battle with his archenemy, Katu unleashed his powers, causing a blast that seemingly killed him and Omega Red. Both survived, but it remains unclear what ill effects, if any, Katu suffers from turning his explosive power on himself.

KATU

POWERS/WEAPONS

- Ability to merge into a single being
- Plasma blasts from hands
- Flight

Real Name:	Harlan, Sven, and Eric Kleinstock
First Appearance:	*Uncanny X-Men* #298 (1993)
Height:	6'2" (all)
Weight:	190 lbs (all)

INTELLIGENCE

STRENGTH

SPEED

DURABILITY

ENERGY PROJECTION

FIGHTING SKILLS

Recruited by <u>Fabian Cortez</u> into the second incarnation of the <u>Acolytes</u>, the Kleinstock brothers engaged in a diabolical and deadly first mission: Along with other Acolytes, the trio helped attack Our Mother of the Sacred Heart School to capture a child whose mutant abilities, though not yet manifested, they hoped would eventually become an asset to the group. During the ensuing melee with the <u>X-Men</u>, Eric was shot and killed. Undeterred by their brother's death, the two remaining Kleinstocks continued to serve as Acolytes.

KLEINSTOCKS

POWERS/WEAPONS

- Phasing

Real Name:	Unrevealed
First Appearance:	*Uncanny X-Men* #300 (1993)
Height:	5'8"
Weight:	150 lbs

INTELLIGENCE

STRENGTH

SPEED

DURABILITY

ENERGY PROJECTION

FIGHTING SKILLS

Found in a church in Switzerland by the <u>Acolytes</u>, a reluctant Neophyte was swayed to join their cause. But once he saw <u>Fabian Cortez</u> torturing <u>Moira MacTaggert</u>, Neophyte had had enough. Using his mutant ability, he betrayed the Acolytes by phasing the <u>X-Men</u> into the Acolytes' stronghold off the coast of France. Infuriated by his betrayal, the Acolytes captured Neophyte and put him on trial for his crimes. Neophyte was spared execution and was instead banished to Earth, ultimately returning to the Acolytes in order to serve their new master, <u>Magneto</u>.

NEOPHYTE

REM-RAM

Real Name: Unrevealed
First Appearance: *X-Men: Magneto War* #1 (1999)
Height: 5'2"
Weight: 120 lbs

POWERS/WEAPONS

• Ability to enter and influence dreams

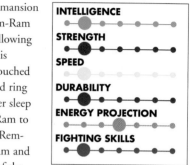

During the Acolytes' attack on Xavier's mansion that was ordered by Fabian Cortez, Rem-Ram was assigned to enter Rogue's dreams, allowing her to touch a man without absorbing his thoughts and feelings. In fact, she had touched Magneto—and even accepted a diamond ring from him—before being jarred out of her sleep by Gambit. When Fabian forced Rem-Ram to invade a conscious Professor X's mind, Rem-Ram failed. Fabian fled, leaving Rem-Ram and the remaining Acolytes on the grounds of the estate to seek asylum from the X-Men. Professor X refused them.

INTELLIGENCE
STRENGTH
SPEED
DURABILITY
ENERGY PROJECTION
FIGHTING SKILLS

SCANNER

Real Name: Unrevealed
First Appearance: *Uncanny X-Men* #300 (1993)
Height: 6'1"
Weight: 159 lbs

POWERS/WEAPONS

• Invisibility
• Intangibility
• Communication via thought projection

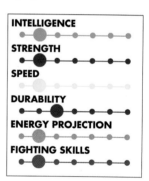

Scanner was among the many mutants recruited by Fabian Cortez to become a member of the second incarnation of the Acolytes. She was one of the few who survived not only the deadly attack by Holocaust, but also the subsequent loss of the Acolytes' orbital base Avalon thanks to an escape pod that also counted Cyclops among its fleeing passengers. Upon their return to Earth, Scanner helped Cyclops find the X-Men's base in the Australian Outback and willingly gave herself up to the authorities who sought her arrest. She later escaped, only to rejoin the Acolytes.

INTELLIGENCE
STRENGTH
SPEED
DURABILITY
ENERGY PROJECTION
FIGHTING SKILLS

SENYAKA

Real Name: Senyaka (full name unrevealed)
First Appearance: *Uncanny X-Men* #300 (1993)
Height: 5'10"
Weight: 173 lbs

POWERS/WEAPONS

• Drains the bio-electrical essence of others upon physical contact
• Accelerated healing powers
• Generation of psionic whips

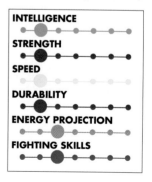

During the mission at Our Mother of the Sacred Heart School, Senyaka critically injured a nurse with his energy coils. An enraged Magneto struck back at the errant mutant, causing Senyaka to crush the life out of himself. But Senyaka survived by siphoning the life energy from the S.H.I.E.L.D. agents who had recovered his body. Seeking revenge, Senyaka set out to kill Lee Forrester, a former paramour of Magneto's. He failed. Senyaka then joined the ranks of former Acolytes who were aiding the Carrion Cove rebellion against Magneto's rule of Genosha.

INTELLIGENCE
STRENGTH
SPEED
DURABILITY
ENERGY PROJECTION
FIGHTING SKILLS

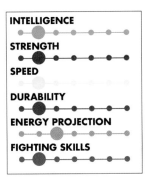

Real Name:
Unrevealed
First Appearance:
X-Men: Magneto War #1 (1999)

Height:
5'6"
Weight:
140 lbs

POWERS/WEAPONS

• Creation of a reaction that solidifies moisture into a hardened shell
• Shoots spray of barnacle-like crust

BARNACLE

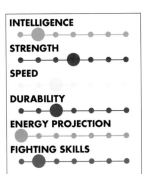

Real Name:
Unrevealed
First Appearance:
Quicksilver #9 (1998)

Height:
3'8"
Weight:
75 lbs

POWERS/WEAPONS

• Enhanced strength, durability, and agility
• Hyper-keen senses
• Natural flight

GARGOUILLE

Real Name:
Javitz (full name unrevealed)
First Appearance:
Uncanny X-Men #300 (1993)

Height:
9'1"
Weight:
1,200 lbs

POWERS/WEAPONS

• Enhanced strength, stamina, and durability

JAVITZ

Real Name:
Kamal (full name unrevealed)
First Appearance:
Magneto #1 (1996)

Height:
6'7"
Weight:
240 lbs

POWERS/WEAPONS

• Ability to absorb the properties of any physical object

KAMAL

SEAMUS MELLENCAMP

Real Name:
Seamus Mellencamp
First Appearance:
Uncanny X-Men #300 (1993)

Height:
6'
Weight:
191 lbs

INTELLIGENCE
STRENGTH
SPEED
DURABILITY
ENERGY PROJECTION
FIGHTING SKILLS

POWERS/WEAPONS

• Super-dense reptilian skin
• Heightened strength, agility, and endurance

MILAN

Real Name:
Milan (full name unrevealed)
First Appearance:
Uncanny X-Men #300 (1993)

Height:
5'10"
Weight:
160 lbs

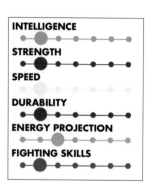

INTELLIGENCE
STRENGTH
SPEED
DURABILITY
ENERGY PROJECTION
FIGHTING SKILLS

POWERS/WEAPONS

• Electropathy, the ability to convert thought waves into electromagnetic signals
• Ability to communicate directly with computers
• Mind reading/mind projection

ORATOR

Real Name:
Unrevealed
First Appearance:
Magneto #1 (1996)

Height:
5'6"
Weight:
135 lbs

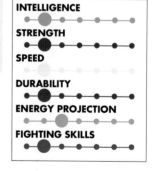

INTELLIGENCE
STRENGTH
SPEED
DURABILITY
ENERGY PROJECTION
FIGHTING SKILLS

POWERS/WEAPONS

• Emotion enhancement
• Heightened empathetic awareness

PROJECTOR

Real Name:
Unrevealed
First Appearance:
Quicksilver #9 (1998)

Height:
6'3"
Weight:
190 lbs

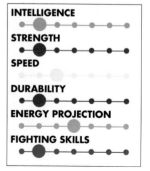

INTELLIGENCE
STRENGTH
SPEED
DURABILITY
ENERGY PROJECTION
FIGHTING SKILLS

POWERS/WEAPONS

• Projection of energy fields of solid light
• Ability to create structures out of energy fields, including ramps, spheres, and pillars

INTELLIGENCE

STRENGTH

SPEED

DURABILITY

ENERGY PROJECTION

FIGHTING SKILLS

Real Name:
Andrew Hamish Graves
First Appearance:
Uncanny X-Men #300 (1993)

Height:
5'6"
Weight:
150 lbs

POWERS/WEAPONS

• Feral mutation granting heightened strength, agility, and stamina

SPOOR

INTELLIGENCE

STRENGTH

SPEED

DURABILITY

ENERGY PROJECTION

FIGHTING SKILLS

Real Name:
Unrevealed
First Appearance:
X-Men: Magneto War #1 (1999)

Height:
5'8"
Weight:
130 lbs

POWERS/WEAPONS

• Ability to fire neuro-synaptic impulses from her fingertips that cause paralysis and temporary negation of any mutant ability

STATIC

INTELLIGENCE

STRENGTH

SPEED

DURABILITY

ENERGY PROJECTION

FIGHTING SKILLS

Real Name:
Carmella Unuscione
First Appearance:
Uncanny X-Men #298 (1993)

Height:
6'2"
Weight:
160 lbs

POWERS/WEAPONS

• Psionic exoskeleton, which serves as reflective body armor and carries a neuro-electric charge that can paralyze opponents

CARMELLA UNUSCIONE

INTELLIGENCE

STRENGTH

SPEED

DURABILITY

ENERGY PROJECTION

FIGHTING SKILLS

Real Name:
Unrevealed
First Appearance:
Uncanny X-Men #366 (1999)

Height:
5'9"
Weight:
160 lbs

POWERS/WEAPONS

• Ability to emit a gel-like liquid and ignite it into a fiery stream of napalm

VINDALOO

ALPHA FLIGHT

Art by Sean Chen

First Appearance:
Uncanny X-Men #120 (1979)

The time was right. The idea was born. And it would draw Canada out of the shadow of the United States once and for all. This is Alpha Flight. And they are the super powers of the Great White North. Born from James MacDonald Hudson's chance reading of a newspaper story recounting the formation of the Fantastic Four, America's team of fabled superhuman adventurers, Alpha Flight was created to aid and benefit Canada.

At first Hudson selected <u>Wolverine</u> to lead the team—but after Wolverine decided to join the <u>X-Men</u>, Hudson took the helm as <u>Guardian</u> and assembled the initial five members: <u>Aurora</u>, <u>Northstar</u>, <u>Sasquatch</u>, <u>Snowbird</u>, and <u>Shaman</u>. Shortly after the five finished training, <u>Marrina</u> and <u>Puck</u> came aboard. Under the direction of Department H, a subunit named after Hudson, Alpha Flight took off. While similar to the X-Men and the Fantastic Four in a number of ways, Alpha Flight differs slightly in its manner of operation: It is a team recognized by the government of Canada. Make no mistake, Alpha Flight is neither military nor menace—it's ultimately the realization of one man's dream for the alignment of Canadian men and mutants against threats to all their humanity. In service to all people of the world, Alpha Flight always maintains its allegiance to all the citizens of our neighbors to the North.

GUARDIAN

James Hudson, a Canadian engineer, invented an armored suit, controlled via a cybernetic helmet, that would enable its wearer to bore through the earth and explore geological resources. When Hudson learned of a plan by his employer to sell the suit to the American military, Hudson quit in disgust, along with executive assistant Heather McNeil (**Vindicator**). Refusing to let his invention be turned into a weapon, Hudson went back to the plant later and donned the armor. He used the suit to break into the company safe and destroy its blueprints. He then abandoned the suit, but took the helmet with him. Knowing he might face jail time for the theft, James and Heather approached the Canadian government and asked for their help. Realizing what a potential asset a man of Hudson's genius would be, the government declared that Hudson had been "retroactively" working for them for six years and that the helmet was indeed his property. James was then invited by the Canadian prime minister to create a top-secret research and development agency within the Canadian Ministry of Defense. The government named this agency Department H after James's last name, Hudson.

After returning from his honeymoon with Heather, James learned of the formation of the team of superhuman champions known as the Fantastic Four. Inspired by the news, Hudson decided to form a team of super-powered agents to protect Canada. Hudson intended **Wolverine** to lead this new team, which he called **Alpha Flight**. Wolverine had other plans, however, and left to join the **X-Men** instead. But his will to see Alpha Flight come to fruition could not be deterred. James decided to lead the team himself. On the advice of his teammate **Shaman**, James adopted the code name Guardian, which Shaman believed befit James's role.

Guardian is the heart of Alpha Flight. A man guided by principles and the compulsion to always do what's right for his team and country—no matter the cost.

Real Name:
James MacDonald Hudson
First Appearance:
X-Men #109 (1977)

Height: 6'2"
Weight: 190 lbs
Eye Color: Brown
Hair Color: Black

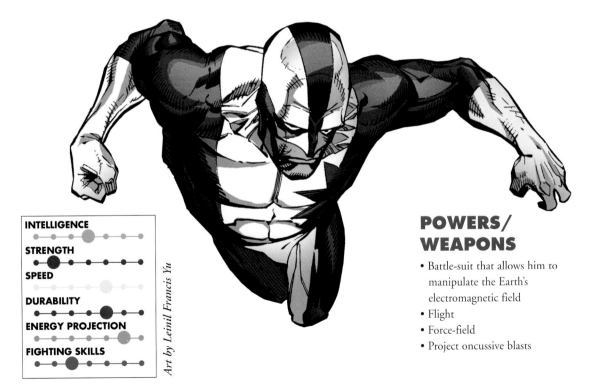

Art by Leinil Francis Yu

INTELLIGENCE

STRENGTH

SPEED

DURABILITY

ENERGY PROJECTION

FIGHTING SKILLS

POWERS/ WEAPONS

- Battle-suit that allows him to manipulate the Earth's electromagnetic field
- Flight
- Force-field
- Project oncussive blasts

PUCK

Real Name:
Eugene Milton Judd
First Appearance:
Alpha Flight #1 (1983)

Height: 3'6"
Weight: 225 lbs
Eye Color: Brown
Hair Color: Black

POWERS/ WEAPONS

- Uncanny gymnastic ability
- Professional-level athlete and fighter

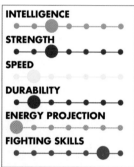

INTELLIGENCE

STRENGTH

SPEED

DURABILITY

ENERGY PROJECTION

FIGHTING SKILLS

Tall, strong, and athletic—Eugene Milton Judd was all of those things in 1939. But one encounter would alter who he was and leave him a man possessed.

When budding soldier-of-fortune Eugene received retainers from antiquities dealers to locate and return the mysterious Black Blade of Baghdad, he accepted the challenge. Further motivated by his own curiosity about the sword's supernatural origins, Eugene eventually tracked down the bounty in the Middle East. Making a fateful decision, he decided to keep the blade for himself. When Eugene touched the Blade, his own selfish thoughts helped unleash the evil within: Razaar, a murderous Persian sorcerer who had been trapped in his own blade long ago by fellow sorcerers who wanted to stop him from using the weapon to kill people. Razaar killed to absorb the life force of his victims to increase his own power and longevity.

When Eugene freed Razaar, the sorcerer began using the Black Blade to steal Eugene's life force, reducing Eugene's height in the process. Using his own previously untested knowledge of sorcery, Eugene fought back and imprisoned Raazer within his now dwarf-like body. Though he was now short in stature, the power of Razaar extended Eugene's life span and greatly slowed his aging process.

Decades passed before Puck came to join **Alpha Flight**, and when the Canadian government temporarily withdrew its funding of the program, Puck was left to seek other employ. But an emotionally turbulent time that involved his increasing guilt over killing a deadly menace and his increased attachment to **Vindicator** caused Puck to release Razaar from his being so he could regain his once tall and strong stature.

With Raazer free, Puck returned to his normal height, but he was now an elderly man. As a ferocious battle broke out between Alpha Flight and Razaar, Puck realized he had to use his own body to imprison Razaar once more for the sake of his team. After struggling for some time with the physical effects of Razaar's entrapment, Puck ultimately freed himself from Razaar's influence entirely through the intervention of magical forces. Despite his newfound freedom, Puck reverted once again to his dwarfish size and youthful appearance.

Puck is devoted to Alpha Flight and its principles, and he will engage in missions with the fervor of a man possessed—even now that he is free of the unwanted spirit within.

Art by Bryan Hitch

SASQUATCH

When Walter Langkowski played professional football for the Green Bay Packers, he independently studied the science of gamma radiation, a subject he fell in love with during college. Once his football career ended, Walter entered M.I.T. and quickly earned his Ph.D.; he went on to teach at McGill University in Montreal.

Accumulating all the information he could about human beings who had been transformed through exposure to gamma radiation, Walter intended to recreate, under controlled circumstances, the conditions that caused Dr. Bruce Banner to change into the Hulk. Walter spent over a million dollars of his own money on his research, and applied to the Canadian government for additional funding. James MacDonald Hudson (Guardian) arranged for the funding and procured an isolated laboratory north of the Arctic Circle for Walter. During a leave of absence from McGill, Walter designed and constructed a device to generate gamma radiation bombardments similar to those which had created the Hulk, but under laboratory conditions.

In his lab, Walter used his equipment to bombard himself with gamma radiation and was transformed into a ten-foot tall, superhumanly powerful creature. The shock of the transformation sent Walter on a savage rampage for hours before he reverted to human form.

Walter called his bestial form "Sasquatch," the Canadian name for the legendary "Bigfoot" creature that he resembled. Once he learned how to maintain his normal personality and intelligence as Sasquatch and had undergone a period of training in his newfound abilities, he joined Alpha Flight. Walter Langkowski continues to be his own successful experiment, a man changed into a superhuman Sasquatch with powers that can benefit all of mutantkind.

Real Name:
Walter Langkowski
First Appearance:
X-Men #120 (1979)

Height:
6'4" (as Langkowski),
10' (as Sasquatch)
Weight:
245 lbs (as Langkowski), 2,000 lbs (as Sasquatch)
Eye Color:
Blue (as Langkowski), red (as Sasquatch)
Hair Color:
Blond (as Langkowski), orange (as Sasquatch)

POWERS/ WEAPONS

- Superhuman strength and resistance to injury
- Ability to leap great distances
- Transformation into superhuman form through act of will

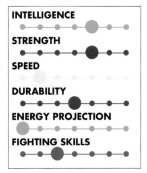

| INTELLIGENCE |
| STRENGTH |
| SPEED |
| DURABILITY |
| ENERGY PROJECTION |
| FIGHTING SKILLS |

Art by David Finch

SHAMAN

Real Name:
Michael Twoyoungmen
First Appearance:
X-Men #120 (1979)

Height:	5'10"
Weight:	175 lbs
Eye Color:	Brown
Hair Color:	Black

POWERS/ WEAPONS

- Powerful magical abilities
- Levitation
- Spirit staff

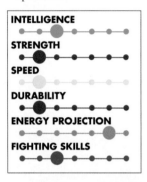

INTELLIGENCE

STRENGTH

SPEED

DURABILITY

ENERGY PROJECTION

FIGHTING SKILLS

Michael Twoyoungman's father believed in the healing and mystical powers of his ancestors' Indian sorcery. Michael believed in the power of Western medicine instead and became a physician with a thriving medical practice. He lived outside his family's reservation in Calgary with his wife, Kathryn, and their young daughter, Elizabeth (**Talisman**). After Michael's father died, his elderly grandfather asked him to become his student in mystical arts, insisting his knowledge could only be passed down to a blood relation. Michael refused, again reiterating his disbelief in ritualized magic.

When Michael discovered Kathryn had cancer, he promised Elizabeth he would dedicate himself to healing her mother. Nevertheless, all his skill couldn't save her. By seeming coincidence, Michael's grandfather died the same day as Kathryn. Elizabeth felt betrayed and went to live with neighbors; she would only reconcile with her father after many years spent hating him. Tormented by grief, Michael became a recluse. One day, compelled to open a gift his grandfather had left for him after he died, he discovered a mystical medicine pouch and the skull of his grandfather, to which his grandfather's spirit was bound. The spirit appeared to Michael and trained him in the mystical arts of the Saracee Indians.

When mystical forces drew Shaman to a desolate area in Canada, the goddess Nelvanna explained the reason for his calling: His help was needed in order for her to give birth to a demigod child. When Shaman helped bring **Snowbird** into the world, he was also called on to raise the child as his own. In a few years, Snowbird aged to full adulthood. At this point, the two were sought out by **Vindicator** and **Guardian** and recruited into **Alpha Flight**.

When Shaman suffered a crisis of confidence, he renounced the use of his medicine pouch. Losing faith in himself caused Shaman to lose his mystical powers. Returning to the life of a hermit, he was again visited by the spirit of his grandfather, who taught him a new approach to native magicks. After passing a number of tests, Michael gained new mystical abilities as well as a "spirit staff" with which he could summon the spirits of nature and ask them to do his bidding.

Art by Ethan Van Sciver

SNOWBIRD

Snowbird was raised by <u>Shaman</u>, whom her mother Nelvanna, the Eskimo god, had summoned to act as a midwife during her demigod-child's birth. When Snowbird was born, Shaman cast a spell that helped bring her into the world. Snowbird aged rapidly, reaching her early 20s in a short span of time. During that time, their neighbors James and Heather Hudson (<u>Guardian</u> and <u>Vindicator</u>) visited them, and Shaman explained his mystical powers and Snowbird's origin to the couple. Guardian then asked both of them to join a team of super-powered agents he was forming. They both accepted and underwent a period of training in the use of their special powers, eventually joining <u>Alpha Flight</u>.

Hudson helped Snowbird create the human cover identity of Anne McKenzie, and she was installed as a records officer for the Royal Canadian Mounted Police. One of McKenzie's fellow officers, Doug Thompson, fell in love with her. Even after she revealed to him that she was Snowbird, the two were married, and she became pregnant with his child. Outraged that she would thus ally herself with a mortal, the Eskimo gods forbade her to return to their realm. When the time came for Snowbird to give birth, she traveled with her husband, Shaman, and other members of Alpha Flight to a mystical place of power in the Canadian Arctic to deliver her child and bind its spirit to the Earth, as had been done for her. Unknown to Shaman, the body of Captain F.R. Crozier lay buried underground for more than 100 years in a state of suspended animation. Crozier was still alive and forced his spirit to take possession of Snowbird's newborn son, transforming the infant's body into a fully mature adult. Crozier fled, and Thompson tracked him to a mining town, where Crozier infected him with a fatal disease. Thompson died after informing Alpha Flight of Crozier's location. Shaman forced Snowbird to assume her sasquatch form and attack Crozier. After Snowbird killed Crozier's body, he attempted to possess hers. Vindicator had no choice but to strike down Snowbird to prevent that from happening.

Years later, resurrected through a combination of science and magic, Snowbird rejoined Alpha Flight. Finally free of her obligation to the gods, Snowbird is able to have the "normal" life and career she had once sought, though lives with the regret that her husband and child are not there to share it with her.

Real Name:
Narya
First Appearance:
X-Men #120 (1979)

Height: 5'10"
Weight: 140 lbs
Eye Color: Blue
Hair Color: Blonde

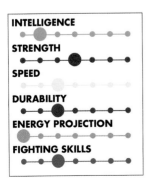

INTELLIGENCE
STRENGTH
SPEED
DURABILITY
ENERGY PROJECTION
FIGHTING SKILLS

POWERS/ WEAPONS

- Mystical ability to assume the form of any animal whose natural habitat is the Canadian arctic north

Art by Phil Noto

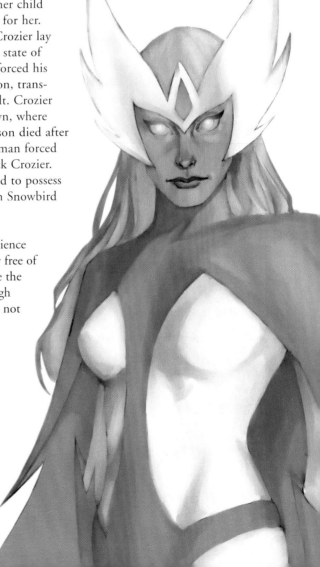

VINDICATOR

Real Name:
Heather McNeil Hudson

First Appearance:
X-Men #139 (1980)

Height: 5'5"
Weight: 120 lbs
Eye Color: Green
Hair Color: Red

By chance—and by choice—she is a woman of great resources: intelligent, powerful, and willing to fight for love and justice, no matter the cost.

To help her family's income, Heather took a full-time job at an early age. At merely 17, thanks to her great organizational talent and intelligence, Heather became the private secretary to Jerome "Jerry" Jaxon, vice president in charge of research and development of the Am-Can Petroleum Company in Edmonton, Alberta.

While working at Am-Can, she fell in love with the much older Dr. James MacDonald Hudson (**Guardian**). After Hudson stole an armored suit he had created to prevent Jaxon from selling it to the American military for purposes it was not intended, Heather helped Hudson seek the aid of the Canadian government in order to avoid prosecution. When Heather and James explained the situation, the government realized they could benefit from Hudson and his inventive genius and created Department H specifically for him.

Within a year, Heather and Guardian were married. While honeymooning in a Canadian national park, the pair encountered a feral **Wolverine**, who came to view the couple as his surrogate parents as they nursed him back to health. But when James tapped Wolverine to lead his fledgling **Alpha Flight** team, Wolverine refused and the trio parted ways. Instead, Guardian assumed the helm of Alpha Flight—until a former associate of Jaxon captured Heather in retaliation for her and her husband's initial betrayal. When Alpha Flight came to her rescue, Heather could do nothing but stand back in horror and watch her husband seemingly die in the ensuing fight.

The members of Alpha Flight subsequently chose Heather to succeed her husband as the team's leader. After a second clash with Jaxon's associate, who was wearing a reconstructed version of her husband's battle-suit, Heather believed she too needed to become an active combatant on the team and also began wearing a modified version of her husband's former battle-suit. After proving herself in combat, Heather became known as the Vindicator.

Much to Vindicator's surprise, Guardian was resurrected, and together the couple continues to lead Alpha Flight; they eagerly anticipate the birth of their first child.

POWERS/ WEAPONS

- Battle-suit that allows her to manipulate the Earth's electromagnetic field
- Flight
- Force-field
- Project oncussive blasts

INTELLIGENCE	
STRENGTH	
SPEED	
DURABILITY	
ENERGY PROJECTION	
FIGHTING SKILLS	

Art by Scott Clark

POWERS/WEAPONS

- Enabled psionically by its operator, the Box robot can lift about 40 tons

INTELLIGENCE

STRENGTH

SPEED

DURABILITY

ENERGY PROJECTION

FIGHTING SKILLS

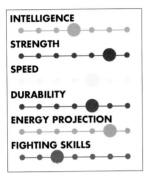

Real Name: Roger Bochs

First Appearance: *Alpha Flight* #1 (1983)

Height: 4'

Weight: 140 lbs

Brilliant engineer and mechanic Roger Bochs was also something else: a paraplegic. Blaming the world for the loss of his legs, he battled against his mental instability. Bochs invented an extremely large and powerful humanoid robot, which he called "Box" as a pun on his own name. For years, Bochs used the powerful device to benefit <u>Alpha Flight</u>. But all the while, his mental health continued its downward spiral, despite many attempts at a cure. On his last mission with the team, Bochs lost more than his mind—he lost his life.

BOX

POWERS/WEAPONS

- Diamond-hard skin resistant to injury

INTELLIGENCE

STRENGTH

SPEED

DURABILITY

ENERGY PROJECTION

FIGHTING SKILLS

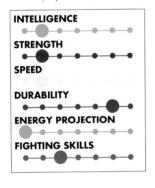

Real Name: Lillian Crawley

First Appearance: *Alpha Flight* #1 (1983)

Height: 6'4"

Weight: 171 lbs

Serving with <u>Alpha Flight</u> and falling in love with teammate <u>Madison Jeffries</u> wasn't enough to satisfy Diamond Lil; she detoured to the wrong side of the law. After stints in prison, Diamond Lil took a hard look at her life and returned to Alpha Flight to rekindle her relationship with Madison. But just when it seemed she had gotten back on track, she found a lump in her breast. Since her skin prevented typical surgery, Diamond Lil discovered a laser that could allow for a biopsy. Learning the mass was benign, she eventually married Madison.

DIAMOND LIL

POWERS/WEAPONS

- Vast innate magical abilities

INTELLIGENCE

STRENGTH

SPEED

DURABILITY

ENERGY PROJECTION

FIGHTING SKILLS

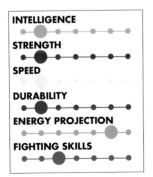

Real Name: Chuck Moss

First Appearance: *Wolverine* #179 (2002)

Height: 6'7"

Weight: 252 lbs

This former hockey player has a power more devastating than anything seen on the ice: shamanism. <u>Wolverine</u> helped Earthmover harness his powers, teaching him that if he were not properly instructed he would become dangerous. Wolverine began instructing his student in the art of bushido, the way of the warrior. It was during this training that Earthmover discovered his shamanistic totem (the natural world's representation of his innate power) was the earthworm, indicative of the power at his command. To further enhance his abilities, Earthmover now seeks guidance from <u>Shaman</u> as a member of Alpha Flight.

EARTHMOVER

FLEX

Real Name: Adrian Corbo
First Appearance: *Alpha Flight: In the Beginning... #-1 (1997)*

Height: 5'7"
Weight: 150 lbs

POWERS/WEAPONS

• Ability to "flex" parts of his body into thin sheets of organic metal which are highly resistant to physical damage

Flex, a shy, withdrawn boy, his brother **Radius** and **Murmur** left the orphanage in which they were raised to join **Alpha Flight**. Fearing that he might hurt someone with his admittedly dangerous ability, Flex is often hesitant to act—but is slowly gaining confidence, thanks in part to his budding relationship with teammate Ghost Girl. After the original members of Alpha Flight rejoined the group, the younger members, including Flex, were reassigned to the training team known as Beta Flight.

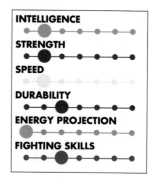

INTELLIGENCE

STRENGTH

SPEED

DURABILITY

ENERGY PROJECTION

FIGHTING SKILLS

MANBOT

Real Name: Bernie Lachenay
First Appearance: *Alpha Flight #1 (1997)*

Height: Variable
Weight: 520 lbs

POWERS/WEAPONS

• Offensive weaponry and defensive systems
• Silent communication via radio link

When Department H salvaged the robot **Box** and reworked it into a new system, they merged one of their employees, Bernie Lachenay, into the robot and called the new machine Manbot. During the newly reassembled **Alpha Flight**'s first few missions, Manbot secretly recorded their activities for later study back at the Department. After the restructuring of the Department that followed the apparent death of a high-ranking official, Manbot was no longer utilized in such a covert manner and has since been reassigned to the training team Beta Flight.

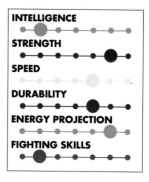

INTELLIGENCE

STRENGTH

SPEED

DURABILITY

ENERGY PROJECTION

FIGHTING SKILLS

MARRINA

Real Name: Marrina Smallwood MacKenzie
First Appearance: *Alpha Flight #1 (1983)*

Height: 6'
Weight: 200 lbs

POWERS/WEAPONS

• Shape-changing
• Creation of water spouts

Found underwater by her adoptive father while fishing, the alien Marrina joined **Alpha Flight** after her 16th birthday when she demonstrated her powers. During a mission, she met, fell in love with, and eventually married Namor, the infamous Atlantean Sub-Mariner. Her alien heritage, however, caused a serious rift in the marriage and ultimately led to a violent confrontation with Namor in which she was thought to have been killed. She later resurfaced as a prisoner of Alpha Flight adversary the Master of the World, but after his base was destroyed, her fate remains unknown.

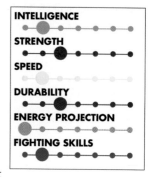

INTELLIGENCE

STRENGTH

SPEED

DURABILITY

ENERGY PROJECTION

FIGHTING SKILLS

POWERS/WEAPONS

- Psionic ability that allows her to manipulate others upon physical contact
- Teleportation

INTELLIGENCE

STRENGTH

SPEED

DURABILITY

ENERGY PROJECTION

FIGHTING SKILLS

Real Name: Arlette Truffaut
First Appearance: *Alpha Flight* #1 (1997)

Height: 5'8"
Weight: 134 lbs

Murmur came to Alpha Flight by way of the same orphanage as her teammate **Flex**. Flirtatious and somewhat vain, Murmur initially proved reluctant to work as a member of a team. Fighting alongside her teammates and watching them risk their lives to save innocents, however, she soon came to realize the inherent value of being a team player and adjusted her attitude. After serving as a valued member of the team, Murmur was reassigned to Department H's second-tier training team Beta Flight following the return of **Alpha Flight**'s original members.

MURMUR

POWERS/WEAPONS

- Circlet of Enchantment that grants her full access to her innate magical powers

INTELLIGENCE

STRENGTH

SPEED

DURABILITY

ENERGY PROJECTION

FIGHTING SKILLS

Real Name: Elizabeth Twoyoungmen
First Appearance: *Alpha Flight* #5 (1983)

Height: 5'8"
Weight: 132 lbs

When her physician father **Shaman** could do nothing to save her mother from dying from cancer, Talisman disowned him. Years afterward, feeling a need for reconciliation, Talisman located her father, who by then was a powerful mystic. When she met up with him, Talisman was asked to draw a magic circlet from his mystical pouch known as the Circlet of Enchantment, and, upon his instruction, put it on her brow. She was transformed into a person of immense mystic ability whose coming had long been prophesied. Soon after, she joined her father in **Alpha Flight**.

TALISMAN

POWERS/WEAPONS

- Ability to create solidified molecules of air
- Transformation of liquids into gases

INTELLIGENCE

STRENGTH

SPEED

DURABILITY

ENERGY PROJECTION

FIGHTING SKILLS

Real Name: Colin Ashworth Hume
First Appearance: *Alpha Flight* #87 (1990)

Height: 6'
Weight: 183 lbs

Ashamed of the villainous deeds he was forced to perform as a special operative for Roxxon Oil, Windshear quit and became an official member of **Alpha Flight**. During his time with Alpha Flight, Windshear gradually became more comfortable with the role of a super hero. When the Canadian government temporarily disbanded Alpha Flight, Windshear retired from the super hero life and returned to his home in England, where he set up a curio shop that sells high-priced objects, created with his mutant power, that are only visible under special lighting.

WINDSHEAR

BROTHERHOOD OF EVIL MUTANTS

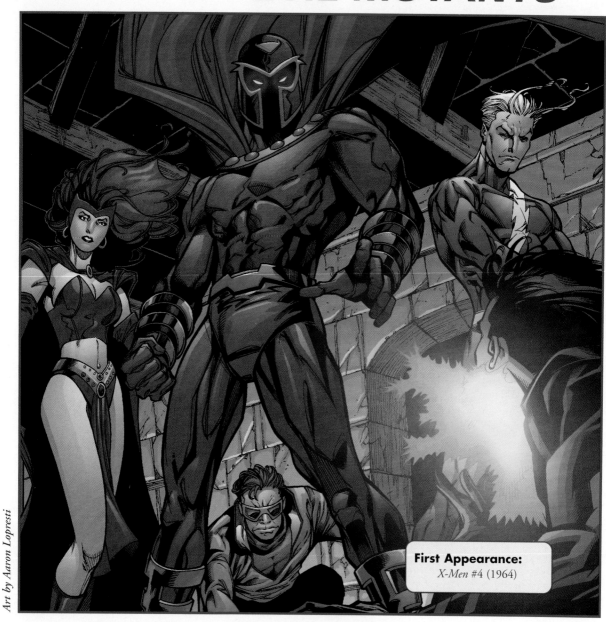

Art by Aaron Lopresti

First Appearance:
X-Men #4 (1964)

It can be defeated, but it will never really go away. It can resurrect itself in many guises—and always does. The players may change, but one thing remains the same: If evil is eternal, then the Brotherhood will always live on.

They are everything the <u>X-Men</u> are not. Terrorists. Murderers. Extortionists. With mutant oppression on the rise, the lost and confused have begun to join the Brotherhood in ever-increasing numbers—seeking family, an escape from human rule, a chance to be themselves, and the freedom to do what they want, whenever they want.

Defeat means nothing to this group of mutant terrorists. If anything, it only fuels their desire to up the ante—and perhaps one day they will successfully orchestrate an act of terror that will finally bring humanity to an end. When the age of evil is ushered in, there is no doubt the Brotherhood will be the one who opens the door.

BLOB

Thinking of himself as nothing more than "an extra-strong freak," Fred J. Dukes used his superhuman powers to make a living for himself as a performer in a carnival, where he earned the nickname "The Blob." At work one day, the original members of the X-Men came to the carnival in their everyday identities to invite the morbidly obese Blob to meet Professor X. Smitten with Jean Grey, Blob accepted and went with the group to the Xavier Mansion. Xavier asked Blob to join the X-Men, but Blob arrogantly refused. Blob's attitude forced Xavier to try and use his mental powers to erase Blob's knowledge of the X-Men's true identities. But the Blob fought off the X-Men, escaped the mansion, and returned to the carnival.

Prior to his meeting with Professor X, Blob had no idea that he possessed superhumanly powerful mutant abilities. Equipped with this knowledge, however, Blob now believed himself to be superior to ordinary humans, and began taking over the carnival. Blob was later approached by Magneto, who was seeking new recruits for his Brotherhood of Evil Mutants. Eager for revenge against the X-Men, Blob agreed to join, but his affiliation with the Brotherhood did not turn out as he expected: During a battle with the X-Men, Magneto launched a powerful torpedo at the heroes—with little concern for the fact that Blob stood right in the weapon's path. The torpedoes did not seriously injure the Blob, but he swore never to trust anyone again and returned to his job with the carnival.

Months later, the Blob relented on his vow when he met another superhumanly powerful mutant, Unus the Untouchable, and the two of them attempted to frame their mutual enemies the X-Men as thieves. Thus began Blob's long and close friendship with Unus, which ended only upon Unus's apparent death several years later.

Eventually, Blob allowed himself to be recruited by Mystique for her reorganized Brotherhood of Evil Mutants. Although the Blob continues to operate independently of Mystique's organization, he remains a member of the group.

Real Name:
Fred J. Dukes
First Appearance:
X-Men #3 (1964)

Height: 8'
Weight: 976 lbs
Eye Color: Brown
Hair Color: Brown

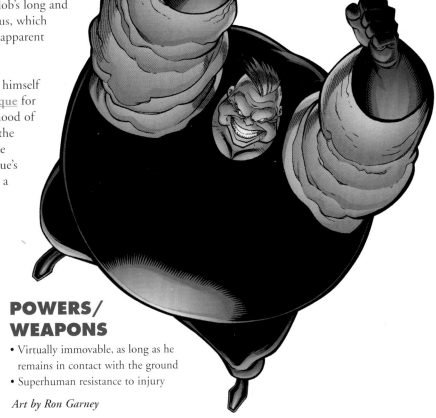

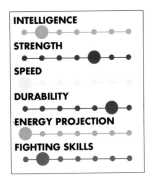

INTELLIGENCE

STRENGTH

SPEED

DURABILITY

ENERGY PROJECTION

FIGHTING SKILLS

POWERS/ WEAPONS

• Virtually immovable, as long as he remains in contact with the ground
• Superhuman resistance to injury

Art by Ron Garney

MAGNETO

Real Name:
Magnus
First Appearance:
X-Men #1 (1963)

Height: 6'2"
Weight: 190 lbs
Eye Color: Bluish-gray
Hair Color: Silver

POWERS/WEAPONS

• Master of magnetism

INTELLIGENCE

STRENGTH

SPEED

DURABILITY

ENERGY PROJECTION

FIGHTING SKILLS

As the only surviving member of his family after an internment at a Nazi prison camp, Magnus saw the kind of inhumanity ruthless, amoral human beings were capable of inflicting upon the world. These brutal events became a black mark forever burned in his memory, fueling his belief that mutants like himself can only be free if they enslave the rest of the human race before it enslaves them. Never again does he want to face the horror and degradation he and his people faced World War II.

After his release from Auschwitz, Magnus married a woman named Magda who gave birth to their first child, Anya. When a mob prevented him from saving his daughter from a fire, Magnus unleashed his powers upon them, killing them all with his mutant ability to manipulate the planet's magnetic forces.

Art by Leinil Francis Yu

Terrified, Magda fled—fearing not just the man's unimaginable power, but his increasing obsession with world mutant domination. She never bothered to tell her husband she was pregnant again. Reaching a safe haven, Magda gave birth to twins (<u>Quicksilver</u> and <u>Scarlet Witch</u>) and turned them over to a gypsy couple to raise as their own. When she took her own life, she took the secret of her children's paternity to her grave.

Crushed by the loss of his child and his wife, Magnus sought solace in Israel and performed volunteer work with Holocaust survivors. He also befriended a young telepath named Charles Xavier, later known as <u>Professor X</u>. As the pair battled terrorists, each was forced to reveal their mutant powers to one another. As they spoke of their mutual mutant status, Charles revealed that

Art by Leinil Francis Yu

he foresaw a planet where *Homo superior* and *Homo sapiens* could peacefully coexist—a viewpoint diametrically opposed to that of Magnus, who believed mutants would merely be the next in a long line of minorities ready to be exploited and persecuted for their differences. Magnus wanted to believe in Charles's philosophy, but his Auschwitz experience kept creeping back to haunt him, and he was unwilling to stand by and watch that terrible history repeat itself all over again with a different set of players.

While Charles chose his path towards peace to accomplish his goals, Magnus chose something else entirely: terrorism. Towards that end, he embraced terrorist dogma and, along with it, a new name: Magneto. During his first attempt to dominate humanity, Magneto tried to take over the Cape Citadel missile base, but found himself thwarted by Charles and his <u>X-Men</u>. Magneto then formed the <u>Brotherhood of Evil Mutants</u>, a terrorist mutant society who acted on his every whim. Among his recruits were Quicksilver and Scarlet Witch. Not until years later would he learn they were his own children.

Countless defeats did nothing to discourage Magneto. He worked just as hard at seeing his ultimate goals come to fruition. But his former friend Professor X held onto the hope that Magneto would one day give up his lethal maneuvers and join the cause for peace. But any chance for change Charles had once thought possible for Magneto dissipated when Magneto temporarily stripped <u>Wolverine</u> of his adamantium implants. Charles felt he had no choice but to temporarily psionically lobotomize his old friend.

Once Magneto regained his full strength and mental capacity, he acted with even more fervor and determination to set in motion a mutant takeover; this time his plan worked. Holding the planet hostage with its own magnetic field, Magneto demanded a sovereign homeland where mutants could govern themselves and face no oppression by humans. Having little choice, the United Nations conceded and turned over the island of Genosha to him. But he paid a dear price for his victory. After taking great care and pride in rebuilding the previously war-torn Genosha, a place where humans had once enslaved mutants turned into a homeland for mutants who for the first time could have a place they could truly call their own, Magneto saw his efforts destroyed. <u>Cassandra Nova</u> sent deadly, mutant-hunting <u>Sentinels</u> to Genosha—who, in short order, slaughtered sixteen million of its citizens. Among them is Magneto, whose body has yet to be recovered. Whatever doubts surround the Master of Magnetism, one thing is certain: Magneto is a survivor. Having survived the Holocaust, he will one day return and continue to prevent the persecution of another race: his very own.

MYSTIQUE

Real Name:
Raven Darkholme
First Appearance:
Ms. Marvel #16 (1978)

Height:	5'10"
Weight:	142 lbs
Eye Color:	Yellow
Hair Color:	Red

She can be a woman. She can be a man. She can be a billionaire. She can be a supermodel. Whatever Mystique deigns to become, she is. But she cannot hide who she truly is: a shape-shifting blue mutant determined to help bring about the end of all humanity.

During one of her stints "passing" for human, Mystique gave birth to a son, Kurt Wagner (<u>Nightcrawler</u>), who was anything but "normal." Born with a prehensile tale and blue skin, Kurt's obvious mutant appearance destroyed Mystique's cover and provoked the ire of the local villagers. Running from the angry mob with the baby in her arms, Mystique knew that to save her own life, she'd have to sacrifice her son's. Her selfish decision culminated with her throwing the boy over a waterfall. Little did Mystique know that as she made a safe getaway, the child made his own, too—into the arms of a local gypsy who would raise him as her own.

This deed was the first in a lifetime of similarly cruel events perpetrated by Mystique.

Never comfortable in her own blue skin, Mystique had for a time tried to manipulate people into forming a peace between man and mutant. But no matter how hard she tried, she always failed. And that failure fueled her greatest belief: that mutants must dominate all mankind. Any human or mutant who disagreed must be destroyed.

In her effort to bring about the demise of humanity, Mystique formed the second incarnation of the <u>**Brotherhood of Evil Mutants**</u>, a terrorist group designed to stamp out all who stood in the way of mutant domination. She even adopted a young <u>**Rogue**</u> to serve her organization's needs. The <u>**X-Men**</u>—Mystique's mortal enemies—always thwarted all of her attempts to realize her goals; even Rogue eventually left her manipulative foster mother to join the X-Men and their cause.

But Mystique is a patient woman. In time, she knows the inevitable war between man and mutant will be fought—and she will not be on the losing side no matter what shape she takes.

POWERS/ WEAPONS

• Shapeshifting

Art by Salvador Larroca

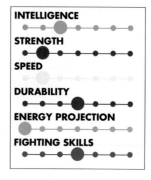

INTELLIGENCE

STRENGTH

SPEED

DURABILITY

ENERGY PROJECTION

FIGHTING SKILLS

QUICKSILVER

While he and his twin sister Wanda (Scarlet Witch) were still in the womb, Pietro's mother Magda fled from their father Magneto. Terrified of her husband's recent manifestation of mutant powers and newly adopted philosophy of world domination, Magda feared she and her unborn children faced grave danger.

Real Name:
Pietro Maximoff
First Appearance:
X-Men #4 (1964)

Height:	6'
Weight:	175 lbs
Eye Color:	Blue
Hair Color:	Silver

Pietro and Wanda were left by their mother to be raised by Django and Marya Maximoff, a loving gypsy couple. Growing up, Pietro discovered he could move at superhuman speeds. Little did he know how soon this superhuman power would come in handy. When his adoptive father stole food to feed his family, hateful villagers converged on their camp and attacked them. Fearing for their lives, Pietro and his sister fled the camp. When the twins were about to be killed in another village they had settled in, they were saved by Magneto. Unaware they were his children, Magneto demanded Pietro and Wanda serve in his Brotherhood of Evil Mutants. Feeling obliged, they agreed. As members of the Brotherhood, the conflicted twins took the names Quicksilver and Scarlet Witch and aided Magneto in his terrorist campaign against humanity.

But Quicksilver wanted out of the cause—fortunately for him, the Brotherhood eventually disbanded. Seeking redemption, he and Scarlet Witch petitioned to join the Avengers, a team of super heroes who protect the planet from any and all threats. He was accepted, and quickly came to relish his role fighting for a cause in which he truly believed. But Magneto came calling again, this time with the news he was Quicksilver's true father. He hoped the revelation would persuade his son to rejoin a new terrorist campaign, but the move backfired. Though stunned, Pietro dismissed Magneto.

Art by Roger Cruz

Plagued by impulsive decisions and rash actions, Quicksilver strives to achieve equilibrium in his life. So far, such balance has eluded him. Undermined by neglect and infidelity, Quicksilver's marriage was doomed to fail despite repeated attempts at reconciliation and the birth of his daughter. Even while Quicksilver continues to bear the burden of his father's legacy, he moves ahead with the fight for peace between man and mutant. Although conflicted, Quicksilver believes in his soul he is the man his father would have been had Magneto opted for tolerance instead of hatred.

INTELLIGENCE

STRENGTH

SPEED

DURABILITY

ENERGY PROJECTION

FIGHTING SKILLS

POWERS/ WEAPONS

• Superhuman speed

SCARLET WITCH

Real Name:
Wanda Django
Maximoff
First Appearance:
X-Men #4 (1964)

Height: 5'7"
Weight: 130 lbs
Eye Color: Blue
Hair Color: Auburn

Abandoned by her mother and born without knowledge of her true father, Wanda Maximoff and her twin brother Pietro (**Quicksilver**) learned of their unique and amazing powers at an early age. While Pietro could move faster than the blink of an eye, young Wanda could cause strange phenomena to occur with probability-altering hex-spheres.

In her adolescence, Wanda's adoptive gypsy father stole food for their family to eat—a crime that did not go unnoticed by the townspeople. As a mob came to exact its vengeance upon the whole family, Wanda fled with Pietro. For years they wandered Europe together, living off the land.

During a visit to a new village, Wanda's uncontrolled powers accidentally set a house ablaze and caused an uproar. When the villagers surrounded Wanda and Pietro, the twins did their best to hold them back—but even their mutant abilities were not enough; there were just too many people against them. At the last minute, they found help in an unlikely ally: **Magneto**, their true father, who appeared and saved them from doom. Magneto, unaware the pair were his children, quickly demanded payback for saving their lives and asked Wanda and Pietro to sign on to his **Brotherhood of Evil Mutants**, a terrorist organization he headed. Partly out of fear, partly out of a sense of obligation, Wanda and Pietro agreed to serve.

When the Brotherhood disbanded, Scarlet Witch could not have been more thrilled. In an effort to redeem the terrible deeds she had done on Magento's behalf, she petitioned for membership in the Avengers, a team of super heroes who protect the planet from any and all threats; both she and Quicksilver were accepted.

Finally fighting for the right cause, Scarlet Witch came out of her shell, valued for her abilities rather than merely exploited. Only after becoming an Avenger did she learn the truth about her parentage. Hoping to sway his children into rejoining his reenergized crusade against humanity, Magneto confronted Scarlet Witch and Quicksilver with the revelation he was their true father. Both denounced him and his cause.

POWERS/ WEAPONS

• Ability to control chaos magick and affect probability fields

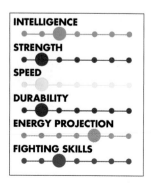

INTELLIGENCE

STRENGTH

SPEED

DURABILITY

ENERGY PROJECTION

FIGHTING SKILLS

Art by J.G. Jones

TOAD

Unlike other mutants whose powers manifested in puberty, Mortimer Toynbee was born a mutant. Abandoned by his parents and knowing nothing of his past, Mortimer was placed in an orphanage, where children continually harassed and tormented him about his freakish appearance, his unusual physique, and his pronounced leaping ability. Traumatized by the continuous rejection and plagued by loneliness, Mortimer developed learning disabilities, which the teachers at the orphanage mistakenly took as a sign of mental retardation. He developed a pathetically subservient personality in order to get anyone to like him, and would unquestioningly obey anyone who even showed him the most remote hint of kindness.

Real Name:
Mortimer Toynbee
First Appearance:
X-Men #4 (1964)

Height: 5'8"
Weight: 169 lbs
Eye Color: Yellow
Hair Color: Brown

After he matured into adulthood, <u>Magneto</u> discovered Toad and recruited him into his <u>Brotherhood of Evil Mutants</u>. But Toad had no idea that Magneto had little use for his powers—he merely wanted to use him as an expendable pawn. True to form, Toad pathetically devoted himself to Magneto, whom he subconsciously regarded as a surrogate father. Toad blinded himself to Magneto's continual verbal and physical abuse, if only because he believed Magneto would defeat the human race and thereby conquer all those who had humiliated Toad in his youth.

But before long, Toad faced a terrible betrayal: When Toad and Magneto were captured and imprisoned on a distant planet, Magneto escaped, callously leaving Toad behind. Though Toad eventually rejoined Magneto, Magneto's relentless bullying caused Toad's resentment to come to a head, and he left Magneto to die in an explosion that followed an encounter with the <u>X-Men</u>. Only later would Toad learn that Magneto had survived the blast.

Though the ensuing years brought him even more depression and despondency, Toad learned how to toughen up and gained enormous confidence in himself—so much so that he even led his own faction of the Brotherhood.

Haunted by the emotional wounds of his past, Toad lives to exact retribution on those who made him what he is today. Either as part of the Brotherhood or on his own, Toad will take whatever extreme measures are needed to make an uncaring society pay for who he has become.

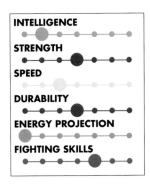

INTELLIGENCE
STRENGTH
SPEED
DURABILITY
ENERGY PROJECTION
FIGHTING SKILLS

POWERS/ WEAPONS

- Superhuman strength
- Leaping ability
- Prehensile tongue, which can reach up to 25 feet in length

Art by Phil Jimenez

AVALANCHE

Real Name:	Dominic Szilard Janos Petros	Height:	5'7"
First Appearance:	*X-Men* #141 (1981)	Weight:	164 lbs

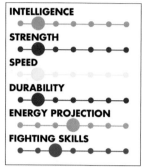

Recruited by <u>Mystique</u> to serve in the <u>Brotherhood of Evil Mutants</u>, Avalanche took part in the organization's first assassination attempt on <u>Senator Kelly</u>. He then briefly left the squad and attempted to blackmail the state of California into paying him a large sum of money by threatening to use his powers to trigger a major earthquake. Avalanche was later forcibly recruited into the paramilitary group X-Corps, which was headed by <u>Banshee</u>. Following the subsequent infiltration of the group by Mystique, Avalanche assisted an attack in Paris, France, where he single-handedly destroyed the Eiffel Tower.

POWERS/WEAPONS
- Generation of powerful vibrations from his hands

INTELLIGENCE

STRENGTH

SPEED

DURABILITY

ENERGY PROJECTION

FIGHTING SKILLS

DESTINY

Real Name:	Irene Adler	Height:	5'7"
First Appearance:	*X-Men* #141 (1981)	Weight:	110 lbs

Though blind, she foresaw the future. Every vision, every prophecy she meticulously detailed in her journals. A lifelong companion to <u>Mystique</u>, Destiny faithfully followed her friend and served the <u>Brotherhood of Evil Mutants</u>. Along for a mission, Destiny was assigned a caretaker, but forced him to leave her so he could participate in the battle. As she foresaw in a vision, <u>Legion</u> found and killed her. It was only after her death that <u>Shadowcat</u> discovered Destiny's journals, which contained pages of cryptic—and thus far accurate—prophecies about the end of the millennium.

POWERS/WEAPONS
- Precognition

INTELLIGENCE

STRENGTH

SPEED

DURABILITY

ENERGY PROJECTION

FIGHTING SKILLS

PHANTAZIA

Real Name:	Eileen Harsaw	Height:	6'2"
First Appearance:	*X-Force* #6 (1992)	Weight:	171 lbs

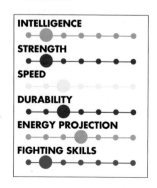

Phantazia was recruited into the <u>Brotherhood of Evil Mutants</u> by <u>Toad</u>. She proved to be an addition Toad would be thankful for: During the Brotherhood's clash with the mutant strike force founded by <u>Nathan Summers</u>, Phantazia scored a big win for her organization when she disrupted the blast field of <u>Cannonball</u>, allowing her teammate <u>Sauron</u> to kill him (or so it seemed). <u>Exodus</u> later approached Phantazia and gave her the opportunity to join the ranks of the <u>Acolytes</u>. Phantazia entertained the invitation but chose to reject the offer, and stayed on with the Brotherhood.

POWERS/WEAPONS
- Projection of a disruptive bioelectric field
- Levitation

INTELLIGENCE

STRENGTH

SPEED

DURABILITY

ENERGY PROJECTION

FIGHTING SKILLS

POWERS/WEAPONS

- Incredible mathematical and analytical skills
- Bio-cybernetic weaponry and body armor

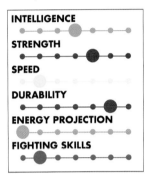

Real Name: Kevin Tremain
First Appearance: *X-Men* #50 (1996)

Height: 8'
Weight: 790 lbs

When government operative Kevin Tremaine lay critically injured after a series of botched experiments performed by the Chinese ultra-nationalist called the Mandarin, Nathan Summers saved his life—but he could not save Kevin from a life lived on the wrong side of Professor X's dream. As Post, Kevin could have fulfilled the promise of the dream of the Brotherhood of Evil Mutants instead: the assassination of Senator Kelly. But when Post was mere seconds away from bringing down his target, the dying Pyro used the last of his strength to kill Post in a single fiery blast.

POST

POWERS/WEAPONS

- Psionic control of fire

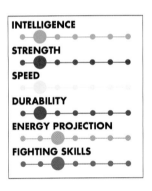

Real Name: St. John Allerdyce
First Appearance: *X-Men* #141 (1981)

Height: 5'10"
Weight: 150 lbs

In his youth, St. John Allerdyce used his mutant abilities only for profit. When Mystique approached him with an invitation to use his powers in the Brotherhood of Evil Mutants, Pyro accepted. Dutifully fighting against the X-Men, Pyro's life would not be lost to combat, but to something worse: the Legacy Virus. Seeking redemption, Pyro halted the Brotherhood's second attempted assassination of Senator Kelly. As Post was about to kill Kelly, Pyro—summoning up one final fiery onslaught—annihilated the mutant before he could carry out the murder.

PYRO

POWERS/WEAPONS

- Impenetrable force-field

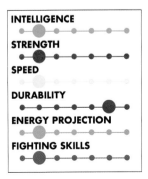

Real Name: Angelo Unuscione
First Appearance: *X-Men* #8 (1964)

Height: 6'1"
Weight: 220 lbs

When the Brotherhood of Evil Mutants recruited the professional wrestler Unus the Untouchable, they forced him to defeat an X-Man as a requirement for membership. As Unus battled Beast, however, Beast employed a device that rendered Unus' power temporarily uncontrollable. Helpless, he surrendered. Unus went on to form a criminal partnership with Blob. When his powers again spun out of control, Unus blacked out and fell into the arms of his friend, who believed him dead. During a search mission on the decimated Genosha, Quicksilver found Unus, shaken but alive. How he made his way to Genosha has yet to be revealed.

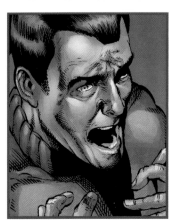

UNUS

EXILES

Art by Mike McKone

First Appearance:
Exiles #1 (2001)

In more ways than one, they are not who they seem to be. They hail from disparate alternate realities where their familiar names do not come with familiar histories. Instead, they come from realities where anything is possible—where good is evil, evil is good, and everything in between is up for grabs.

And now, assembled as the Exiles, they live as outcasts who have fallen through the cracks of reality and have been charged with fixing rifts in time. Only when they repair the damage can they return to the people they once were and the places where they once lived. They have little choice: if they don't fulfill their mission, each will suffer a terrible fate that was never meant to be.

Traveling to the far corners of Earths even stranger than their own, the Exiles are often called on to align themselves with those whom they once thought were enemies—and kill those whom they once called friends. They live in a world where "what ifs" and "what nows" happen daily. Their mission can only be a success when they cease to be Exiles.

BLINK

Born in the alternate reality where Apocalypse ruled supreme, young Clarice Ferguson's parents and brother were killed in the death camp of Mr. Sinister, a Horseman of Apocalypse. Rescued by Sabretooth and Weapon X, two members of Magneto's X-Men, Blink eventually became a member of the team and came to view Sabretooth as her surrogate father. Under Magneto's tutelage, she learned to control her powers.

During the final days of the X-Men's fight against Apocalypse, Sabretooth asked Blink to teleport him to the Horseman Holocaust so he could delay the Horseman long enough to ensure the X-Men would arrive in time to free the people in the death camps. She reluctantly agreed, knowing that his act could save them all—and that he would face a mighty foe alone. Indeed, when Sabretooth fought Holocaust, Holocaust easily defeated him. Believing Sabretooth to be dead, Blink sought revenge on Holocaust and managed to best the villain in combat, teleporting him into a corrosive pool.

The X-Men's ultimate victory set off a chain of events that would end Blink's universe. But Blink would not see that happen. Moments before her universe evaporated, she was plucked from her reality. She emerged in a strange location outside both time and space and soon discovered she was not alone; five other mutants were also present. **Timebroker** explained to the group that they had all fallen through the cracks in reality caused by breaks in the chain of time itself. The only way they could return to their lives was to travel to other realities and repair those breaks. If they failed, however, they would return to their now-altered home reality, each suffering a fate that was never meant to be. In Blink's case, she would cease to exist, as her reality had changed to the point where she had never been born.

The assembled heroes agreed to help repair time, and Blink became the leader of the team—the **Exiles**. The Timebroker gave her a device known as the Tallus, which would use her teleportation powers to transport the team from reality to reality, as well as give them instructions on what they needed to accomplish in each dimension to achieve their goal. After a successful mission in which Blink and the Exiles freed a world plagued by the deadly mutant-killing Legacy Virus, Blink was teleported away, having fulfilled her obligation to the team. Her current whereabouts are unknown.

Real Name:
Clarice Ferguson
First Appearance:
X-Men: Alpha (1994)

Height: 5'6"
Weight: 127 lbs
Eye Color: Green
Hair Color: Pinkish-purple

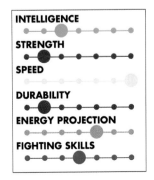

INTELLIGENCE
STRENGTH
SPEED
DURABILITY
ENERGY PROJECTION
FIGHTING SKILLS

POWERS/ WEAPONS

• Teleportation

Art by Chris Bachalo

MIMIC

Real Name:
Calvin Montgomery Rankin

First Appearance:
Exiles #1 (2001)

Height: 6'3"
Weight: 196 lbs
Eye Color: Blue
Hair Color: Blond

Calvin Rankin's father was a brilliant scientist but a bad businessman whose discoveries and creations were stolen from him. As a result, Calvin grew up poor under the discipline of a bitter, dejected man. Despite his own innate intellect, Calvin gravitated towards the wrong crowd and would have become a petty thief were it not for a chance meeting with his reality's version of the X-Men. Calvin's own mutant power had manifested in his late teens, but now he had a chance to use his abilities on people worthy of mimicking. As he copied their abilities, the X-Men's powers surged through Calvin's body. The changes physically manifested as a pair of angelic wings and enlarged hands and feet. Mimic used his newfound power to begin a criminal career and joined the Brotherhood of Evil Mutants. On their first mission to kidnap mutant-hating Senator Robert Kelly, the Brotherhood clashed with the X-Men, who were surprised by Mimic and his use of powers that reflected their own. Unfortunately for Mimic, his lack of training sealed the Brotherhood's defeat. The Brotherhood abandoned Mimic, who was captured and imprisoned. During his incarceration, Mimic met Professor X, who extended him an invitation to join the X-Men. Seeing no other choice, Mimic accepted and soon came to consider the X-Men valued teammates and friends. He also learned to look upon Professor X as a surrogate father figure and eventually became team leader.

Soon, however, Mimic was pulled from his reality to join the **Exiles**. Mimic was told that if they failed in their quest to repair the breaks in the chain of time, he would return to a reality where the Brotherhood had successfully murdered Senator Kelly, along with a busload of innocent people. Mimic would be tried for the crime and sentenced to death. The strain of constantly being forced to battle alternate reality counterparts of people who were his dearest friends in his own reality began to tell on Mimic, and for weeks he became distant and stoic. After a harrowing mission in which the Exiles were forced to kill Jean Grey, a romance began to blossom between Mimic and **Blink**. The plight of being an Exile left them little time to explore the depth of their feelings for each other, though, and it wasn't long before it was time for Blink to leave the team. Mimic is now forced to lead a team he may not even want to be part of.

POWERS/ WEAPONS

• Ability to mimic the powers of other super-beings

Art by Mike McKone

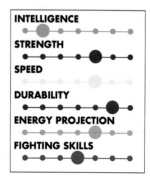

INTELLIGENCE

STRENGTH

SPEED

DURABILITY

ENERGY PROJECTION

FIGHTING SKILLS

MORPH

As a child, Kevin Sidney hid his shape-shifting ability, allowing him to live a well-adjusted childhood free of the scorn that plagued mutantkind. Following the death of his mother from lung cancer when he was just thirteen, Kevin chose humor as an outlet for his emotions.

Kevin eventually obtained a master's degree in computer engineering. After graduation, he came to the attention of his reality's Professor X, who invited the young man to study at his School for Gifted Youngsters. Morph's enthusiasm coupled with his irreverent brand of humor both charmed and annoyed his fellow New Mutants; still, Morph eventually graduated to the ranks of the X-Men, becoming a valued member of the team. He also served as a member of the Avengers, Earth's mightiest heroes.

On a mission with the X-Men, Morph was teleported away by a ripple in the time stream. He emerged in a strange location outside both time and space, joined by five other similarly displaced mutants. When **Timebroker** charged them with their mission, Morph learned how critical it was: If he and the others did not successfully repair the breaks in time, Morph would fall victim to an accident where his physical composition would be disrupted and he'd have to live out his life in a comatose, liquid state in a beaker in Beast's laboratory. Not exactly thrilled by that fate, Morph decided it might be in his best interest to do everything in his power to help the team succeed.

Real Name:
Kevin Sidney
First Appearance:
Exiles #1 (2001)

Height: Variable, 5'11"
(in human form)
Weight: Variable, 155 lbs
(in human form)
Eye Color: White
Hair Color: None

POWERS/ WEAPONS

• Shapeshifting

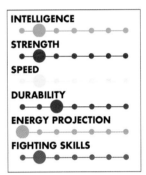

INTELLIGENCE					
STRENGTH					
SPEED					
DURABILITY					
ENERGY PROJECTION					
FIGHTING SKILLS					

Art by Mike McKone

NOCTURNE

Real Name:
Talia Josephine Wagner
First Appearance:
X-Men: Millennial Visions 2000 (2000)

Height:	5'7"
Weight:	135 lbs
Eye Color:	Yellow
Hair Color:	Indigo

In the alternate universe from which she hails, Nocturne was born with indigo skin, three fingers and toes on each hand and foot, and a prehensile tail, all thanks to her dad. And somewhere down the line, she developed great musical ability. If she wants to return to her band, the Butt Monkeys, and her cherished father, she'll have to put all her skills to the test—or face dire consequences.

T. J. Wagner grew up under the watchful eye of her parents, Nightcrawler and Scarlet Witch, and eventually sought tutelage from Xavier's School for Gifted Youngsters. Inheriting much of Nightcrawler's ability and bravado, as well as his likeness, she quickly moved up through the ranks of Xavier's School to become an X-Man and fight alongside Nightcrawler. But Nocturne wasn't able to serve the X-Men for long. She and five other mutants found themselves ripped out of their realities by the Timebroker.

Nocturne, like all the other Exiles, had been called upon to mend the breaks in the chain of time— or else she would face a tragic fate. If Nocturne did not satisfy her mission, she would have to live in a reality where her beloved father would have been slain by her own grandmother, Mystique. Nocturne, unwilling to lose her father in such a terrible manner, joined the other fate-fearing Exiles as they set out on their urgent quest.

Before being plucked from her home reality, Nocturne had fallen in love with the brother of that world's Thunderbird, now her Exiles teammate. But in their new time-tossed existence, she felt a closer bond with Thunderbird, and the two quickly became lovers. During a mission with the Exiles on an Earth that had been conquered by the shape-shifting alien Skrulls, Nocturne learned that she was pregnant with Thunderbird's child. When Thunderbird was critically injured in the ensuing clash with the world-eater Galactus, he remained in a coma in that reality after the other Exiles had been teleported to their next mission.

Nocturne was devastated—and her devastation turned into utter, unrelenting despair, causing her to lose the baby. After losing her baby, the normally free-spirited Nocturne became withdrawn and depressed for a time, refusing to discuss her feelings with her teammates. She has since managed to come to terms with losing both Thunderbird and her only physical link to him. Nocturne knows that setting aside a broken heart and broken spirit is necessary for the task at hand, where greater pain faces her in a possible reality: a murdered father. No matter the risk, no matter the pressure, the mission—and Nocturne—must go on.

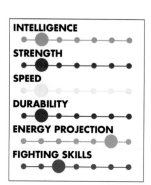

Art by Jim Calafiore

POWERS/ WEAPONS

- Possession of another person for no longer than one lunar cycle, or approximately 12 hours
- Hex bolts
- Ability to open small dimensional portals

INTELLIGENCE

STRENGTH

SPEED

DURABILITY

ENERGY PROJECTION

FIGHTING SKILLS

Real Name: Heather Hudson   **Height:** 5'9"(as Hudson),   **Weight:** 133 lbs (as Hudson),
First Appearance: *Exiles* #10 (2002)   10' (as Sasquatch)   2,000 lbs (as Sasquatch)

SASQUATCH

POWERS/WEAPONS

- Superhuman strength and a large degree of resistance to injury
- Exceptional leaping ability

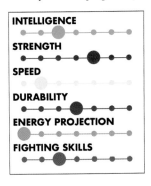

INTELLIGENCE
STRENGTH
SPEED
DURABILITY
ENERGY PROJECTION
FIGHTING SKILLS

Though not an original Exiles member, her duty to fulfill their mission is every bit as critical. Like the others, Sasquatch can't afford to face life in a reality where all that awaits her is pain and loss.

Heather Hudson didn't know what hit her. One day she's the field leader and chief medical officer for an alternate-reality Alpha Flight—and the next she's barreling through a crack in her reality that she will be called upon to fix. If she cannot, she will face another, more frightening reality in which her husband James burns to death.

Called up to the Exiles to replace their comatose teammate **Thunderbird**, Sasquatch shocked the others when she reverted from her hulking, hairy bestial form to her human form, an attractive female. But their surprise faded, and Sasquatch took her place on the team, eagerly accepting her mission in order to stave off a fate she can barely even imagine.

Art by Mike McKone

POWERS/WEAPONS

- Creation and projection of firey plasma
- Flight

INTELLIGENCE
STRENGTH
SPEED
DURABILITY
ENERGY PROJECTION
FIGHTING SKILLS

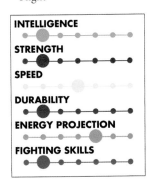

Real Name: Mariko Yashida   **Height:** 5'5"
First Appearance: *Exiles* #2 (2001)   **Weight:** 120 lbs

Mariko Yashida knew all about shame. In the alternate reality from which she hailed, her strict Japanese parents where ashamed of not only her mutant ability but also by her announcement of her homosexuality. Rebellious and free-spirited, Mariko refused to be subjugated and took off for America to join the Xavier School for Gifted Mutants at Professor X's invitation. She quickly ascended through the ranks at the school and joined the X-Men.

Mariko was yanked from her reality by a defect in the time stream and joined the **Exiles**. Her mission with them was critical. If she and the other Exiles failed, Sunfire would face a return trip to her home reality, where her powers would manifest as uncontrollable atomic radiation.

While serving the Exiles' mission, Sunfire developed a very close friendship with **Morph**, who developed a crush on her. On a rare break from their frenetic dimension hopping, Sunfire invited Morph for a day of shopping, capped off by dinner. Confessing she knew about his crush, Sunfire gently explained her sexual preference to Morph and the two now enjoy a mutually platonic friendship.

SUNFIRE

Art Georges Jeanty

WEAPON X

Art by Jim Calafiore

First Appearance:
Exiles #5 (2001)

The good. The bad. The deadly. They're all here and all fighting for the same cause in a reality not their own. As Weapon X, these alternate-reality heroes have a critical mission: repair the breaks in time. Then and only then can they return to their home realities and their own individual destinies. Along with the **Exiles**, the ragtag team of Weapon X has been charged by **Timebroker** to repair cracks in the timestream itself so they can return to the lives they once knew.

While Weapon X and the Exiles have the same objective, their methods could not be more different. The Weapon X team possesses the aggression necessary to complete entirely different tasks from the Exiles' missions. Weapon X is not quantified as "good" or "bad;" they are simply needed to help repair the time stream. The team's lineup has included Sabretooth, Kane, Deadpool, Spider, Storm, the Vision, and She-Hulk.

Weapon X teamed up with the Exiles to liberate a young mutant named David Richards from a detainment camp guarded by Sentinels. After David was freed, Weapon X learned that their mission in that reality had not ended yet: They needed to kill David to prevent him from growing up to become a callous dictator. But Sabretooth could not accept his orders; in an effort to save David's life, he betrayed his team to prevent them from fulfilling their mission. It was an act that cost Deadpool his life. Timebroker intervened, reminding Sabretooth and the Exiles that they must complete their missions, regardless of their own feelings. Disengaging from Weapon X, Sabretooth stayed in that reality to raise young David himself and change the course of the boy's future, ensuring he would not become a dictator and thus negating the need to kill him. Sabretooth's act allowed for the mission to draw successfully to a close and Weapon X, minus Sabretooth, moved on to other realities. The newest incarnation of Weapon X is led by Gambit, and includes Archangel.

Mission after mission, it is up to Weapon X to continue to complement the Exiles' efforts to repair the time stream so that they may all return to their home realities someday.

POWERS/WEAPONS

- Master of magnetism
- Ability to transform another's flesh into cold unliving steel through touch

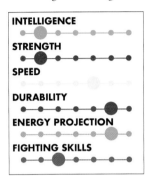

INTELLIGENCE

STRENGTH

SPEED

DURABILITY

ENERGY PROJECTION

FIGHTING SKILLS

Real Name: Magnus (full name unrevealed)
First Appearance: *Exiles* #1 (2001)

Height: 6'
Weight: 177 lbs

The son of his reality's Magneto and Rogue, Magnus was summoned by the Exiles. He learned that if he and the others did not repair the cracks in time, he would return to a life where he had accidentally killed his mother, resulting in his grief-stricken father resuming his war against humanity. When the Exiles were transported to a world where Magneto had to be freed from a detention facility about to be destroyed by an atomic bomb, Magnus surrounded the facility with a magnetic shield to contain the explosion; the force of the blast ultimately killed him.

MAGNUS

POWERS/WEAPONS

- Enhanced strength, speed, and endurance

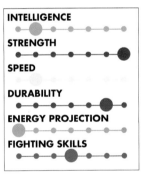

INTELLIGENCE

STRENGTH

SPEED

DURABILITY

ENERGY PROJECTION

FIGHTING SKILLS

Real Name: John Proudstar
First Appearance: *Exiles* #1 (2001)

Height: 7'
Weight: 1,200 lbs

In his home reality, Thunderbird was captured by Apocalypse, who remade him as his cybernetically enhanced disciple. But Thunderbird's indomitable spirit enabled him to escape—only to see him ripped from his reality. He had no choice but to help the Exiles complete their mission; if he did not, he faced a life where he would never have broken free from Apocalypse's control. Thunderbird fell in love with his teammate Nocturne and learned she was carrying his child, but a brutal battle ended his hopes for the future. Thunderbird now lies in a coma, unaware Nocturne lost the baby.

THUNDERBIRD

POWERS/WEAPONS

- Not known

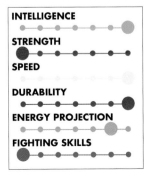

INTELLIGENCE

STRENGTH

SPEED

DURABILITY

ENERGY PROJECTION

FIGHTING SKILLS

Real Name: Inapplicable
First Appearance: *Exiles* #1 (2001)

Height: 5'5"
Weight: 180 lbs

Timebroker doesn't exist in the conventional sense. Akin to a "living verb," Timebroker is a construct created from the collective consciousnesses of two teams, the Exiles and Weapon X. When the members of the teams had accepted their missions to repair the breaks in time, Timebroker gave a Tallus to one member of each. The Tallus acts as a guide, instructing the teams as best it can on what is needed to repair the breaks in a particular reality. Once each repair is made, the Tallus then transports the teams to their next reality and their next mission.

TIMEBROKER

HELLFIRE CLUB

Art by Adam Kubert

First Appearance:
Uncanny X-Men #129 (1980)

It is at once austere and revered, a place where only the unimaginably wealthy and powerful are welcome. But behind its stately guise, something else lurks: something diabolical, something deadly, and something seemingly unstoppable. Founded in the 1760s in London, England, the Hellfire Club began as a meeting place for the highest ranks of British society. Within the confines of the exclusive club, members could meet to make deals and secretly indulge in pleasures forbidden by the morality of the time. In the 1770s, two of the club's leading members emigrated to New York City, where they founded the American branch of the Hellfire Club.

Throughout the ensuing centuries, the Hellfire Club continued to attract the world's wealthiest and most socially prominent people. Its exclusive membership invitations were coveted by nearly everyone who was anyone and were thought to be one of the highest compliments a human being could ever receive. By its very nature, it was an invitation rarely turned down. To most of the members—and to society at large— the Hellfire Club was merely a respectable, upper-class social organization principally devoted to giving spectacular parties where members of the social, economic, and political elite could meet unofficially to discuss matters of mutual interest, and to forge political or business alliances.

But there was something held secret—not just from society, but from the majority of Hellfire Club members as well—a super-secret upper echelon of the Hellfire membership called the Inner Circle, whose subversive members engage in a conspiracy to dominate the world through the accumulation of economic power and political influence. Members of the Inner Circle hold positions named after chess pieces to denote their standing within the organization. The most powerful positions are the King and Queen; below them are their Bishops, Rooks, and Pawns. The infighting for King and Queen titles is fierce, and frequently leads to uprisings and power struggles. Regardless of their ongoing power struggles, the goal of the Inner Circle remains clear and focused: Don't back down until the world is your hands.

Welcome to the Hellfire Club, where membership is the ultimate status symbol—and membership in the Inner Circle signifies ultimate evil.

Sebastian Shaw was born into an impoverished family, but his superb business skills made him a millionaire by the age of 20. He eventually became the head of Shaw Industries, a multinational corporation heavily involved with United States defense contracts and the production of munitions. His vast wealth and power allowed him entrance into the Hellfire Club; after a while his ruthlessness peaked and he killed its Inner Circle leader. After taking the reigns as the Black King, Shaw worked closely with Emma Frost, the Club's new White Queen.

Having killed to achieve his coveted position, Shaw knew he'd face similar attempts to displace him as the Black King. And indeed, the renegade White Bishop Donald Pierce challenged him—as did his own son, Shinobi Shaw, who attempted to assassinate his father so he could earn the title of Black King for himself. Eventually, Sebastian Shaw fled underground, allowing the Club's Black Queen, Selene, to take control.

Regardless of his deposed status, nothing threatens Shaw's opportunism, and he continues with his plans to dominate the world through his force, money, and power, with or without the title of Black King.

SEBASTIAN SHAW

Real Name:
Sebastian Hiram Shaw
First Appearance:
X-Men #129 (1980)

Height:	6'2"
Weight:	210 lbs
Eye Color:	Black
Hair Color:	Gray

Art by Salvador Larroca

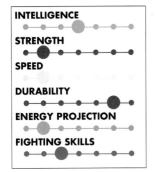

INTELLIGENCE

STRENGTH

SPEED

DURABILITY

ENERGY PROJECTION

FIGHTING SKILLS

POWERS/WEAPONS

• Ability to absorb kinetic energy on impact and rechannel it into physical strength, speed, and stamina

---

EMMANUEL DaCOSTA

Real Name: Emmanuel DaCosta
First Appearance: *Marvel Graphic Novel* #4 (1982)

Height: 6'
Weight: 190 lbs

Once a poor, barefoot houseboy, Emmanuel DaCosta swore his mother would become the mistress of the estate where she was once a maid. By the age of twenty, he saw his dream become reality. After Emmanuel had become a millionaire and the head of his own corporation, DaCosta International, he also became a one-man economic and political force. The Hellfire Club came calling and invited him to become a member. Seizing this opportunity to expand his power and influence, Emmanuel dumped his wife Nina and son Roberto DaCosta (Sunspot). His diabolical ways caught up with him, though, and a mutant eventually poisoned and killed Emmanuel to pave the way for Roberto to gain access to his father's fortunes.

HARRY LELAND

Real Name: Harry Leland
First Appearance: *X-Men* #129 (1980)

Height: 5'10"
Weight: 235 lbs

Corporate lawyer Harry Leland helped **Sebastian Shaw** overthrow the leader of the **Hellfire Club** and become its Black Bishop. During the Inner Circle's clash with the **X-Men**, the rival teams were forced to join together to defeat **Sentinels**. Leland suffered a heart attack in battle, yet still managed to greatly increase the mass of Shaw, who had been thrown into the upper atmosphere by the Sentinel Nimrod. Shaw returned to Earth with the force of a small meteor, smashing Nimrod to pieces and saving the lives of both the Inner Circle and the X-Men. But Leland's heart attack proved fatal.

POWERS/WEAPONS

- Geometrically increase the mass of any person or object within 350 feet of his person

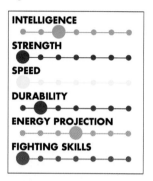

MASTERMIND

Real Name: Jason Wyngarde
First Appearance: *X-Men* #4 (1964)

Height: 5'10"
Weight: 140 lbs

After his stint with the **Brotherhood of Evil Mutants**, Mastermind left to pursue a career of his own and was invited to apply for admission to the Inner Circle of the **Hellfire Club**. Mastermind used his mutant powers to alter the personality of **Jean Grey** so she would willingly become the Inner Circle's new Black Queen. His plan backfired: Jean, possessed by the Phoenix Force, broke free of Mastermind's control and opened his mind to the cosmos. Unable to cope, Mastermind fell into a catatonic state. While he recovered, Mastermind eventually succumbed to the mutant-targeting Legacy Virus.

POWERS/WEAPONS

- Psionic ability to cast illusions, causing people to see, hear, touch, smell, or taste things which do not actually exist

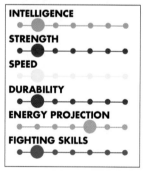

DONALD PIERCE

Real Name: Donald Pierce
First Appearance: *X-Men* #129 (1980)

Height: 5'11"
Weight: 240 lbs

After a catastrophic injury left Donald Pierce mortally wounded, he was turned into a cyborg by **Sebastian Shaw**. When Shaw assumed control of the Inner Circle of the **Hellfire Club**, he invited Pierce to become the Circle's White Bishop. During his affiliation with the Inner Circle, Pierce frequently clashed with the **X-Men**. After a particularly brutal defeat, he sought revenge against both Shaw and **Professor X** for the failure. Unsuccessful, he was subsequently expelled from the Inner Circle, later teaming up with the **Reavers** to combat the X-Men.

POWERS/WEAPONS

- Technological implants that provide augmented strength, endurance, and reflexes

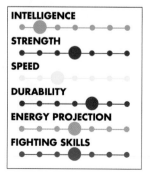

POWERS/WEAPONS

- Psionic ability to drain the life force of others, using the energy to restore her youth and beauty

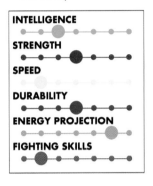

INTELLIGENCE

STRENGTH

SPEED

DURABILITY

ENERGY PROJECTION

FIGHTING SKILLS

Real Name: Selene (full name unrevealed)
First Appearance: *New Mutants* #9 (1983)

Height: 5'10"
Weight: 144 lbs

The powerful sorceress Selene can never grow old or ugly—so long as she drains the life force of others to replenish her youth and beauty. Her anti-aging regime served her well: Following a restructuring of the Hellfire Club by its then-leader Sebastian Shaw, Selene was recruited into the Club's Inner Circle along with her high priest, Friedrich von Roehm, and eventually ascended to the position of Black Queen. Her most recent maneuver was blackmailing an unwilling Roberto DaCosta (Sunspot) into joining the Club's ranks as its new Black Rook.

SELENE

POWERS/WEAPONS

- Manipulation of the density of his body's molecular structure

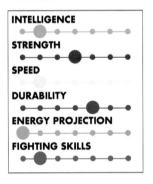

INTELLIGENCE

STRENGTH

SPEED

DURABILITY

ENERGY PROJECTION

FIGHTING SKILLS

Real Name: Shinobi Shaw
First Appearance: *X-Factor* #67 (1991)

Height: 5'11"
Weight: 165 lbs

The spoiled son of billionaire Sebastian Shaw, Shinobi Shaw managed to accumulate his own personal fortune, using it to buy out Shaw Industries from under his father. In the confrontation that followed, Shinobi seemingly killed his father. Shinobi then usurped his father's position as Black King of the Hellfire Club and sought to reform the Club's Inner Circle by recruiting a myriad of new members. But soon Shinobi learned that his father was still alive, and the elder Shaw reclaimed his title of Black King.

SHINOBI SHAW

POWERS/WEAPONS

- Enhanced lupine features as well as heightened senses and agility

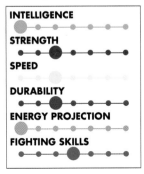

INTELLIGENCE

STRENGTH

SPEED

DURABILITY

ENERGY PROJECTION

FIGHTING SKILLS

Real Name: Friedrich von Roehm
First Appearance: *New Mutants* #22 (1984)

Height: 5'8"
Weight: 190 lbs.

Friedrich von Roehm was bred and programmed by Selene to enter a semi-lycanthropic state at her command. After Selene came calling on Friedrich in his jewelry store in Manhattan, he helped her secure a stateside residence from which she could bring her plans to fruition; he also suggested she join the Hellfire Club. When Selene was accepted as the new Black Queen of the Club's Inner Circle, Friedrich became Black Rook. During a battle between the Club's Inner Circle and the X-Men, a mutant-hunting Sentinel disintegrated Friedrich.

FRIEDRICH VON ROEHM

HELLIONS

They were the Hellions: trained in secret to serve in secret.

The White Queen, <u>Emma Frost</u>, brought them together to serve the <u>Hellfire Club</u>'s Inner Circle.

Frost secretly trained her young mutants to utilize their powers at her Massachusetts Academy, a private school located in Snow Valley in the Berkshire Mountains, where Frost acted as the school's headmistress.

Once unleashed, the Hellions would serve the interests of the Inner Circle and further their agenda to amass political and economic power through both legal and illegal means, frequently coming into conflict with the <u>New Mutants</u>.

But they would fail to meet their goals.

Only the lucky would survive a horrible encounter at the Hellfire Club with <u>Trevor Fitzroy</u>.

The dead survive only as memories now—terrible ghosts of an idea too awful to come to fruition. And the living are left to bear the legacy of all the young who died too soon.

Art by Jim Cheung

First Appearance:
New Mutants #16 (1984)

POWERS/WEAPONS

- Transforms herself into a lavender feline humanoid form with enhanced strength, senses, and agility

INTELLIGENCE

STRENGTH

SPEED

DURABILITY

ENERGY PROJECTION

FIGHTING SKILLS

Real Name: Unrevealed
First Appearance: *New Mutants* #16 (1984)

Height: 6'
Weight: 140 lbs

Abandoned at birth by her human parents, Catseye was raised by a cat. Emma Frost found her and convinced her she was a mutant, and Catseye soon became emotionally attached to the woman she came to regard as her surrogate mother. Under Frost's tutelage, Catseye progressed from illiteracy to upper grade-school reading levels in less than a year. But after Catseye joined Frost's Hellions, Trevor Fitzroy's assault on the Hellfire Club claimed her life. She later reappeared, seemingly reborn.

CATSEYE

POWERS/WEAPONS

- Psionically detects and alters the emotional state of other sentient beings in his immediate vicinity

INTELLIGENCE

STRENGTH

SPEED

DURABILITY

ENERGY PROJECTION

FIGHTING SKILLS

Real Name: Manuel Alfonso Rodrigo de la Rocha
First Appearance: *New Mutants* #16 (1984)

Height: 5'11"
Weight: 160 lbs

During the Hellions' frequent clashes with the New Mutants, Empath and Magma developed a mutual attraction. After Emma Frost captured the New Mutants and brainwashed them into swelling the Hellions' ranks, Empath and Magma's attraction blossomed into romance. Surviving the massacre of the Hellions at the hands of Trevor Fitzroy, the couple traveled to Magma's former home in the Amazon jungle. But their relationship soured when Magma became uncertain whether her feelings were her own or the result of Empath's power.

EMPATH

POWERS/WEAPONS

- Generation of thermo-chemical energy within his body
- Flight

INTELLIGENCE

STRENGTH

SPEED

DURABILITY

ENERGY PROJECTION

FIGHTING SKILLS

Real Name: Haroun ibn Sallah al-Rashid
First Appearance: *New Mutants* #16 (1984)

Height: 5'7"
Weight: 145 lbs

Jetstream's body was unable to withstand the tremendous energies he generated, and one day his flesh caught fire as he flew. To save him and still allow him to use his power, the Hellions equipped Jetstream with a bionic system that enabled him to contain, focus, and control the power he generated. As a result, Jetstream felt bound by his sense of honor to serve the Hellfire Club for life—a life that, as it turned out, would not last much longer. Jetstream was the first Hellion to be killed by Trevor Fitzroy during his assault on the Hellfire Club.

JETSTREAM

BEEF

Real Name:
Unrevealed
First Appearance:
New Warriors #9 (1991)

Height:
6'6"
Weight:
250 lbs

POWERS/WEAPONS
• Augmented muscle mass that grants him superhuman size, strength, endurance, and durability

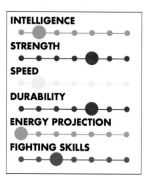

INTELLIGENCE
STRENGTH
SPEED
DURABILITY
ENERGY PROJECTION
FIGHTING SKILLS

BEVATRON

Real Name:
Unrevealed
First Appearance:
New Warriors #9 (1991)

Height:
5'8"
Weight:
150 lbs

POWERS/WEAPONS
• Increases the storage of bioelectricity within his body's cells, then channels the electricity into radiant discharges of high-voltage energy from his hands

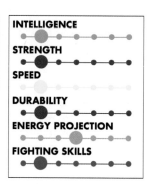

INTELLIGENCE
STRENGTH
SPEED
DURABILITY
ENERGY PROJECTION
FIGHTING SKILLS

ROULETTE

Real Name:
Jennifer Stavros
First Appearance:
New Mutants #16 (1984)

Height:
5'1"
Weight:
90 lbs.

POWERS/WEAPONS
• Generation of black energy disks that create bad luck and white energy disks that create good luck

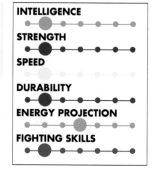

INTELLIGENCE
STRENGTH
SPEED
DURABILITY
ENERGY PROJECTION
FIGHTING SKILLS

TAROT

Real Name:
Marie-Ange Colbert
First Appearance:
New Mutants #16 (1984)

Height:
5'7"
Weight:
115 lbs.

POWERS/WEAPONS
• Psionically causes figures and objects to materialize on the tarot cards she carries

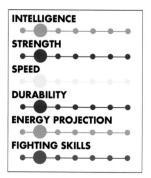

INTELLIGENCE
STRENGTH
SPEED
DURABILITY
ENERGY PROJECTION
FIGHTING SKILLS

MARAUDERS

Art by Joe Madureira

First Appearance:
Uncanny X-Men #210 (1986)

Where there is killing, where there is chaos, where there is terror, where there is mayhem, there is always something else: Marauders. In their wake, these mutant assassins leave nothing but devastation; slaughtered innocents, demolished homesteads, shattered lives. And then they go back for more.

They embody the deadly combination of sycophant and killer, enacting their terrorist agenda on behalf of a single master, <u>Mr. Sinister</u>. From the annihilation of a weak race of underground dwellers to the destruction of the <u>Xavier Mansion</u>, the Marauders' deadly and meticulous handiwork is vicious and swift. They tally their victories by the number of body bags left behind. No life is sacred. No home is secure. No man or mutant is safe. In the absence of goodness and mercy there are Marauders.

Let the killing begin.

MR. SINISTER

Real Name:
Nathaniel Essex
First Appearance:
Uncanny X-Men #213
(1987)

Height: 6'3"
Weight: 255 lbs
Eye Color: Red
Hair Color: Black

A geneticist of unparalleled genius living in Victorian England, Dr. Nathaniel Essex began conducting experiments to learn more about mutants. Nathaniel engaged in unorthodox trials, earning him the outrage of his peers and ultimately ejection from the Royal Society. Repudiated, Nathaniel found his way to **Apocalypse**, who granted him the ability to control his body's molecules, allowing him to pass energy blasts through himself and change his appearance at will. Reenergized by his new abilities, Mr. Sinister plotted the course of certain gene pools for over a century, and found that the combination of the genes of both Scott Summers (**Cyclops**) and **Jean Grey** would eventually generate a mutant of incredible power. Acting on his discovery, Mr. Sinister found young Scott in a hospital the night after Scott's fall from the airplane accident that took away his parents. Adopting a human guise, Mr. Sinister arranged for both Scott and his brother Alex (**Havok**) to be transferred to an orphanage, where he maintained a secret basement complex.

After outfitting Scott with ruby quartz lenses that would hold back his optic beams, Mr. Sinister buried Scott's memories of the year spent experimenting on the young mutant, so that Scott believed he had lain unconscious in a coma for that time. Mr. Sinister also arranged for Alex's eventual adoption, though he continued to keep track of the boy. Once **Professor X** recruited Cyclops, however, Mr. Sinister's plans to use the mutant as his own pawn were thwarted; he considered the experiment a personal failure. Undeterred in his pursuit of genetic perfection, Mister Sinister duped **Gambit** into assembling a group of assassins known as the **Marauders** to wipe out the **Morlocks**, whom he considered genetically useless. His Marauders murdered every Morlock they encountered, leaving few to survive and flee to new cities.

Mr. Sinister later led the Marauders in battle against the **X-Men** and demolished the **Xavier Institute**. In the midst of this attack, Mr. Sinister revealed to Cyclops the true story of what had happened to him as a boy. But it wasn't until Mr. Sinister threatened the life of Jean Grey that Cyclops obliterated Mr. Sinister with a massive optic blast. Mr. Sinister survived, thanks in large part to his malleable form.

POWERS/ WEAPONS

- Control over every molecule in his body
- Telepathy

Art by Tom Raney

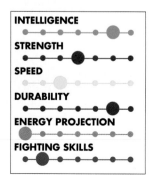

INTELLIGENCE				
STRENGTH				
SPEED				
DURABILITY				
ENERGY PROJECTION				
FIGHTING SKILLS				

POWERS/WEAPONS

- A being of pure psionic energy that can merge with the mind of another sentient creature

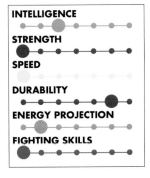

| INTELLIGENCE |
| STRENGTH |
| SPEED |
| DURABILITY |
| ENERGY PROJECTION |
| FIGHTING SKILLS |

Real Name: Unrevealed
First Appearance: *Uncanny X-Men* #210 (1986)

Height: Inapplicable
Weight: Inapplicable

Art by Marc Silvestri

MALICE

The psionic entity Malice was recruited by **Mr. Sinister** to join his **Marauders**. As a member of that organization, Malice body-hopped through a number of female **X-Men**, including **Dazzler**, **Rogue**, and **Storm**. But Storm's will was too strong, and she forcibly ejected Malice from her body. During a Marauders' attack on **Polaris**, Malice possessed the powerful mutant. As their two energy matrices interwove, the two women became permanently bound together. Mr. Sinister had known this union would occur, but failed to warn Malice of it because he had specific plans for the now-blended entity: using the Malice-possessed Polaris to attack the X-Men, who counted among their team members Polaris's lover, **Havok**.

Malice was later freed from Polaris's body when **Zaladane** temporarily stole Polaris' magnetic powers. Freedom for Malice turned out to be fleeting: Mr. Sinister had tired of her presence and decided to kill her rather than keep her around.

POWERS/WEAPONS

- Psionic disorientation of any sentient being's equilibrium

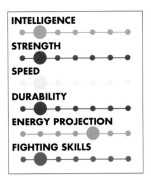

| INTELLIGENCE |
| STRENGTH |
| SPEED |
| DURABILITY |
| ENERGY PROJECTION |
| FIGHTING SKILLS |

Real Name: Unrevealed
First Appearance: *Marvel Fanfare* #1 (1982)

Height: 5'6"
Weight: 128 lbs

Art by Joe Madureira

VERTIGO

A native of the hidden prehistoric Antarctic jungle known as the Savage Land, Vertigo received her great powers with the help of **Brainchild**'s genetic engineering. Once empowered, Vertigo joined the **Savage Land Mutates** and used her new skills to help her compatriots battle their enemies the **X-Men**.

But life outside the Antarctic jungle called, and Vertigo traded her life in the Savage Land for another kind of savage existence with the **Marauders**. Willingly using her powers to advance her new team's murderous agenda, Vertigo took great pleasure in wiping out the **Morlocks** in their tunnels beneath Manhattan. When her own life was taken during a demonic invasion of Manhattan, she once again enjoyed the benefits of genetic engineering: **Mr. Sinister** cloned her from DNA he had taken from her body.

Her resurrection complete—and her voracious desire for killing returned—Vertigo left the Marauders for some time to serve as a member of the all-female superhuman army known as the Femizons. Eventually, Vertigo returned home to fight alongside the Savage Land Mutates.

ARCLIGHT

| **Real Name:** | Philippa Sontag | **Height:** | 5'8" |
| **First Appearance:** | *Uncanny X-Men* #210 (1986) | **Weight:** | 139 lbs |

Deep in an underground tunnel in New York City, Arclight plunged headfirst into the most notorious of all <u>Marauder</u> missions: finding and slaughtering the <u>Morlocks</u>. After the triumphant completion of her genocidal duties, Arclight's superhuman abilities failed to save her during a demonic invasion of aboveground Manhattan. But dying turned out to be a mere blip to Arclight: <u>Mr. Sinister</u>, using DNA he had previously extracted from her, cloned and resurrected the fierce girl. Afterwards, Arclight served for a brief time in the all-female superhuman army called the Femizons.

POWERS/WEAPONS

- Ability to focus seismic energy though her hands to create shock waves or earth tremors

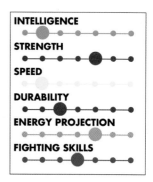

INTELLIGENCE
STRENGTH
SPEED
DURABILITY
ENERGY PROJECTION
FIGHTING SKILLS

HARPOON

| **Real Name:** | Kodiak Noatak | **Height:** | 5'7" |
| **First Appearance:** | *Uncanny X-Men* #210 (1986) | **Weight:** | 173 lbs |

Relentlessly deadly and fiercely devoted, Harpoon invaded the <u>Morlocks</u>' underground tunnels in New York City, intent on wiping out their entire population. Despite fierce resistance from the <u>X-Men</u>, they were merely distractions from the task at hand. While the other <u>Marauders</u> murdered Morlocks, Harpoon plunged his spear into <u>Archangel</u>'s wings, necessitating their later amputation. He also caused <u>Shadowcat</u> to become trapped in a phased state and seriously injured <u>Colossus</u>, temporarily preventing the mutant's body from turning back into flesh from its steel form.

POWERS/WEAPONS

- Creation of projectile weapons by transforming long, narrow objects into a form of bio-energy

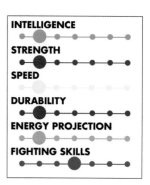

INTELLIGENCE
STRENGTH
SPEED
DURABILITY
ENERGY PROJECTION
FIGHTING SKILLS

RIPTIDE

| **Real Name:** | Janos Quested | **Height:** | 5'10" |
| **First Appearance:** | *Uncanny X-Men* #210 (1986) | **Weight:** | 158 lbs |

Riptide, though possessed of the ability to whirl and twirl at frenetic, mind-jostling speeds, was further genetically engineered by <u>Mr. Sinister</u>. During his murderous mission in the <u>Morlocks</u>' tunnels, Riptide used his ability to severely injure <u>Nightcrawler</u>—a feat not gone unpunished by <u>Colossus</u>, who broke Riptide's neck in return. Though he managed to bounce back from his comeuppance, Riptide did not survive a demonic invasion that swept through Manhattan. Since Mr. Sinister retained his DNA, however, Riptide remains cloneable and may yet return.

POWERS/WEAPONS

- Ability to spin at high velocities
- Secretes a calcium-based substance that hardens into super-dense throwing stars

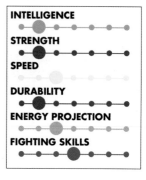

INTELLIGENCE
STRENGTH
SPEED
DURABILITY
ENERGY PROJECTION
FIGHTING SKILLS

BLOCKBUSTER

INTELLIGENCE
STRENGTH
SPEED
DURABILITY
ENERGY PROJECTION
FIGHTING SKILLS

Real Name:
Michael Baer
First Appearance:
X-Factor #10 (1986)

Height:
6'10"
Weight:
386 lbs

POWERS/WEAPONS
- Superhuman strength, endurance, and durability

PRISM

INTELLIGENCE
STRENGTH
SPEED
DURABILITY
ENERGY PROJECTION
FIGHTING SKILLS

Real Name:
Unrevealed
First Appearance:
Uncanny X-Men #210 (1986)

Height:
5'10"
Weight:
260 lbs

POWERS/WEAPONS
- Energy refraction, allowing him to augment power and reflect it back to its source

SCALPHUNTER

INTELLIGENCE
STRENGTH
SPEED
DURABILITY
ENERGY PROJECTION
FIGHTING SKILLS

Real Name:
Grey Crow
First Appearance:
Uncanny X-Men #210 (1986)

Height:
6'6"
Weight:
205 lbs

POWERS/WEAPONS
- Technoforming, the ability to manipulate mechanical components and assemble them into a variety of different configurations by modifying their shape and construction

SCRAMBLER

INTELLIGENCE
STRENGTH
SPEED
DURABILITY
ENERGY PROJECTION
FIGHTING SKILLS

Real Name:
Kim Il Sung
First Appearance:
Uncanny X-Men #210 (1986)

Height:
5'9"
Weight:
145 lbs

POWERS/WEAPONS
- Generation of a disruptive form of energy that alters the function of any living or mechanical system he touches

MORLOCKS

Art by Shaun Martinbrough

First Appearance:
Uncanny X-Men #169 (1983)

They are mutants. They do not want to be heroes. They do not want to be villains.

They just want to be let alone—and left in peace.

It remains a wish cruelly unfulfilled.

Comprised of mutants ostracized from society, the Morlock community took its name from the subterranean race depicted in H. G. Wells's *The Time Machine*. Fleeing a society that viewed them as objects of scorn and ridicule, the Morlocks took to the long-abandoned military tunnels underneath New York City in an effort to hide themselves away from the hateful world above.

It would not be long before their hiding place became their graveyard.

Having decided the Morlocks were the most disdainful genetic product on the planet, <u>Mr. Sinister</u> orchestrated their annihilation. In an act of unparalleled brutality, the <u>Marauders</u> entered the tunnels and killed every Morlock they could find. Even the <u>X-Men</u> sent to rescue the helpless social outcasts were powerless to halt the Marauder murder machine.

When the madness subsided, the few surviving Morlocks made their way out of the underground wasteland and scattered across the country. Living under the streets of major cities across the country, the Morlocks live in continual fear of a different menace to their safety: the <u>Sentinels</u>.

CALLISTO

When Callisto was young and beautiful, her life seemed so perfect, so enviable. But catastrophe struck, blinding her in her right eye and leaving her horribly disfigured. Forced to hold up a mirror to her new reality, Callisto realized that society had little use for a beautiful woman who was beautiful no more.

Scared and alone, she decided to go underground where it was safe, and where she could escape prying, peering eyes. She quickly made a huge abandoned military tunnel built underneath Manhattan in the 1950s her home.

With help from Caliban, Callisto brought together other mutant outcasts. Discovering she was not alone in her desire to escape the aboveground world, Callisto dubbed the growing group of mutants who came to live under her leadership in the tunnels the Morlocks.

In the course of her duties, Callisto met the X-Men—and took quite a shine to Archangel. Taking extreme measures to ensure his affection, Callisto kidnapped him, hoping to make him her consort. But the X-Men pursued their teammate, and Callisto was forced to battle Storm in an effort to keep her man. Callisto lost the battle—and Archangel.

Not long after, Callisto and her growing band of outcasts became the victims of the Marauders' genetic massacre. Though she lost the majority of those who lived with her in the tunnels, she and a few others managed to survive. Tending to her own injuries, Callisto left the tunnels to recuperate—and Masque immediately seized the opportunity to take control of the group.

Having resumed her leadership of the group following the death of Masque, Callisto realizes that while her physical beauty was fleeting, her true beauty can never be taken away: her infinite compassion and concern for other outcasts from society not as strong as she.

Real Name:
Unrevealed, presumed Callisto
First Appearance:
Uncanny X Men #169 (1983)

Height: 5'9"
Weight: 140 lbs
Eye Color: Blue
Hair Color: Black

INTELLIGENCE
STRENGTH
SPEED
DURABILITY
ENERGY PROJECTION
FIGHTING SKILLS

POWERS/ WEAPONS

• Superhumanly keen senses of sight, hearing, smell, touch, and taste

Art by Joe Madureira

ANGEL DUST

Real Name: Christine (full name unrevealed)
First Appearance: *Morlocks* #1 (2002)
Height: 5'5"
Weight: 126 lbs

When the scared young mutant Angel Dust ran away to join the Chicago faction of the Morlocks, she left behind frantic parents who had no idea where she went or why she had left. After Angel Dust and the other Morlocks swore to help each other resolve one "aboveground" issue, she returned home to tell her parents the truth she thought would turn her out of the family forever: She was a mutant. To Angel Dust's surprise, her parents accepted her for who she was, but it was only after she had helped her compatriots defeat a Sentinel base that Angel Dust finally returned home for good.

POWERS/WEAPONS

- Superhuman strength temporarily granted by her ability to chemically supercharge her adrenaline levels

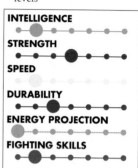

INTELLIGENCE
STRENGTH
SPEED
DURABILITY
ENERGY PROJECTION
FIGHTING SKILLS

ARTIE

Real Name: Arthur Maddicks
First Appearance: *X-Factor* #2 (1986)
Height: 4'2"
Weight: 67 lbs

Disfigured and rendered mute when his powers manifested, young Artie rejected his father's diabolical, though well-intentioned, plans to return him back to his normal human form. Only through the intervention of the original X-Men was Artie saved. After his father was killed in the aftermath, the orphan Artie went on to spend time with the X-Men and met Leech, a member of the Morlocks. Together the pair would later be officially enrolled in the Massachusetts Academy as students, where they learned to further hone their abilities.

POWERS/WEAPONS

- Communication via creation of visual images of whatever or whomever he conceives

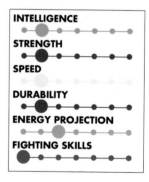

INTELLIGENCE
STRENGTH
SPEED
DURABILITY
ENERGY PROJECTION
FIGHTING SKILLS

CALIBAN

Real Name: Unrevealed
First Appearance: *Uncanny X-Men* #148 (1981)
Height: 5'8"
Weight: 150 lbs

Even among fellow outcasts the Morlocks, the childlike Caliban battles constantly against loneliness. After Shadowcat rebuffed Caliban in a New York nightclub, the Morlocks kidnapped her and attempted to force her to marry Caliban. Caliban, realizing that she truly did not wish to live with him, released Shadowcat from her captivity—and the two became friends. Possibly believing an increase in power would alleviate his troubles, Caliban allowed himself to be transformed into a Horseman of Apocalypse. But after Apocalypse was finally defeated, Caliban reverted back to his childlike self.

POWERS/WEAPONS

- Psionically senses the presence of other mutants within a 25-mile radius
- Superhuman strength as a minion of Apocalypse

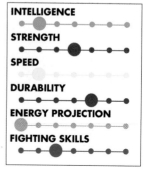

INTELLIGENCE
STRENGTH
SPEED
DURABILITY
ENERGY PROJECTION
FIGHTING SKILLS

CELL

POWERS/WEAPONS

- Digestive acids that burn matter upon contact

INTELLIGENCE	
STRENGTH	
SPEED	
DURABILITY	
ENERGY PROJECTION	
FIGHTING SKILLS	

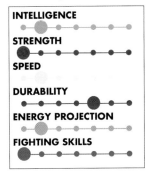

Real Name: Unrevealed
First Appearance: *Morlocks* #1 (2002)

Height: 5'8"
Weight: Indeterminate

As a tough and hardened Chicago gang member, Cell thought he had experienced everything—until the night a policeman's bullet ripped through his body and caused him to turn into a single-celled organism that oozed into the city sewers below. The Morlocks rescued the mutant from the police, who were still in pursuit, and a grateful Cell joined their group. After the Morlocks invaded a Sentinel base, Cell engulfed the base commander so his friends could escape. As they safely exited, a Sentinel killed Cell and the commander in an explosion that wiped out the entire base.

ELECTRIC EVE

POWERS/WEAPONS

- Absorb, store, and discharge electricity

INTELLIGENCE	
STRENGTH	
SPEED	
DURABILITY	
ENERGY PROJECTION	
FIGHTING SKILLS	

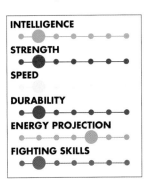

Real Name: Eve (full name unrevealed)
First Appearance: *X-Men: Millennial Visions* 2001 (2000)

Height: 5'11"
Weight: 140 lbs

As a schoolgirl in Chicago, Eve fell in love with two dangerous things: heroin and her dealer, Ricky. Eve would do anything to get either—and greedy Ricky knew it. After Ricky pushed Eve into prostitution, Eve's powers manifested during an encounter with a customer, killing him. Scared straight by the experience, Eve fled the scene and turned to the Morlocks for help. With their assistance, Eve exacted revenge on Ricky. At his penthouse, she electrocuted her former dealer and lover in his rooftop swimming pool. Shortly thereafter, Eve, along with the other Morlocks, left Chicago for good.

LEECH

POWERS/WEAPONS

- Can cancel out others' superhuman abilities, mutant or otherwise

INTELLIGENCE	
STRENGTH	
SPEED	
DURABILITY	
ENERGY PROJECTION	
FIGHTING SKILLS	

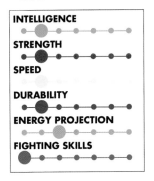

Real Name: Unrevealed
First Appearance: *Uncanny X-Men* #179 (1984)

Height: 4'2"
Weight: 67 lbs

Leech lived a lonely existence with the Morlocks until he used his powers to prevent Annalee from experiencing the suicidal anguish caused by her children's murder. They drew close, and Leech came to regard her as his mother. After the Marauders slaughtered Annalee, a devastated Leech was saved by the original X-Men and met fellow orphan Artie; the two formed a lifelong friendship. The pair eventually enrolled as students at the Massachusetts Academy, where they learned to further hone their abilities. Leech later was abducted by the Weapon X program, which used his powers to hold captive other mutants.

LITTERBUG

| **Real Name:** | Unrevealed | **Height:** | 6'5" |
| **First Appearance:** | *X-Men: Millennial Visions* 2001 (2000) | **Weight:** | 326 lbs |

POWERS/WEAPONS

• Chitinous exoskeleton that protects him from injury

As a mechanic in the United States Army, Litterbug utilized his skills to help the Army construct Sentinels. But when his mutant power manifested, Litterbug went AWOL, knowing both the Army and the Sentinels would soon be after him. Finding his way to the streets of Chicago, he eventually sought out the safety of the Morlock underground. Knowing his new friends lived in fear of Sentinel attacks, Litterbug was instrumental in allowing them to capture a Sentinel, which they used as a Trojan horse to infiltrate a Sentinel base. Once they destroyed the base, the Morlocks fled Chicago.

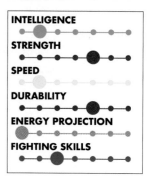

INTELLIGENCE

STRENGTH

SPEED

DURABILITY

ENERGY PROJECTION

FIGHTING SKILLS

MASQUE

| **Real Name:** | Unrevealed | **Height:** | 5'6" |
| **First Appearance:** | *Uncanny X-Men* #169 (1983) | **Weight:** | 140 lbs |

POWERS/WEAPONS

• Ability to psionically rearrange the flesh of organic substances to create any physical effect possible

While most Morlocks are content to live peacefully away from society, Masque wanted something more: power. When the Morlocks' leader, Callisto, left her group to help take care of members wounded in the Marauders' massacre, Masque quickly usurped her position and took control of the group. With Callisto temporarily out of the way, Masque allied his band of Morlocks with the Brotherhood of Evil Mutants to combat the mutant strike force founded by Nathan Summers. But Masque was killed by Shatterstar in the ensuing battle.

INTELLIGENCE

STRENGTH

SPEED

DURABILITY

ENERGY PROJECTION

FIGHTING SKILLS

POSTMAN

| **Real Name:** | David (full name unrevealed) | **Height:** | 5'10" |
| **First Appearance:** | *Morlocks* #1 (2002) | **Weight:** | 170 lbs |

POWERS/WEAPONS

• Telepathically reach into another being's cerebral cortex and erase it

Living life aboveground, the bespectacled David had everything society expected of him: a good job working at the post office and a wonderful wife, Erica. But all expectations evaporated the moment his mutant powers activated and he found he had accidentally erased his wife's mind. Panicked, Postman sought refuge with the Chicago-area Morlocks. To make penance for Erica's accident, Postman penned a farewell note to her. With the help of the Morlocks, Postman delivered his heartfelt letter to his comatose wife in her hospital room but could do nothing to save her from her vegetative state.

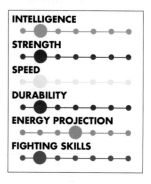

INTELLIGENCE

STRENGTH

SPEED

DURABILITY

ENERGY PROJECTION

FIGHTING SKILLS

POWERS/WEAPONS

- Ability to open up portals in the dimensional barrier to allow travel between realities

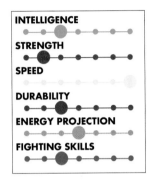

INTELLIGENCE			●				
STRENGTH		●					
SPEED							○
DURABILITY			●				
ENERGY PROJECTION		●					
FIGHTING SKILLS			●				

Real Name: Mikhail Rasputin
First Appearance: *Uncanny X-Men* #285 (1992)

Height: 6'1"
Weight: 225 lbs

As a Russian cosmonaut, Mikhail Rasputin—brother of <u>Colossus</u> and <u>Magik</u>—was thought dead after his spacecraft was lost. But Mikhail had survived—though not without great damage to his psyche. For years he loitered in strange dimensions where time and circumstances eroded his mind. Once back on Earth, Mikhail was driven insane by the terrible voices and images of his past, but eventually found some solace in the tunnels beneath Manhattan with the <u>Morlocks</u>, even controlling his emotional instability enough to become their leader for a time.

MIKHAIL RASPUTIN

POWERS/WEAPONS

- Ability to crystallize liquids

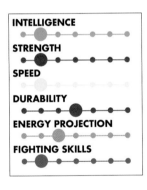

INTELLIGENCE		●					
STRENGTH		●					
SPEED	○						
DURABILITY			●				
ENERGY PROJECTION		●					
FIGHTING SKILLS	●						

Real Name: Unrevealed
First Appearance: *Morlocks* #1 (2002)

Height: 5'7"
Weight: 150 lbs

For Shatter, there was only one plausible way to come to terms with his life as a mutant: suicide. After his power molecularly crystallized the cells of his body, Shatter pointed a gun to his head and pulled the trigger. But the bullet did not kill him—it merely cracked his crystalline form. Unwilling to live among people who hated and feared him, Shatter took up with the <u>Morlocks</u> who made their home in the Chicago underground. With their help, Shatter fulfilled one last aboveground wish: to save his best friend, a dog named Hank, from being put to sleep.

SHATTER

POWERS/WEAPONS

- Retina clouding of anyone who sees him, allowing him to blend near-invisibly into shadows and walls

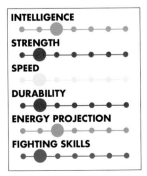

INTELLIGENCE		●					
STRENGTH		●					
SPEED		●					
DURABILITY		●					
ENERGY PROJECTION	●						
FIGHTING SKILLS		●					

Real Name: Unrevealed
First Appearance: *Morlocks* #1 (2002)

Height: 6'1"
Weight: 175 lbs

Hiding his mutant abilities, Trader lived and worked as a successful stockbroker. Trader enjoyed all the trappings of his six-figure income—until a conniving stockbroker decided to "out" Trader as a mutant. Unwilling to face the scorn of his employers and clients, he fled. Finding refuge with the <u>Morlocks</u>, Trader asked them to help him avenge his betrayal. His desire never came to fruition. When Chicago police entered the tunnels to flush out the Morlocks, they shot at <u>Electric Eve</u>. Trader leapt in front of the girl to protect her—and took the bullet that ended his life.

TRADER

ANNALEE

Real Name:
Annalee (full name unrevealed)
First Appearance:
Power Pack #12 (1985)

Height:
5'2"
Weight:
165 lbs

POWERS/WEAPONS

- Emotional projection on other sentient beings, causing them to feel whatever she feels

INTELLIGENCE
STRENGTH
SPEED
DURABILITY
ENERGY PROJECTION
FIGHTING SKILLS

APE

Real Name:
Unrevealed
First Appearance:
Power Pack #12 (1985)

Height:
5'10"
Weight:
150 lbs

POWERS/WEAPONS

- Malleable molecular structure that enables restructuring of his physical appearance to change his shape into that of any solid object he can imagine

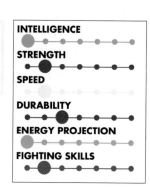

INTELLIGENCE
STRENGTH
SPEED
DURABILITY
ENERGY PROJECTION
FIGHTING SKILLS

BEAUTIFUL DREAMER

Real Name:
Unrevealed
First Appearance:
Power Pack #12 (1985)

Height:
5'1"
Weight:
115 lbs

POWERS/WEAPONS

- Psionic alteration of the memories of other sentient beings

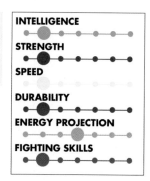

INTELLIGENCE
STRENGTH
SPEED
DURABILITY
ENERGY PROJECTION
FIGHTING SKILLS

BLOWHARD

Real Name:
Unrevealed
First Appearance:
X-Factor #11 (1986)

Height:
5'11"
Weight:
220 lbs

POWERS/WEAPONS

- Generation of gale force winds

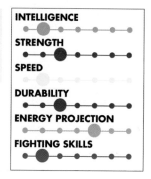

INTELLIGENCE
STRENGTH
SPEED
DURABILITY
ENERGY PROJECTION
FIGHTING SKILLS

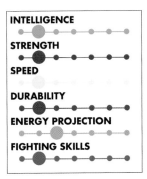

Real Name:
Cybelle
First Appearance:
Uncanny X-Men #211 (1986)

Height:
5'5"
Weight:
129 lbs

POWERS/WEAPONS

• Pore secretion of a fast-acting acidic sweat

CYBELLE

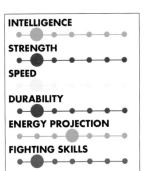

Real Name:
Unrevealed
First Appearance:
Power Pack #12 (1985)

Height:
6'6"
Weight:
192 lbs

POWERS/WEAPONS

• Absorption of various forms of ambient- and focused-energy into his body's cells that he metabolizes into electricity and releases from his left eye

ERG

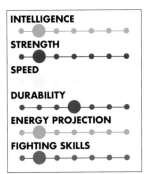

Real Name:
Unrevealed
First Appearance:
Uncanny X-Men #179 (1984)

Height:
6'3"
Weight:
210 lbs

POWERS/WEAPONS

• Taps into the specific gene that causes mutations and rapidly heals wounds or diseases

HEALER

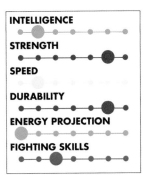

Real Name:
Unrevealed
First Appearance:
Generation X #5 (1995)

Height:
7'10"
Weight:
480 lbs

POWERS/WEAPONS

• Indestructible exoskeletal body that grants him superhuman strength and endurance

HEMINGWAY

PIPER

Real Name:
Unrevealed
First Appearance:
Power Pack #11 (1985)

Height:
5'9"
Weight:
170 lbs

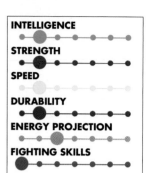

INTELLIGENCE
STRENGTH
SPEED
DURABILITY
ENERGY PROJECTION
FIGHTING SKILLS

POWERS/WEAPONS

• Possesses the psionic ability, aided by music he plays on his pipe, to control animals

---

PLAGUE

Real Name:
Unrevealed
First Appearance:
Uncanny X-Men #169 (1983)

Height:
5'5"
Weight:
130 lbs

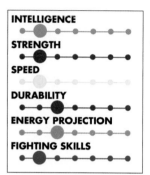

INTELLIGENCE
STRENGTH
SPEED
DURABILITY
ENERGY PROJECTION
FIGHTING SKILLS

POWERS/WEAPONS

• Adaptation of her immune system to any virus or disease that allows her to mutate the virus and transmit it to another living being by touch

---

SACK

Real Name:
Unrevealed
First Appearance:
Uncanny X-Men #323 (1995)

Height:
5'7"
Weight:
Indeterminate

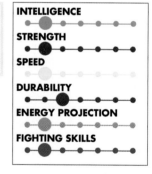

INTELLIGENCE
STRENGTH
SPEED
DURABILITY
ENERGY PROJECTION
FIGHTING SKILLS

POWERS/WEAPONS

• Amorphous form that affords him a high degree of resistance to penetrating weapons

---

SCALEFACE

Real Name:
Unrevealed
First Appearance:
X-Factor #11 (1986)

Height:
5'7"
Weight:
139 lbs

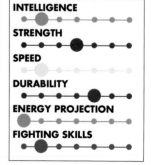

INTELLIGENCE
STRENGTH
SPEED
DURABILITY
ENERGY PROJECTION
FIGHTING SKILLS

POWERS/WEAPONS

• Transformation into a large dragon-like reptilian form with a fanged mouth, clawed hands and feet, and a ridge of spines along her back

SUNDER

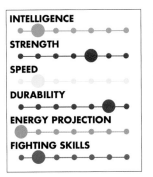

INTELLIGENCE
STRENGTH
SPEED
DURABILITY
ENERGY PROJECTION
FIGHTING SKILLS

Real Name:
Unrevealed
First Appearance:
Uncanny X-Men #169 (1983)

Height:
7'1"
Weight:
245 lbs

POWERS/WEAPONS
• Superhuman strength

TAR BABY

INTELLIGENCE
STRENGTH
SPEED
DURABILITY
ENERGY PROJECTION
FIGHTING SKILLS

Real Name:
Unrevealed
First Appearance:
Power Pack #12 (1985)

Height:
6'1"
Weight:
163 lbs

POWERS/WEAPONS
• Secretion of a powerful adhesive through the pores of his skin that causes objects to permanently stick to him on contact

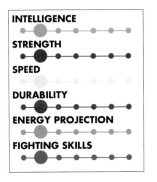

TOMMY

INTELLIGENCE
STRENGTH
SPEED
DURABILITY
ENERGY PROJECTION
FIGHTING SKILLS

Real Name:
Tommy (full name unrevealed)
First Appearance:
Uncanny X-Men #210 (1986)

Height:
5'3"
Weight:
110 lbs

POWERS/WEAPONS
• Ability to become two-dimensional

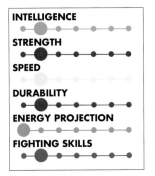

VESSEL

INTELLIGENCE
STRENGTH
SPEED
DURABILITY
ENERGY PROJECTION
FIGHTING SKILLS

Real Name:
Unrevealed
First Appearance:
Uncanny X-Men #323 (1995)

Height:
6'6"
Weight:
320 lbs

POWERS/WEAPONS
• Can siphon psionic residue from his victims and transmute it into raw physical power

NEW MUTANTS

Art by Josh Middleton

First Appearance:
Marvel Graphic Novel #4 (1982)

They were adolescents—kids—too young to be <u>X-Men</u>, but old enough to start the training that would allow them to fully understand and harness their profound mutant powers. <u>Professor X</u> brought together <u>Cannonball</u>, <u>Karma</u>, <u>Moonstar</u>, <u>Wolfsbane</u>, and <u>Sunspot</u> to become the first New Mutants team. Over time, <u>Cypher</u>, <u>Warlock</u>, and <u>Magik</u> were added to the team and, as they learned to become more powerful mutants together, they learned another important lesson: It's okay to act like normal kids. The New Mutants enjoyed their status as mutants, but they also enjoyed their youth. As with all kids their age, they fought and fell in love with one another, partied together, and argued with teachers and parents alike. But when duty called, maturity set in, and the New Mutants went into action—though sometimes not without consequence. During an assignment, Cypher was shot and killed after leaping into the path of a bullet destined for his teammate Wolfsbane.

Eventually, the team came under the direction of <u>Nathan Summers</u>, who used them to start up a paramilitary organization of his own. But they floundered under Summers's command and eventually, all the members went off on their own, effectively disbanding the New Mutants. Now, years later, the surviving New Mutants are all grown up. Some of them have resurrected the New Mutants, this time as teachers—not students—who are committed to training a new generation of young mutants. Working feverishly to gather young mutants from around the country who will face terrible fates if left alone among the mutant-hating populace, the leaders of the New Mutants know that the students of today are tomorrow's only hope for helping Professor X realize his dream of peace.

KARMA

The daughter of a Vietnamese Army colonel who served during the Vietnam War, Xi'an Coy Manh's fierce devotion to her family began when an enemy soldier threatened her elder brother Tran. Acting impulsively, Karma tapped into her latent mutant powers and took possession of the soldier's mind, stopping him from killing Tran. Tran then successfully attempted the same feat and forced the soldier to kill himself. While he took great delight in this use of his newfound power, Karma was frightened of hers. She tried to keep their powers secret, but Tran told their uncle Nguyen Coy, who was delighted by the news.

Real Name:
Xi'an "Shan" Coy Manh
First Appearance:
Marvel Team-Up #100 (1980)

Height: 5'4"
Weight: 110 lbs
Eye Color: Blue
Hair Color: Black

After the war, Nguyen, who had become a powerful and prosperous United States criminal, arranged for Karma's family to leave Vietnam. Tran was sent ahead first; eventually, Karma and the rest of the family followed, leaving Vietnam on a small, crowded boat. But the voyage was doomed. Though Xi'an and her younger siblings Leong and Nga were rescued by the U.S. Navy, her parents did not survive the trip. Reunited with her brother and uncle, Karma discovered to her horror that Tran had been using his powers to serve their uncle's criminal network. When Nguyen asked Karma to do the same, she refused, which enraged her uncle. He kidnapped Leong and Nga in an effort to blackmail her into working for him. Frantic, Karma sought the help of Spider-Man and the Fantastic Four, but Tran used his powers to take control of the heroes. Karma had no choice but to kill her brother to save what was left of her family—and to save the people who had come to aid her.

Feeling great empathy for the orphaned girl, the Fantastic Four contacted Professor X, who invited Xi'an to enroll in his school and learn to better use her powers. Xi'an accepted, and went on to become the first leader of Xavier's team of New Mutants. Karma had to leave the New Mutants when Leong and Nga disappeared. She discovered that Shinobi Shaw, then Black King of the Hellfire Club, had made the siblings the subjects of genetic experiments, and then turned them over to Spiral. Karma, along with Beast and Cannonball, defeated Spiral and rescued the two children. With the last remaining members of her family now in safe hands, Karma has enrolled in college to pursue a normal life.

INTELLIGENCE
STRENGTH
SPEED
DURABILITY
ENERGY PROJECTION
FIGHTING SKILLS

POWERS/ WEAPONS

- Psionic ability to take possession of others' minds

Art by Josh Middleton

MAGMA

Real Name:
Allison Crestmere
First Appearance:
New Mutants #8 (1983)

Height:	5'6"
Weight:	128 lbs
Eye Color:	Brown
Hair Color:	Blonde

Magma grew up as Amara Aquilla, the daughter of the first senator of Nova Roma, a hidden city in the Amazon jungle of Brazil whose citizens believed they were descendants of ancient Romans. To save his daughter from becoming a potential human sacrifice to the Black Priestess Selene, Magma's father sent Magma to live in the jungles outside Nova Roma. Magma remained in hiding for years until she was discovered by the New Mutants. But both Magma and the New Mutants were soon captured by Selene, and Magma was readied for sacrifice. When Selene used her mutant powers to drain Magma's life energy into her own body, a momentary distraction caused the Black Priestess to knock Magma into a nearby pit of lava. Rather than harming Magma, her immersion in the lava awakened the latent mutant powers that helped her defeat Selene. Magma's father instructed her to go to the United States with the New Mutants and learn more about their modern civilization.

At first, Magma had trouble adjusting to this strange civilization. Time and patience prevailed, and eventually Magma adapted to 20th century inventions and lifestyles. She proved herself a worthy asset to the New Mutants, but left the team after she met and fell in love with the Hellion Empath. The pair left for Nova Roma so Magma could introduce her boyfriend to her father. But her homecoming was anything but happy when Magma learned the terrible truth about her life in Nova Roma: It had all been a lie.

As it turned out, the city had not been founded by ancient Roman settlers after all. Instead, it was populated by the kidnapped and mind-wiped victims of Selene, who had created the city as a testament to the times she loved most and desperately wanted to relive. Along with the other citizens of Nova Roma, Magma eventually regained the memory of who she really was. As it turned out, her real name had been Allison Crestmere and she was, in fact, the mutant daughter of a British ambassador. Equipped for the first time with the truth, Magma's time spent in the modern world came in handy when she and Empath decided to stay and help the people of Nova Roma acclimate to their true reality. Though she was intent on helping the citizens of Nova Roma recover, Magma was understandably reluctant to believe in anything again, including her relationship with Empath. Convinced that Empath had used his abilities to force her to love him, Magma broke up with him and ultimately left for England to search for her true parents.

POWERS/ WEAPONS

• Generation and projection of intense heat from her body

Art by Jim Cheung

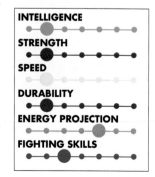

INTELLIGENCE		
STRENGTH		
SPEED		
DURABILITY		
ENERGY PROJECTION		
FIGHTING SKILLS		

MELTDOWN

Tabitha Smith had not gotten along with her parents for most of her life, and they were revolted when her mutant power emerged at age 13. Resentful toward her father, she placed a small explosive ball of energy in his lasagna. In retaliation, he beat her severely. Desperate to escape her parents' scorn and disgust, she learned of Professor X's School for Gifted Youngsters in Westchester, New York—headquarters to the X-Men and New Mutants—and set off by train for more friendly environs.

Tabitha eventually encountered the Vanisher, who made her a member of his gang of thieves, the Fallen Angels, and taught her to steal. Believing the Vanisher was treating her badly, Tabitha alerted Cyclops, Jean Grey and the other original X-Men—whom she believed to be a group of mutant hunters— about the Vanisher's activities. But when Beast and Iceman arrived, Tabitha changed her mind about turning in the Vanisher and used her "time bomb" on Iceman as a prank. When Beast and Iceman caught up to her, she agreed to leave the Vanisher's gang and live at their headquarters instead.

Later, after Tabitha set off another of her "time bombs" in the X-Men's laboratory as a prank, Iceman pursued her through the headquarters. Another member of the Vanisher's gang, Ariel, used her powers to enable Tabitha to escape. Thereafter, Tabitha remained for a time with the Fallen Angels. After an adventure on another planet, Tabitha returned to the X-Men's headquarters only to be captured by the anti-mutant organization known as the Right. Tabitha and other mutants associated with the original X-Men regained their freedom, however, and she went into action with her fellow trainees as the X-Terminators, later joining the New Mutants.

As a member of the New Mutants, Tabitha became enamored with Cannonball. She served as a member until the New Mutants came under the tutelage of Nathan Summers, who forged them into a proactive mutant strike force. Possessed of greater control over her powers, Meltdown was now no longer afraid to use them in nearly lethal ways. Under the guidance of Pete Wisdom, who introduced her teammates to the world of covert operations, Meltdown learned to expand her powers to be able to fire beams of concussive force. When Wisdom was seemingly killed, the team continued his crusade until they all appeared to die in a colossal explosion. They later resurfaced, and Meltdown joined Nathan Summers in a revolution against Weapon X and the Neverland mutant concentration camp.

Real Name:
Tabitha Smith
First Appearance:
Secret Wars II #5 (1985)

Height: 5'5"
Weight: 120 lbs
Eye Color: Blue
Hair Color: Blonde

Art by Jim Cheung

POWERS/ WEAPONS

• Creation of "time bombs," balls of explosive energy

INTELLIGENCE
STRENGTH
SPEED
DURABILITY
ENERGY PROJECTION
FIGHTING SKILLS

MOONSTAR

Real Name:
Danielle Moonstar
First Appearance:
Marvel Graphic Novel #4
(1982)

Height:	5'6"
Weight:	124 lbs
Eye Color:	Brown
Hair Color:	Black

Dani Moonstar was the happy child of Cheyenne Indian parents until her emerging mutant powers started causing uncontrollable nightmares—including one where she envisioned her parents' deaths. Shortly after the dream, Moonstar's parents disappeared. Believing them to have been killed, Moonstar had dreams that were haunted by the appearance of a demonic bear, which she believed to be responsible for her parents' deaths. But Moonstar was mistaken; her parents had, in fact, been transformed into the bear itself. When the bear intended the same fate for Moonstar, only her grandfather's spells could keep the demon at bay.

As her powers continued to manifest, her grandfather contacted <u>Professor X</u>, a friend of Moonstar's father, for help. But after <u>Donald Pierce</u> murdered Moonstar's grandfather, the demon bear was free to seek her out and tracked her to the <u>Xavier Mansion</u>, where it attacked her outside her new home. Nearly killed, she was saved by her teammates. With Moonstar out of harm's way, <u>Magik</u> used her mystical Soulsword to break the spell that trapped Moonstar's parents in the bear's form. As she recovered from the injuries she had sustained in the battle, Moonstar enjoyed a reunion with her newly freed mother and father.

Moonstar and the other <u>New Mutants</u> were soon kidnapped and sent to Asgard, the extra-dimensional home of the gods of Norse mythology. While there, Moonstar rescued a winged

horse, with which she felt an immediate psychic rapport. The bond endowed her with the Valkyries' power to perceive the coming of death. When Hela, Goddess of Death, attempted to usurp control of Asgard, she used Moonstar to gather mutants to her forces to defeat Thor, God of Thunder. Under Hela's sway, Moonstar nearly killed Odin, Lord of Asgard. Hela was defeated by the combined forces of the New Mutants and the Asgardians, but Moonstar remained in Asgard to repair the damage she had unwittingly caused.

Now back on Earth and free of the tormenting nightmares of her youth, Moonstar went to work for the <u>X-Men</u> for a short time before deciding to further her education by attending college. College didn't suit her though, and she is now living on her own.

Art by Josh Middleton

POWERS/ WEAPONS

- Psionic ability to create three-dimensional images from concepts within the minds of herself and others

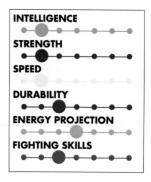

INTELLIGENCE

STRENGTH

SPEED

DURABILITY

ENERGY PROJECTION

FIGHTING SKILLS

SUNSPOT

Son of Brazilian millionaire Emmanuel DaCosta and his American wife Nina, Roberto, playing in a championship soccer match for his school team in Rio de Janiero, was deliberately knocked to the ground by a member of the opposing team. The hot-tempered Roberto retaliated by tackling the boy and brutally beating him. Roberto's superhuman strength began to turn his body and clothing black, but he had no idea what was happening to him. Tossing the other boy away from him, Roberto sought help, but the other players and most of the spectators panicked and fled. Only Roberto's girfriend Juliana stood by Roberto in his time of need. When Roberto's mutant powers came to the attention of Donald Pierce, the Hellfire Club's renegade White Bishop, Pierce sent a team of mercenaries to seize the boy. Though Pierce's operatives failed to abduct Roberto, they did kidnap Juliana. When Roberto tracked down their whereabouts, he attempted to use his mutant powers on her captors. When they fired at him, Juliana threw herself in front of Roberto—saving her boyfriend, but dying herself. Roberto vowed revenge on Pierce. He joined Professor X and several other young mutants to make good on his word, and Professor X succeeded in defeating Pierce.

Even when Roberto decided to stay with Professor X and receive training in the use of his superhuman powers as a member of the New Mutants, his hatred of the Inner Circle never faded—even after his father became the organization's White Rook. After his father died, Sunspot faced his greatest challenge when he was abducted and subjected to a barrage of unwanted experiments. After his powers were increased substantially, Sunspot was found and freed by the mutant strike force founded by Nathan Summers, a team largely composed of former members of the New Mutants. Suns subsequently joined forces with them.

For a time, Sunspot put his life as a hero on hold when Selene blackmailed him into joining the Hellfire Club, on the promise to grant Juliana a second lease on life. Forced to become the Club's new Black Rook, Sunspot welcomed her insidious effort and entered the Inner Circle intent on finally bringing down the organization—this time from the inside. Putting his lust for vengeance aside, Sunspot now heads up the Los Angeles branch of the X-Corporation.

Real Name:
Roberto DaCosta
First Appearance:
Marvel Graphic Novel #4 (1982)

Height: 5'8"
Weight: 170 lbs
Eye Color: Brown
Hair Color: Black

INTELLIGENCE
STRENGTH
SPEED
DURABILITY
ENERGY PROJECTION
FIGHTING SKILLS

POWERS/ WEAPONS

- Absorption and conversion of solar energy into physical strength
- Concussive force blasts

Art by Adam Pollina

WARLOCK

Real Name:
Warlock (English approximation of his name in his native tongue)

First Appearance:
New Mutants #18 (1984)

Height:	Variable
Weight:	Variable
Eye Color:	Black
Hair Color:	Black

Hailing from outer space, Warlock claims the heritage shared by other members of his race, the Technarchy. Though taking a human form, Warlock is actually a techno-organic life form whose biology comprises more circuitry and machinery than DNA code; he eats by infecting other life forms with the transmode virus, making them techno-organic like himself and draining their life energies. As he grew older, Warlock found he could not fulfill the legacy of the children of the Technarchy, who were expected to either kill their parents or be killed by them. Finding both outcomes equally appalling, Warlock fled, but his escape route sent him crashing into **Magneto**'s orbiting space station, Asteroid M, before he hurtled to Earth and landed near the mansion owned by **Professor X**.

Warlock was disoriented by his new surroundings and became terribly frightened. In his anxious state, unable to speak the native tongue of this strange new place, Warlock could do nothing more than lash out against the nearby **New Mutants**. While in battle mode, the young alien lost control over his innate life energies, which began ebbing out of him; Warlock fell to the floor, slowly dying. Unable to communicate with their visitor, the New Mutants summoned **Cypher**, another of Professor X's students, to help. Cypher had the ability to master any form of language and broke through to Warlock, allowing him to articulate in English the nature of his trouble. Once Cypher discovered Warlock's reason for malfunctioning, he called on **Wolfsbane** to assist in recharging Warlock's energy.

Warlock befriended the New Mutants, and Cypher helped Warlock understand what it means to be human. In return, Warlock literally developed a unique bond with his friend: During battle, he physically merged with Cypher, covering him with his own "living circuitry." This act allowed Cypher to perceive his environment in the same way Warlock did.

When Cypher took a bullet intended for Wolfsbane during battle, the shot killed him instantly. Warlock, still childlike in many ways, had a hard time understanding the concept of death. Incapable of comprehending the finality, and assuming the state was somehow reversible, Warlock merged himself with Cypher's corpse in an attempt to revive his best friend. Though powerful and poignant, Warlock's last act of friendship could not resurrect Cypher. From that moment on, the devastated and grief-stricken Warlock would never be the same again.

POWERS/ WEAPONS

- Body structure that resembles machinery
- Ability to shape change into any solid or liquid form

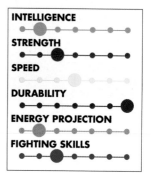

INTELLIGENCE

STRENGTH

SPEED

DURABILITY

ENERGY PROJECTION

FIGHTING SKILLS

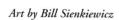

Art by Bill Sienkiewicz

WOLFSBANE

Abandoned at birth, Rahne Sinclair was turned over to Reverend Craig, a fire-and-brimstone minister who raised the child with an iron hand under the belief that all that was not normal was the work of the devil. Matters went from bad to worse when, at age 14, Wolfbane's lycanthropic mutant abilities first manifested.

Horrified at what this aberration he called a daughter had turned into, Reverend Craig immediately prepared to have the girl exorcised to expel the apparent demon within, but Wolfsbane escaped from her home. Her father eagerly led a lynch mob to track her down.

Wolfsbane managed to escape her pursuers and ran to Moira MacTaggert, the woman who had presided over her birth. Once in the safe arms of the understanding woman, Wolfsbane reverted back to her human form. Recognizing her as the child she helped birth years ago, Moira saved the frightened Rahne from the mob and took her in as her ward.

Moira saw in Wolfsbane an inherent goodness and power, and decided to send her to Professor X in America so Wolfsbane could join the New Mutants and gain a better understanding of the powers she possessed. A doting Moira visited Wolfsbane frequently, and the girl came to view the doctor as her surrogate mother.

As a member of the New Mutants, Wolfsbane's physical prowess grew. Though she had finally escaped her overly dogmatic father's control, she still suffered emotional repercussions from all the guilt and fear he had heaped upon her in her youth. So deep was the sense of shame brought on by her ingrained religious beliefs that Wolfsbane could never develop a healthy relationship with any boy to whom she became attracted.

When Mystique's Brotherhood of Evil Mutants swarmed Muir Island in an attempt to destroy Moira's reseach on a cure for the Legacy Virus, Wolfsbane tried to stave off the attack. After being shot by a gun that neutralized her powers, Wolfsbane could only helplessly watch as the one person in the world who ever loved her died at the Brotherhood of Evil's hands.

Distraught and devastated, Wolfsbane returned to the Xavier Institute clinging to the memory of Moira—her guide, her savior, her mother.

POWERS/ WEAPONS

• Lycanthropic shapeshifting

Real Name:
Rahne Sinclair
First Appearance:
Marvel Graphic Novel #4 (1982)

Height: 5'2" (in human form), up to 8' (in transitional form), up to 12' (in lupine form, standing erect)
Weight: 110 lbs (in human form), up to 410 lbs (in transitional form), up to 1050 lbs (in lupine form)
Eye Color: Blue-green
Hair Color: Red (in human form), reddish-brown (in transitional/lupine forms)

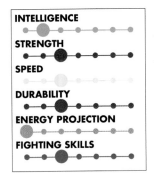

Art by Josh Middleton

CYPHER

| **Real Name:** | Douglas Aaron Ramsey | **Height:** | 5'9" |
| **First Appearance:** | *New Mutants* #13 (1984) | **Weight:** | 150 lbs |

Art by Jim Calafiore

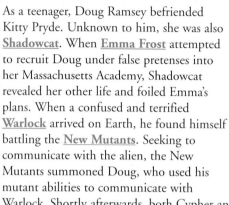

As a teenager, Doug Ramsey befriended Kitty Pryde. Unknown to him, she was also Shadowcat. When Emma Frost attempted to recruit Doug under false pretenses into her Massachusetts Academy, Shadowcat revealed her other life and foiled Emma's plans. When a confused and terrified Warlock arrived on Earth, he found himself battling the New Mutants. Seeking to communicate with the alien, the New Mutants summoned Doug, who used his mutant abilities to communicate with Warlock. Shortly afterwards, both Cypher and Warlock joined the team. Cypher soon became fast friends with Warlock, and the alien came to aid Doug in battle situations by covering him with his "living circuitry," allowing Doug to perceive his environment in the same way Warlock did. At first, Cypher's and Warlock's consciousnesses remained separate, but the more the pair merged, the more their personalities rapidly began to resemble one another. Following the capture of the New Mutants by the mad scientist Frederick Animus, Cypher dove in front of a bullet fired by Animus at Wolfsbane: an act that cost him his life.

POWERS/WEAPONS

• Translation of all languages, spoken or written, human or alien in origin

INTELLIGENCE
STRENGTH
SPEED
DURABILITY
ENERGY PROJECTION
FIGHTING SKILLS

MAGIK

| **Real Name:** | Illyana Nikolievna Rasputin | **Height:** | 5'5" |
| **First Appearance:** | *Giant-Size X-Men* #1 (1975) | **Weight:** | 120 lbs |

Art by Randy Green

While spending time at the Xavier Institute with her brother Colossus, Illyana and the other X-Men were taken to Limbo, the other-dimensional realm of Belasco. Although they tried everything in their power, the X-Men were unable to wrest Illyana away from Belasco when they made their escape. Held against her will for seven years under Belasco's spell, Illyana was imbued with tremendous magical powers, which she used to do his bidding. Finally, after a fierce struggle, Illyana defeated Belasco to become Mistress of Limbo and returned to Earth to discover only seconds had passed on the X-Men's journey. The now 14-year-old joined the New Mutants, adjusting to her newfound powers and age among other teenage mutants. When her demon servant S'ym tried to usurp her power in Limbo and helped orchestrate a demonic invasion of Earth, she used her magic to alter time and reconfigure Limbo as if she had never been there. This caused her to revert back to her original age of seven. She later tragically succumbed to the deadly Legacy Virus.

POWERS/WEAPONS

• Teleportation through time and space
• Trained sorceress

INTELLIGENCE
STRENGTH
SPEED
DURABILITY
ENERGY PROJECTION
FIGHTING SKILLS

REAVERS

Art by Salvador Larroca

First Appearance:
Uncanny X-Men #229 (1988)

Originally a band of garden-variety criminals, the Reavers first claimed residency in an abandoned town in the Australian outback. Fortune smiled on them in the form of <u>Gateway</u>, a proud and powerful aboriginal mutant whom the Reavers had kidnapped. Threatening to destroy his people's homeland, the Reavers forced Gateway to use his powers to transport them to and from the robberies they planned throughout the South Pacific.

Not just content to merely rob a Hong Kong bank, the Reavers deemed it necessary to murder the family who owned it. To curtail further bloodshed, the <u>X-Men</u> stepped in and easily crushed the group, taking over the Reavers' outback outpost.

While they found foes in the X-Men, the Reavers found a friend in <u>Donald Pierce</u>, the deposed White King of the <u>Hellfire Club</u>. Pierce reorganized the group, turning them into cybernetically enhanced soldiers with the sole desire to seek out and destroy mutants—specifically, the X-Men. Newly regrouped and refreshed with cybernetic skills, the Reavers reclaimed their lost base.

Their subsequent battle at the genetic research station on Muir Island, however, would be quite another matter entirely. A clash with a government-sponsored team of mutants saw heavy casualties on both sides. However, Pierce was able to rebuild those Reavers lost in the battle—an accomplishment he would repeat when they were seemingly destroyed in a later struggle with the <u>Sentinels</u>.

LADY DEATHSTRIKE

Art by Jim Lee

Real Name:
Yuriko Oyama
First Appearance:
Daredevil #197
(1983)

Height: 5'9"
Weight: 136 lbs
Eye Color: Black
Hair Color: Brown

Yuriko Oyama's kamikaze father, Lord Dark Wind, was not supposed to survive his mission against an American battleship. But despite grievous injuries, he did. Ashamed, Lord Dark Wind bore the scars of his defeat on his soul—and on his face. Forcing his children into the same fate, Lord Dark Wind carved ritual designs into the faces of Yuriko and her two brothers. He then turned his attention to a means for bonding the virtually indestructible steel alloy adamantium to human bone, hoping to create an army of superhuman soldiers for Japan. But his plans were stolen, leaving his dreams to flounder.

As the years passed, Yuriko's lover Kira and her brothers were employed as members of her father's private army. After her brothers were killed in her father's service, Yuriko grew increasingly hateful towards her father. She was determined to save Kira from facing that same death. Seizing upon the first available opportunity, Lady Deathstrike lashed out and killed Lord Dark Wind. But she could not have anticipated that Kira's loyalty to her father was greater than his love for her. Kira, despairing over Lord Dark Wing's death, committed suicide. Reeling over the loss of her lover and desperate to understand his fervor, Lady Deathstrike adopted her late father's radical views. Her first vengeful task: find the one responsible for stealing her father's adamantium plans.

Lady Deathstrike's quest led her to **Wolverine**, who'd had adamantium forcibly bonded to his skeleton. But **Vindicator** prevented her from fulfilling her need for retribution. After her defeat, Lady Deathstrike struck a deal with **Donald Pierce**, who helped turn her into a cyborg in exchange for her service in the **Reavers**. Using her now cybernetically enhanced body, Lady Deathstrike felt confident she could defeat Wolverine. As it turns out, her confidence was greatly misplaced, and Wolverine easily defeated her in battle. Not content to wallow in defeat, Lady Deathstrike maintains her focus and her mission: murder and mayhem as a means towards all ends.

POWERS/WEAPONS

- Skilled marital artist
- Unbreakable bones created with help from adamantium molecules

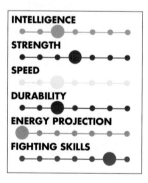

INTELLIGENCE
STRENGTH
SPEED
DURABILITY
ENERGY PROJECTION
FIGHTING SKILLS

COLE, MACON & REESE

Real Name: Wade Cole, Angelo Macon, Murray Reese
First Appearance: *X-Men #133* (1980)

Originally soldiers of the **Hellfire Club**'s Inner Circle, Wade Cole, Angelo Macon, and Murray Reese barely survived a savage encounter with **Wolverine**. Fortunately for them, **Donald Pierce** stepped in, willing to save their lives in exchange for their eternal service against the **X-Men**. They agreed, and Pierce reengineered them into cybernetically enhanced assassins.

POWERS/WEAPONS

- Cybernetic augmentation giving them enhanced strength, endurance, accuracy, and reaction time

BONEBREAKER

INTELLIGENCE
STRENGTH
SPEED
DURABILITY
ENERGY PROJECTION
FIGHTING SKILLS

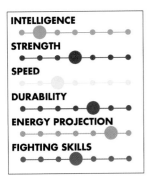

Real Name:
Unrevealed
First Appearance:
Uncanny X-Men #229 (1988)

Height:
4'6"
Weight:
410 lbs

POWERS/WEAPONS
• Motorized chassis propelled by tank treads in place of his legs

PRETTY BOY

INTELLIGENCE
STRENGTH
SPEED
DURABILITY
ENERGY PROJECTION
FIGHTING SKILLS

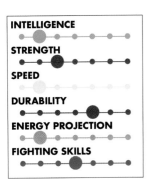

Real Name:
Unrevealed
First Appearance:
Uncanny X-Men #229 (1988)

Height:
5'8"
Weight:
235 lbs

POWERS/WEAPONS
• Augmented cybernetic body
• Ability to extend fiber-optic filaments from his eyes that can reach into victims' brains and reprogram their minds

SKULLBUSTER

INTELLIGENCE
STRENGTH
SPEED
DURABILITY
ENERGY PROJECTION
FIGHTING SKILLS

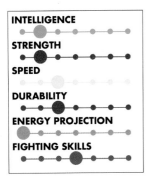

Real Name:
Unrevealed
First Appearance:
Uncanny X-Men #229 (1988)

Height:
6'
Weight:
260 lbs

POWERS/WEAPONS
• Cybernetic legs that enable him to kick with the force of a pile driver

SKULLBUSTER II

INTELLIGENCE
STRENGTH
SPEED
DURABILITY
ENERGY PROJECTION
FIGHTING SKILLS

Real Name:
Cylla Markham
First Appearance:
Uncanny X-Men #260 (1990)

Height:
5'8"
Weight:
245 lbs

POWERS/WEAPONS
• Numerous cybernetic augmentations
• Molybdenum steel claws on her wrists
• Targeting computer
• Infrared detectors
• Pulse-Doppler radar system

SAVAGE LAND MUTATES

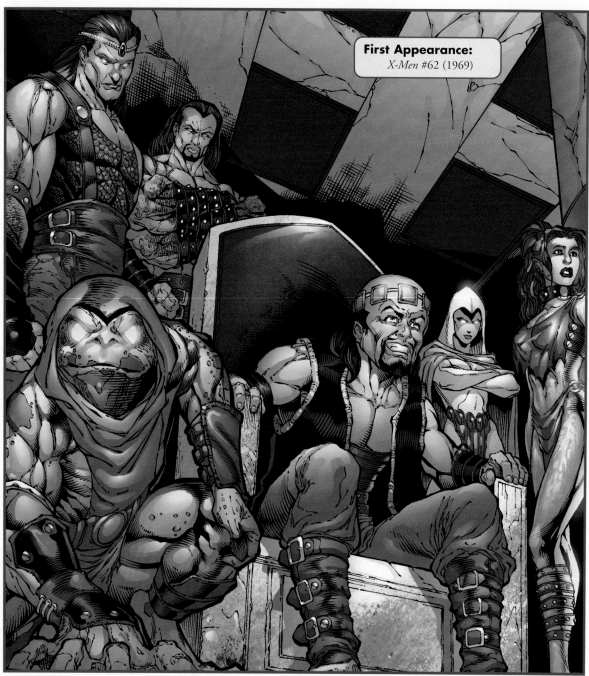

Art by Kevin Sharpe

First Appearance:
X-Men #62 (1969)

In the vast frozen wasteland of Antarctica, there lies an unexpected place: a lush, tropical jungle teeming with vegetation, native peoples—and dinosaurs. It is the Savage Land. A prehistoric place that time may have forgotten—but, fortunately for one tribe, **Magneto** had not.

After arriving in the Savage Land, Magneto artificially mutated the primitive Swamp People, granting them superhuman powers. These people became the Savage Land Mutates, and used their newly acquired powers to aid Magneto in his ongoing conflict with the **X-Men**.

But once Magneto abandoned them, the Mutates were left to their own devices, frequently engaging in clashes with the X-Men, the Avengers, and even Spider-Man. Brutal, violent, and willing to do anything necessary to have their way, the Savage Land Mutates exist in a time and place all their own.

POWERS/WEAPONS

- Computer-like superhuman intelligence

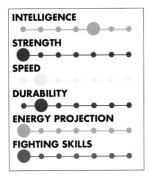

INTELLIGENCE

STRENGTH

SPEED

DURABILITY

ENERGY PROJECTION

FIGHTING SKILLS

Real Name:	Unrevealed	**Height:**	5'4"
First Appearance:	*X-Men* #62 (1969)	**Weight:**	125 lbs

Brainchild was one of several denizens of the Savage Land whom Magneto artificially mutated through technological means to battle the X-Men. After Magneto abandoned the Mutates, Brainchild assumed leadership of the group. Ready to settle a score with his old nemesis, Storm, Brainchild brainwashed her into battling her teammates. But the X-Men defeated him, and Sage later reversed the effects of Brainchild's mental manipulation of Storm. Consequently, the X-Men turned over Brainchild and his tribe of Mutates to the leaders of the Savage Land tribes.

BRAINCHILD

POWERS/WEAPONS

- Emission of mutated pheromones that allow her to place bestial creatures in her thrall

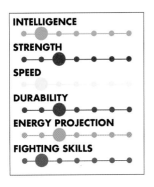

INTELLIGENCE

STRENGTH

SPEED

DURABILITY

ENERGY PROJECTION

FIGHTING SKILLS

Real Name:	Unrevealed	**Height:**	5'11"
First Appearance:	*X-Treme X-Men: Savage Land* #2 (2001)	**Weight:**	161 lbs

Unlike many of the Savage Land Mutates, Lupa was genetically altered from her normal state not by Magneto, but Brainchild. Lupa's first test came when Brainchild asked her to help him settle an old score with his enemy, Storm. Calling on her newly endowed powers, Lupa enslaved Beast, hoping he would turn on his teammates, who had come to Storm's aid. But her newly created abilities were no match against the much more skilled and trained Beast. He broke free of Lupa's control and helped the other X-Men defeat the Mutates.

LUPA

POWERS/WEAPONS

- Sorcery
- Superhuman strength and enhanced durability

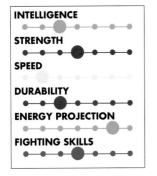

INTELLIGENCE

STRENGTH

SPEED

DURABILITY

ENERGY PROJECTION

FIGHTING SKILLS

Real Name:	Zala Dane	**Height:**	5'9"
First Appearance:	*Astonishing Tales* #3 (1970)	**Weight:**	141 lbs

When she took over control of the Savage Land Mutates from Brainchild, the sorceress Zaladane quickly cemented her seat of power by raiding Antarctic research stations and plundering Chilean cities. Thus successful, Zaladane dispatched the Mutates to kidnap Polaris, who, unknown to Zaladane, was her sister. Siphoning Polaris's mutant powers, Zaladane infused them into her own body. Zaladane used these stolen powers to battle Ka-Zar and the X-Men—and, finally, Magneto. Ending the threat she posed once and for all, Magneto slew Zaladane.

ZALADANE

AMPHIBIUS

Real Name:
Unrevealed
First Appearance:
X-Men #62 (1969)

Height:
6'
Weight:
145 lbs

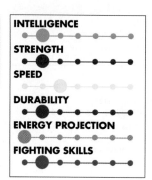

INTELLIGENCE
STRENGTH
SPEED
DURABILITY
ENERGY PROJECTION
FIGHTING SKILLS

POWERS/WEAPONS

• Frog-like legs that allow him to leap superhuman distances

BARBARUS

Real Name:
Unrevealed
First Appearance:
X-Men #62 (1969)

Height:
6'2"
Weight:
235 lbs

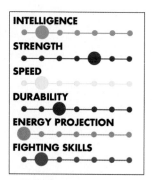

INTELLIGENCE
STRENGTH
SPEED
DURABILITY
ENERGY PROJECTION
FIGHTING SKILLS

POWERS/WEAPONS

• Superhuman strength in all four of his arms that allows him to lift at least 30 tons

EQUILIBRIUS

Real Name:
Unrevealed
First Appearance:
X-Men #62 (1969)

Height:
5'11"
Weight:
175 lbs

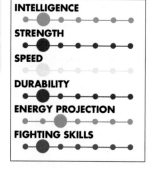

INTELLIGENCE
STRENGTH
SPEED
DURABILITY
ENERGY PROJECTION
FIGHTING SKILLS

POWERS/WEAPONS

• Hypnotic eyes that induce a state of vertigo-like imbalance in those who look in them

GAZA

Real Name:
Unrevealed
First Appearance:
X-Men #62 (1969)

Height:
6'9"
Weight:
290 lbs

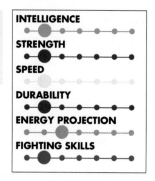

INTELLIGENCE
STRENGTH
SPEED
DURABILITY
ENERGY PROJECTION
FIGHTING SKILLS

POWERS/WEAPONS

• Psionic ability that allows him to "see" mentally, which compensates for his blindness

INTELLIGENCE

STRENGTH

SPEED

DURABILITY

ENERGY PROJECTION

FIGHTING SKILLS

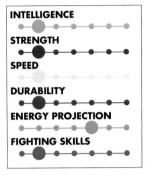

Real Name:
Unrevealed
First Appearance:
X-Treme X-Men:
Savage Land #3 (2002)

Height:
6'1"
Weight:
153 lbs

POWERS/WEAPONS

- Psionic ability to summon the astral self from her intended victim, and mentally imprison the victim's psyche and soul

LEASH

INTELLIGENCE

STRENGTH

SPEED

DURABILITY

ENERGY PROJECTION

FIGHTING SKILLS

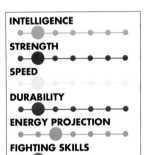

Real Name:
Unrevealed
First Appearance:
X-Men #63 (1969)

Height:
5'6"
Weight:
125 lbs

POWERS/WEAPONS

- Generation of hypersonic pitches that affect the sexual drive of a human male and completely paralyzes him

LORELEI

INTELLIGENCE

STRENGTH

SPEED

DURABILITY

ENERGY PROJECTION

FIGHTING SKILLS

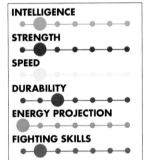

Real Name:
Unrevealed
First Appearance:
X-Men #62 (1969)

Height:
5'6"
Weight:
135 lbs

POWERS/WEAPONS

- Can summon and control mammalian carnivores, notably wolves

LUPO

INTELLIGENCE

STRENGTH

SPEED

DURABILITY

ENERGY PROJECTION

FIGHTING SKILLS

Real Name:
Unrevealed
First Appearance:
X-Men #62 (1969)

Height:
5'1"
Weight:
135 lbs

POWERS/WEAPONS

- Psionic ability to summon and control animals

PIPER

SHI'AR

Art by Ivan Reis

First Appearance:
X-Men #97 (1976)

This is the Shi'ar Empire, where the path to peace is paved with many obstacles: Murder. Chaos. Upheaval. Insanity. Betrayal. Possession. Plagued by deadly infighting in the last quarter century, the royal Neramani family—from which all ruling Emperors and Empresses hail—desperately tries to hold together the one million worlds that comprise the empire. It's a tough job, considering they can't even hold themselves together for long.

After <u>Deathbird</u>'s murder of her mother and sister led to her exile, her brother D'Ken assumed the throne. But D'Ken's own quest for power left him insane. After D'Ken became mentally incapacitated, his sister <u>Lilandra</u> took control of the throne—until Deathbird organized a coup d'état that deposed her. But leading one million worlds wasn't all that it was cracked up to be, and Deathbird, sick of her administrative duties, eventually ceded the throne back to Lilandra. As Majestrix of the Shi'ar empire, Lilandra is only loyal to the people under her reign. Though she maintains a positive working relationship with the <u>X-Men</u> and the <u>Starjammers</u>, she will work against both teams with her <u>Shi'ar Imperial Guard</u> if she feels that doing so is in the best interest of the galaxy. Nonetheless, the X-Men's headquarters brims with advanced Shi'ar technology, perhaps as much of a testament to the quality of the advanced Shi'ar technological capabilities as it is to their continued good relations.

Ruling from the Imperial Throneworld, the artificial planet Chandilar, Lilandra grants the worlds she rules differing degrees of autonomy depending on various factors, notably their loyalty to the empire. Some worlds have virtual independence and are allowed to send representatives to serve on the Shi'ar High Council; some are kept under martial law to protect themselves and the empire at large. Like the people of Earth, the Shi'ar would prefer to live in peace, but wars among the millions of worlds must be fought and battles must be won to ensure the Shi'ar empire maintains its status in the universe.

LILANDRA

After Lilandra's sister <u>Deathbird</u> was exiled for the murder of her mother and other sister, Lilandra contentedly served as the Grand Admiral of the <u>Shi'ar Imperial Guard</u>, and her brother D'Ken became the Majestor of the <u>Shi'ar</u> empire. When Lilandra discovered D'Ken's dangerous plan to grant himself omniscience, however, she desperately tried to stop him. Arresting Lilandra for treason, D'Ken sentenced her to death. While Lilandra awaited execution, <u>Professor X</u> subconsciously caused a psychic link to form between the two. Knowing Earth was home to super heroes who could help her stop D'Ken, Lilandra escaped captivity and made her way to Professor X. An agent of D'Ken's quickly caught up with her and took Lilandra to her brother. The <u>X-Men</u> followed right behind, arriving just in time to witness D'Ken's plans implode on him, rendering him incurably insane and catatonic.

After the Shi'ar High Council decided Lilandra would become Majestrix, she took Professor X as her royal consort. When the Phoenix Force impersonated <u>Jean Grey</u> and presented a threat to the galaxy, Lilandra had to extinguish it. Professor X opposed her decision and sent the X-Men to battle the Guard. In the end, a remnant of Jean's psyche caused the Phoenix Force to commit suicide to prevent untold destruction. Lilandra attended the funeral as a sign of respect to her husband and his X-Men.

Meanwhile, Deathbird staged a successful coup, sending Lilandra into exile. Lilandra took up with the <u>Starjammers</u>, fighting to reclaim her throne. Eventually Deathbird, despising the responsibilities of ruling an Empire as large as the Shi'ar's, willingly stepped down.

While Lilandra was successful at regaining the throne, a greater threat loomed: <u>Cassandra Nova</u>. Cassandra took possession of Lilandra's mind and body to force the Shi'ar Imperial Guard to annihilate the X-Men. The damage to Lilandra's mind was so great that she later attempted to assassinate Xavier, whom she believed was Cassandra. Members of Professor X's <u>X-Corporation</u> foiled the plot, but Lilandra's marriage to Xavier was annulled and she returned to her people to recover.

Real Name:
Lilandra Neramani
First Appearance:
X-Men #97 (1976)

Height: 5'11"
Weight: 150 lbs
Eye Color: Blue
Hair Color: Black

Art by Bryan Hitch

INTELLIGENCE

STRENGTH

SPEED

DURABILITY

ENERGY PROJECTION

FIGHTING SKILLS

DEATHBIRD

Real Name:
Cal'syee Neramani
First Appearance:
Ms. Marvel #9 (1977)

Height:	5'8"
Weight:	136 lbs
Eye Color:	White
Hair Color:	Purple and blue

Deathbird's deadly mix of self-absorption and unchecked ferociousness exploded at a young age. In one unholy act she lashed out against her mother and her sister, killing them both. Though destined to become Majestrix, she was exiled into space for this crime and her true name was stricken from all Shi'ar historical records. Her brother D'ken, being the next oldest, took the throne instead.

In her exile, Deathbird seethed with jealousy, believing that her title and position had been stolen from her without just cause, Deathbird had no intention of quietly disappearing. She aligned herself with a treacherous member of the Shi'ar High Council who helped her stage a successful coup against her sister Lilandra, to whom the throne passed after D'Ken went insane. Putting her scheme into action, Deathbird captured Lilandra, her consort Professor X, and the X-Men. Lilandra and her allies soon found themselves prisoners on the home world of the Brood, leaving the way clear for Deathbird to seize the throne. Lilandra and the X-Men escaped with help from the Starjammers. By then Deathbird had consolidated her power, and even the Shi'ar Imperial Guard had sworn fealty to her. Swiftly branding her sister a traitor and a rebel, Deathbird banished Lilandra.

The hassles and the headaches that come with managing more than one million worlds proved far too difficult to the battle-weary and administration-hating Deathbird. She decided to step down and watched as Lilandra took the throne once again. Surprising all, Deathbird offered her services to her sister to help her battle a Phalanx invasion of the Shi'ar Throneworld. In the course of the battle, one particular X-Man caught her attention: Bishop. The attraction was mutual, but while escorting the X-Men back to Earth the two were separated from the rest of the group, and any real affection between them soon began to crumble. After sharing a few exhilarating adventures in their time-tossed states, Deathbird went back to her old ways and ultimately decided to betray Bishop by aligning herself with Apocalypse as his new Horseman, War. After the X-Men defeated Apocalypse, Deathbird fled.

Resurfacing aboard a deep-space Shi'ar starstation, driven mad by the cold and oxygen deprivation, Deathbird killed the station's entire crew. Her madness never abated even when Bishop turned up; Deathbird and her former lover engaged in a fierce struggle where the helmet of Deathbird's spacesuit was smashed open and she decided to cast herself out into the frigid, ceaseless void of space rather than face capture at Bishop's hand.

POWERS/ WEAPONS

- Wings enabling her to fly at speeds of up to 60 mph
- Talon-like fingernails that can slice through glass and brick and even score steel

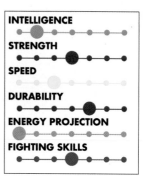

INTELLIGENCE	
STRENGTH	
SPEED	
DURABILITY	
ENERGY PROJECTION	
FIGHTING SKILLS	

Art by Chris Bachalo

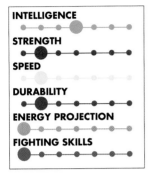

INTELLIGENCE

STRENGTH

SPEED

DURABILITY

ENERGY PROJECTION

FIGHTING SKILLS

Real Name: Araki (full name unrevealed)

First Appearance: *X-Men* #109 (1977)

Height: 6'1"

Weight: 160 lbs

Araki is both the Prime Minister of the intergalactic <u>Shi'ar</u> Imperium and the Lord Chancellor to the Empire's ruling emperor or empress. When Araki defended the Shi'ar throne against an impending coup, the rebellion's leader killed him. But Araki's services had proven so valuable to the Empire that <u>Lilandra</u> had his body cloned by means of the Shi'ar's advanced technology and ordered his consciousness transferred into a new body.

In the years that followed, Araki remained an easy target for adversaries of the Empire. A greater sage than a fighter, Araki went down four more times. While on his fifth cloned body, Araki discovered that his Empress was possessed by <u>Cassandra Nova</u> and tried to intervene before her orders to the <u>Shi'ar Imperial Guard</u> to annihilate the <u>X-Men</u> could be carried out. Choosing to believe Lilandra's repeated denials of Araki's heretical words, the Guardsman <u>G-Type</u> was forced by his Empress to kill Araki.

But death mattered little to this wise old Shi'ar: After Cassandra was expelled from Lilandra's mind, a sixth Araki arrived to help his Empress recover and return her to her people once again.

Art by Igor Kordey

ARAKI

POWERS/WEAPONS

• Generation of malleable energy fields of coherent crimson light that grant her flight, concussive blasting ability, and generation of solid energy constructs that she can shape into any form imaginable

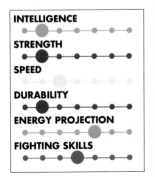

INTELLIGENCE

STRENGTH

SPEED

DURABILITY

ENERGY PROJECTION

FIGHTING SKILLS

Real Name: Cerise (full name unrevealed)

First Appearance: *Excalibur* #46 (1992)

Height: 5'11"

Weight: 148 lbs

As part of a recruitment team from the intergalactic <u>Shi'ar</u> empire, Cerise traveled from planet to planet, offering other civilizations the opportunity to join the Empire. Cerise grew frantic, however, when her team's commander decided to decimate the races they met instead of recruiting them. Not wanting to take part in such mass genocide, Cerise set the ship on a collision course with the nearest star. After escaping before her ship was destroyed, Cerise sought to return to the Shi'ar Throneworld of Chandilar to report her commander's crimes—but a spatial anomaly skewed her journey and brought her to the planet Earth. When news of her so-called crime reached her home world, Cerise was quickly tried and convicted in absentia for the deaths of her fellow crew members. On Earth, Cerise was never aware of the conviction until the <u>Starjammers</u> captured her and took her to a prison planet to serve her sentence. Eventually, the Shi'ar Majestrix <u>Lilandra</u> arrived at the jail and agreed to allow Cerise to explain her actions. After listening to Cerise's terrible tale, Lilandra immediately pardoned her and offered Cerise an advisory position on her staff.

Art by Leinil Francis Yu

CERISE

SHI'AR IMPERIAL GUARD

First Appearance:
X-Men #107 (1977)

Art by José Ladronn

The members of the Imperial Guard are akin to legions of Roman soldiers who would sooner die than see their emperor ruined. The Guardsmen have fought to the death to protect their ruler and ensure their empire's survival.

Assembled from the far reaches of the **Shi'ar** empire, the Imperial Guard is composed of a garrison of super-powered beings charged with the enforcement of galactic law. Due to their varied origins and disparate home worlds, the members of the Guard collectively control every form of energy and matter known to exist.

Responsible for keeping the peace in thousands of worlds within the vast Shi'ar Empire, the members of the Imperial Guard must also protect and carry out the decrees of the Shi'ar Majestrix, **Lilandra**. Since Lilandra has a close relationship with **Professor X**, the Guard has encountered the **X-Men** on numerous occasions. Not all of these meetings were friendly. When the Phoenix Force entered **Jean Grey** and caused a grave threat to the universe, Lilandra called up the Guard and ordered them to execute the mutant. The members of the Guard defeated the X-Men who were trying to protect her—but ultimately, the Phoenix Force committed suicide before the Guard could finish its mission.

Fierce fighters and intense warriors, the Shi'ar Imperial Guard know no adversary capable of defeating them, including the mighty X-Men. All too aware of their awesome powers, the Guard routinely overpower the Earth's most mighty mutants—but only in the name of service to their Empire.

The Guard acts as the Shi'ar's first line of defense and has helped the Empire in military actions against both the Skrull and the Kree, who—along with the Shi'ar—make up the triumvirate of major interstellar empires.

Because of the demanding nature of their duties, every member of the guard is a well-trained warrior capable of myriad superhuman feats. In service to the entire universe, the warriors of the Shi'ar Imperial Guard have the distinct privilege of fighting for their empire and their emperor—no matter the cause or cost.

Art by José Ladronn

GLADIATOR

He is Gladiator, a fiercely proud and wise warrior who leads the Shi'ar Imperial Guard. Bound by his duty to his empire, Guardian serves all of his rulers without hesitation, without question, and with complete and total obedience. In his obsessively patriotic and loyal servitude to his Empire, Gladiator unswervingly followed even its most objectionable leaders without regard to questions of their character or motivation. Gladiator was there to do D'Ken's bidding during his spiral into power-fueled madness, and even served Deathbird, who had overthrown her sister Lilandra to earn the crown she so coveted.

True to form, Gladiator is steadfastly devoted to his current ruler, Lilandra, confident that Lilandra's directives are always made with the best interests of the Empire at heart. He is sworn to protect and preserve stellar harmony—and will do so at any cost. So when Lilandra commanded him to wipe out the carriers of a psi-virus that would soon ravage and destroy the universe, Gladiator complied, even though those carriers were the X-Men. He had no reason to question his Empress—and, of course, he had no idea that Cassandra Nova had taken possession of Lilandra to manipulate the Guard into doing her bidding.

Gladiator and his Guardsmen tore through the mansion and stood poised to deal a killing blow when Plutonia revealed Cassandra's deception. Devastated that his Empire had been polluted, Gladiator vowed to stop the menace. As he battled Cassandra, the powerful mutant temporarily stripped Gladiator of his powers. A stricken Gladiator was left in a collapsed heap on the lawn of the Xavier Mansion and never witnessed the defeat of Cassandra.

In the end, Gladiator learned a hard lesson in following commands without question. Now a new challenge lies ahead: whether he will so willingly follow his leader in the future or allow caution to supersede compliance.

Real Name:
Kallark
First Appearance:
X-Men #107 (1977)

Height: 6'6"
Weight: 595 lbs
Eye Color: Blue
Hair Color: Dark blue

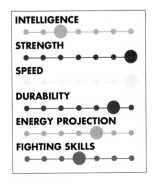

INTELLIGENCE

STRENGTH

SPEED

DURABILITY

ENERGY PROJECTION

FIGHTING SKILLS

POWERS/ WEAPONS

- Ability to lift over 100 tons
- Flight at faster-than-light speeds
- Incredible lung capacity that allows him to draw in large amounts of air and then expel it to create a gale force wind
- Projection of high-intensity beams from his eyes

Art by Ethan Van Sciver

ARC

| Real Name: | Unrevealed | Height: | 6'4" |
| First Appearance: | *New X-Men* #123 (2002) | Weight: | 225 lbs |

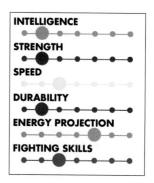

Like all members of the <u>Shi'ar Imperial Guard</u>, Arc lives to serve their Empress, Lilandra. Arc spearheaded the Guard's first strike on the <u>X-Men</u> after <u>Lilandra</u>, under the mental control of <u>Cassandra Nova</u>, had ordered the destruction of all mutants on Earth. Without question or hesitation, Arc rounded up his squad and captured <u>Cyclops</u> and <u>Xorn</u>. The Guard took them to the orbiting Shi'ar superdestroyer to await execution—but these X-Men's date with death was never to be. The pair escaped, and <u>Beast</u> subsequently defeated Arc in battle.

POWERS/WEAPONS

• Generation of heightened levels of bio-electricity within his body which project outwards

INTELLIGENCE
STRENGTH
SPEED
DURABILITY
ENERGY PROJECTION
FIGHTING SKILLS

DELPHOS

| Real Name: | Unrevealed | Height: | 5'9" |
| First Appearance: | *Inhumans* #3 (2000) | Weight: | 137 lbs |

A warrior in the <u>Shi'ar</u> Imperial Army, Delphos always dreamed of becoming a member of the <u>Shi'ar Imperial Guard</u>. She got her chance when she learned that <u>Oracle</u> was soon to be married, thus creating an open post in the Guard. Delphos sought to claim that position for herself and volunteered for a dangerous mission to quell a rebellion on a frontier moon. Following the successful completion of her mission, Delphos's skills were recognized and she was initiated into the Guard.

POWERS/WEAPONS

• Precognition

INTELLIGENCE
STRENGTH
SPEED
DURABILITY
ENERGY PROJECTION
FIGHTING SKILLS

FANG

| Real Name: | Unrevealed | Height: | Varies |
| First Appearance: | *X-Men* #107 (1977) | Weight: | Varies |

Though killed time and again in <u>Shi'ar Imperial Guard</u> battles, those who bear the name Fang always return—though not always as the same sex or in the same body. All three bearers of the name Fang hail from a race of alien beings who possess lupine traits similar to those found in wolves. From this race, one member is chosen to bear the name and wear the costume of Fang in the Imperial Guard. Though a great enigma, whoever bears the name of Fang is always a fierce Guard warrior, willing to go down in battle in order to serve Empress <u>Lilandra</u>.

POWERS/WEAPONS

• Heightened strength, speed, agility and hyper-keen senses

INTELLIGENCE
STRENGTH
SPEED
DURABILITY
ENERGY PROJECTION
FIGHTING SKILLS

POWERS/WEAPONS

- Ability to supercharge the his body with bio-electricity and project lightning-like bolts

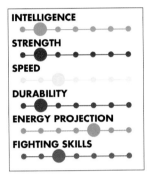

INTELLIGENCE

STRENGTH

SPEED

DURABILITY

ENERGY PROJECTION

FIGHTING SKILLS

Real Name: Grannz
First Appearance: *X-Men* #107 (1977)

Height: 5'11"
Weight: 195 lbs

Choosing a name that reflected his hotheaded personality, Flashfire has served the Shi'ar Imperial Guard with great strength and courage in battles both against and alongside the X-Men and Starjammers. Flashfire took a break from battle when he fell in love with his teammate Oracle. After their wedding and Oracle's retirement from the team, Flashfire went back into service, defending Lilandra against an assassination attempt by the Kree, Ronan the Accuser, and Ronan's unwilling agents, the royal family of the Earth race known as the Inhumans.

FLASHFIRE

POWERS/WEAPONS

- Ability to focus his body's intense energy (up to 6000° F) through wrist-mounted flamethrowers

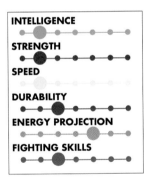

INTELLIGENCE

STRENGTH

SPEED

DURABILITY

ENERGY PROJECTION

FIGHTING SKILLS

Real Name: Unrevealed
First Appearance: *New X-Men* #124 (2002)

Height: 6'2"
Weight: Indeterminate

As a member of the Shi'ar Imperial Guard, G-Type has little trouble taking the lives of those who appear to threaten his Empress. Even when Lilandra was under the spell of Cassandra Nova and ordered G-Type to atmospherically cremate Cyclops and Xorn, G-Type complied. Before they could be incinerated, however, Xorn induced a minor reactor failure in G-Type's plasma core. G-Type quickly recovered; when he took Araki's life, as the Cassandra-possessed Lilandra had commanded, Xorn appeared once more—this time causing a reactor failure in G-Type from which he might never recover.

G-TYPE

POWERS/WEAPONS

- Projection of consciousness from one exo-body form to another

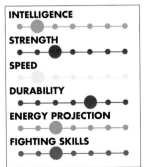

INTELLIGENCE

STRENGTH

SPEED

DURABILITY

ENERGY PROJECTION

FIGHTING SKILLS

Real Name: Unrevealed
First Appearance: *New X-Men* #124 (2002)

Height: 4'6"
Weight: 82 lbs

Neosaurus is an artificial brain able to project his consciousness into a series of physical exo-bodies. When instructed by Lilandra, acting under the spell of Cassandra Nova, to wipe out the X-Men, Neosaurus willingly sprung into action like any member of the Guard. But Neosaurus picked the wrong X-Man to challenge: Wolverine. During the battle, the more ferocious Wolverine viciously fought Neosaurus, seemingly killing him. Yet Wolverine had only killed one of Neosaurus's many exo-body forms, and Neosaurus later went back into action with the Guard.

NEOSAURUS

ORACLE

Real Name:	Sybil	**Height:**	5'5"
First Appearance:	*X-Men* #107 (1977)	**Weight:**	125 lbs

As a member of the <u>Shi'ar Imperial Guard</u>, Oracle met and fell in love with her teammate <u>Flashfire</u>. After deciding to marry him, Oracle resigned from active duty and <u>Delphos</u> stepped in to take her place. But something went awry, and Oracle's dreams went up in flames. For reasons never fully explained, Oracle and Flashfire ultimately broke up. And when Oracle went back to her post on the Guard, she didn't return as the impeccably put-together beauty she had once been. Instead, she now fights in the guise of a disheveled, naked harridan.

POWERS/WEAPONS
- Varying degrees of telepathic ability

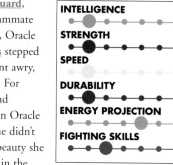

INTELLIGENCE

STRENGTH

SPEED

DURABILITY

ENERGY PROJECTION

FIGHTING SKILLS

PLUTONIA

Real Name:	Unrevealed	**Height:**	6'
First Appearance:	*New X-Men* #124 (2002)	**Weight:**	160 lbs.

Under the spell of <u>Cassandra Nova</u>, <u>Lilandra</u> commanded Plutonia to battle the "virus-carrying" <u>X-Men</u>. But before engaging in the fight, Plutonia discovered her fellow Guardsman and lover, <u>Smasher</u>, who had been sent to Earth by Lilandra prior to her possession to warn the X-Men of Cassandra's actions. Rescuing him, Plutonia took Smasher to the <u>Xavier Institute</u> just in time to convince the <u>Shi'ar Imperial Guard</u>'s leader, <u>Gladiator</u>, of the true threat. Together, Plutonia, the Guard, and the X-Men then managed to defeat Nova and free Lilandra.

POWERS/WEAPONS
- Generation of intense levels of an unknown form of radiation

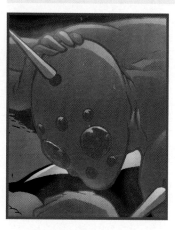

INTELLIGENCE

STRENGTH

SPEED

DURABILITY

ENERGY PROJECTION

FIGHTING SKILLS

STUFF

Real Name:	Unrevealed	**Height:**	Variable
First Appearance:	*New X-Men* #123 (2002)	**Weight:**	Variable

Unaware he was taking orders from <u>Cassandra Nova</u> and not <u>Lilandra</u>, Stuff assumed a human form to infiltrate the <u>Xavier Institute</u> and covertly gauge its defenses prior to a full Guard invasion. Stuff also managed to dupe Esme, a <u>Stepford Cuckoo</u>, into falling in love with him. But once his form was broken, so, too, was Esme's heart. Heralding the arrival of the invading Guardsman, Stuff mocked the girl for her foolishness. After the Guard's initial attack, the Cuckoos took over Stuff's mind and used his body to trap Cassandra in a childlike state.

POWERS/WEAPONS
- An alien bio-computer able to transform his synthetic form into virtually any conceivable shape

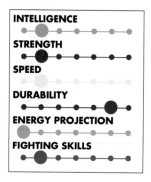

INTELLIGENCE

STRENGTH

SPEED

DURABILITY

ENERGY PROJECTION

FIGHTING SKILLS

ASTRA

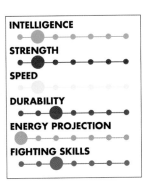

INTELLIGENCE

STRENGTH

SPEED

DURABILITY

ENERGY PROJECTION

FIGHTING SKILLS

Real Name:
Unrevealed
First Appearance:
X-Men #107 (1977)

Height:
5'10"
Weight:
140 lbs

POWERS/WEAPONS
- Alteration of her body's molecular density, allowing physical attacks to pass through her without harm

BLACKTHORN

INTELLIGENCE

STRENGTH

SPEED

DURABILITY

ENERGY PROJECTION

FIGHTING SKILLS

Real Name:
Unrevealed
First Appearance:
Uncanny X-Men #157 (1982)

Height:
6'
Weight:
190 lbs

POWERS/WEAPONS
- Communication with plant life like himself to command them to do his bidding

BLIMP

INTELLIGENCE

STRENGTH

SPEED

DURABILITY

ENERGY PROJECTION

FIGHTING SKILLS

Real Name:
Unrevealed
First Appearance:
New X-Men #124 (2002)

Height:
5'9"
Weight:
Indeterminate

POWERS/WEAPONS
- Bio-helium body contained within a specially constructed space suit

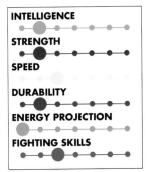

COMMANDO

INTELLIGENCE

STRENGTH

SPEED

DURABILITY

ENERGY PROJECTION

FIGHTING SKILLS

Real Name:
M-Nell
First Appearance:
Imperial Guard #1 (1997)

Height:
5'10"
Weight:
185 lbs

POWERS/WEAPONS
- Mega-radiation that works to augment his physical attributes, including his strength, endurance, and intellect

EARTHQUAKE

Real Name:
Unrevealed
First Appearance:
X-Men #137 (1980)

Height:
6'
Weight:
220 lbs

POWERS/WEAPONS

• Seismic energy projection that creates tremors beneath the surface of a planet

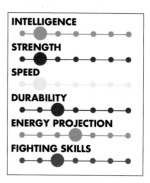

ELECTRON

Real Name:
Unrevealed
First Appearance:
X-Men #107 (1977)

Height:
5'10"
Weight:
180 lbs

POWERS/WEAPONS

• Generation of an electromagnetic charge within his body used to shock others, power electrical devices, or create defensive magnetic fields

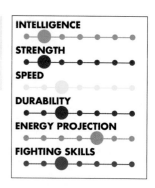

FADER

Real Name:
Unrevealed
First Appearance:
New X-Men #124 (2002)

Height:
3'3"
Weight:
45 lbs

POWERS/WEAPONS

• Light refraction ability that renders him invisible to the naked eye

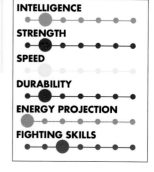

HARDBALL

Real Name:
Unrevealed
First Appearance:
Quasar #32 (1992)

Height:
5'3"
Weight:
210 lbs

POWERS/WEAPONS

• Extraordinarily strong legs that allow him leap great distances
• Rubbery body that allows him rebound off any surface, object or being he strikes

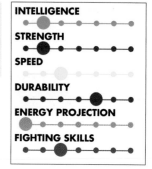

HOBGOBLIN

INTELLIGENCE

STRENGTH

SPEED

DURABILITY

ENERGY PROJECTION

FIGHTING SKILLS

Real Name:
Unrevealed
First Appearance:
X-Men #107 (1977)

Height:
6'1"
Weight:
165 lbs

POWERS/WEAPONS

- Shape-shifting into any form possible

HUSSAR

INTELLIGENCE

STRENGTH

SPEED

DURABILITY

ENERGY PROJECTION

FIGHTING SKILLS

Real Name:
Unrevealed
First Appearance:
X-Men #137 (1980)

Height:
5'5"
Weight:
120 lbs

POWERS/WEAPONS

- Channeling of bioelectricity into other living beings to shock their nervous system and paralyze their motor functions

IMPULSE

INTELLIGENCE

STRENGTH

SPEED

DURABILITY

ENERGY PROJECTION

FIGHTING SKILLS

Real Name:
Unrevealed
First Appearance:
X-Men #107 (1977)

Height:
5'10"
Weight:
Indeterminate

POWERS/WEAPONS

- Concussive energy blasts via a special containment suit

MAGIQUE

INTELLIGENCE

STRENGTH

SPEED

DURABILITY

ENERGY PROJECTION

FIGHTING SKILLS

Real Name:
Unrevealed
First Appearance:
X-Men #107 (1977)

Height:
5'7"
Weight:
126 lbs

POWERS/WEAPONS

- Utilizes ambient magic energy already existing within the universe and psionically focuses it to create three-dimensional intangible holographic illusions

MANTA

Real Name:
Unrevealed
First Appearance:
X-Men #137 (1980)

Height:
5'6"
Weight:
125 lbs

POWERS/WEAPONS

• Generates a blinding flash of blue-white light with her life force to dazzle her opponents

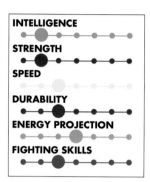

INTELLIGENCE
STRENGTH
SPEED
DURABILITY
ENERGY PROJECTION
FIGHTING SKILLS

MENTOR

Real Name:
Unrevealed
First Appearance:
X-Men #107 (1977)

Height:
5'9"
Weight:
150 lbs

POWERS/WEAPONS

• Instantaneous processing of vast amounts of information

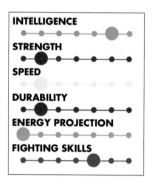

INTELLIGENCE
STRENGTH
SPEED
DURABILITY
ENERGY PROJECTION
FIGHTING SKILLS

MONSTRA

Real Name:
Unrevealed
First Appearance:
New X-Men #123 (2002)

Height:
6'8"
Weight:
516 lbs

POWERS/WEAPONS

• Enhanced strength and a heightened resistance to physical injury

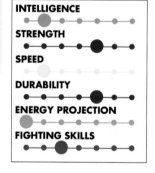

INTELLIGENCE
STRENGTH
SPEED
DURABILITY
ENERGY PROJECTION
FIGHTING SKILLS

NEUTRON

Real Name:
Unrevealed
First Appearance:
X-Men #107 (1977)

Height:
6'2"
Weight:
680 lbs

POWERS/WEAPONS

• Ability to absorb ambient electromagnetic energy into his body cells to enhance physical strength

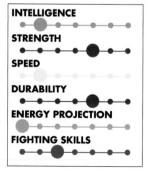

INTELLIGENCE
STRENGTH
SPEED
DURABILITY
ENERGY PROJECTION
FIGHTING SKILLS

NIGHTSIDE

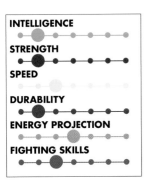

INTELLIGENCE
STRENGTH
SPEED
DURABILITY
ENERGY PROJECTION
FIGHTING SKILLS

Real Name:
Unrevealed
First Appearance:
X-Men #107 (1977)

Height:
5'6"
Weight:
125 lbs

POWERS/WEAPONS

• Utilizes a dark energy source to enshroud her opponents in a cloak of darkness, and causes beings and objects to plunge into a nightmarish void

SCINTILLA

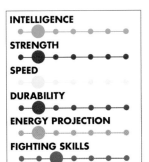

INTELLIGENCE
STRENGTH
SPEED
DURABILITY
ENERGY PROJECTION
FIGHTING SKILLS

Real Name:
Unrevealed
First Appearance:
X-Men #107 (1977)

Height:
5'1"
Weight:
100 lbs

POWERS/WEAPONS

• Can shrink to as little as 1/20 her normal size

SMASHER

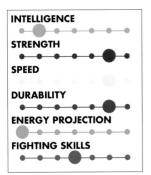

INTELLIGENCE
STRENGTH
SPEED
DURABILITY
ENERGY PROJECTION
FIGHTING SKILLS

Real Name:
Vril Rokk
First Appearance:
X-Men #107 (1977)

Height:
6'2"
Weight:
290 lbs

POWERS/WEAPONS

• Ability to absorb ambient cosmic energies to augment his strength and resistance to physical injury
• Exo-spex glasses that allow him to "download" various powers and abilities

SQUORM

INTELLIGENCE
STRENGTH
SPEED
DURABILITY
ENERGY PROJECTION
FIGHTING SKILLS

Real Name:
Unrevealed
First Appearance:
New X-Men #123 (2002)

Height:
6'
Weight:
Indeterminate

POWERS/WEAPONS

• Specially created spacesuit that contains his alien form: a hive of thousands of vastly intelligent tiny worm-like creatures

STARBOLT

Real Name:
Unrevealed
First Appearance:
X-Men #107 (1977)

Height:
5'1"
Weight:
Indeterminate

POWERS/WEAPONS

• Body is composed of an unknown form of energy that resembles fire
• Ability to fire bolts of energy from his hands

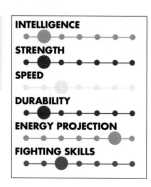

INTELLIGENCE
STRENGTH
SPEED
DURABILITY
ENERGY PROJECTION
FIGHTING SKILLS

TITAN

Real Name:
Unrevealed
First Appearance:
X-Men #107 (1977)

Height:
6'
Weight:
183 lbs

POWERS/WEAPONS

• Growth to gigantic size

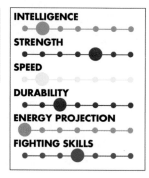

INTELLIGENCE
STRENGTH
SPEED
DURABILITY
ENERGY PROJECTION
FIGHTING SKILLS

WARSTAR

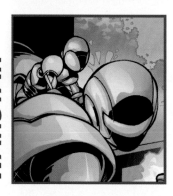

Real Name:
B'nee and C'cil
First Appearance:
X-Men #137 (1980)

Height: 2'2" (B'nee)
7'2" (C'cil)
Weight: 75 lbs (B'nee)
340 lbs (C'cil)

POWERS/WEAPONS

• C'cil possesses enhanced strength and durability
• B'nee has the ability to electrically shock an opponent with his touch

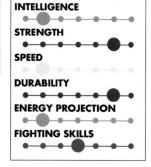

INTELLIGENCE
STRENGTH
SPEED
DURABILITY
ENERGY PROJECTION
FIGHTING SKILLS

WEBWING

Real Name:
Unrevealed
First Appearance:
Uncanny X-Men #157 (1982)

Height:
8'1"
Weight:
145 lbs

POWERS/WEAPONS

• Numerous suckered tentacles that exude a powerful narcotic sedative

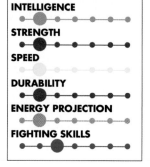

INTELLIGENCE
STRENGTH
SPEED
DURABILITY
ENERGY PROJECTION
FIGHTING SKILLS

STARJAMMERS

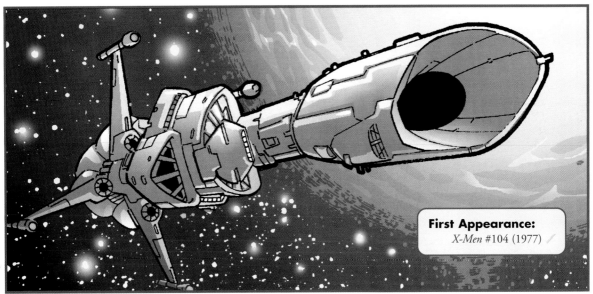

Art by Carlos Pacheco

First Appearance:
X-Men #104 (1977)

Five ex-prisoners. One starship. And the unwavering desire to strike out against the <u>Shi'ar</u> empire, which they blamed for their wrongful incarcerations.

They are the Starjammers, intergalactic pirates led by <u>Corsair</u>. Though they were once bound and determined to exact vengeance on the Shi'ar who had subjugated them, they have always been excessively cautious about letting innocents get caught up in their wrath.

The sentient computer Waldo oversees their base of operations, the starship Starjammer. The four original members—Corsair, <u>Ch'od</u>, <u>Hepzibah</u>, and <u>Raza</u>—eventually brought onboard the insect-like being <u>Sikorsky</u>, who came to serve as the Starjammers' physician.

After the Starjammers aided <u>Lilandra</u> in her struggle against her mad brother D'ken, the Shi'ar Empress put an unofficial end to her empire's opposition to the Starjammers. Although they sometimes fall out of favor with Lilandra over their decisions, the Starjammers always continually strive to break the yoke of oppression that they once toiled under. Because there are still missions to fight and innocents to be saved, when there is trouble in the galaxy, there are Starjammers to the rescue.

POWERS/WEAPONS

- Resistance to physical injury due to his thick scaly skin
- Can breathe on land and underwater

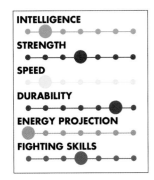

INTELLIGENCE

STRENGTH

SPEED

DURABILITY

ENERGY PROJECTION

FIGHTING SKILLS

Real Name: Ch'od
First Appearance: *X-Men #104 (1977)*

Height: 9'
Weight: 430 lbs

Scientist-philosopher Ch'od was once content to willingly serve the <u>Shi'ar</u> empire as a mercenary. But once he was sent to kill a village of helpless innocents, Ch'od flatly refused. To save the people of the village, he killed the Shi'ar commanding officer instead. His act of compassion was branded treason, and Ch'od was sentenced to the Slave Pits. Unwilling to accept his fate, he used his brute strength and keen scientific mind to help his fellow prisoners reach freedom. This team of five banded together to help serve their Empire, calling themselves the <u>Starjammers</u>.

CH'OD

CORSAIR

Real Name:
Christopher Summers
First Appearance:
X-Men #104 (1977)

Height:	6'3"
Weight:	175 lbs
Eye Color:	Brown
Hair Color:	Brown

It should have been a routine flight for Christopher Summers at the controls, his wife Katherine Anne beside him, and their two young sons Scott (**Cyclops**) and Alex (**Havok**) as passengers, but the family's journey went terribly awry. A **Shi'ar** starship attacked Christopher's plane, firing on the wooden aircraft and causing it to burst into flames. As Christopher struggled to keep the plane in the air, a frantic Katherine Anne searched for parachutes but could only find one. Strapping the lone parachute onto Scott, she told him to hold onto Alex, and pushed them out of the burning plane's door in order to save them from the Shi'ar.

Their children were saved, but Christopher and Katherine Anne were eventually teleported aboard the Shi'ar starship and taken to the Shi'ar Imperial Throneworld where the mad Shi'ar Emperor D'ken tried to rape Katherine Anne. D'ken murdered her in full view of Christopher and ordered him sent to the Slave Pits with the other political prisoners and criminals. There, Christopher's sprit was slowly being broken. But as he witnessed **Hepzibah** being brutalized by guards, his fighting spirit returned in force. He lashed out against the barbaric guards, and two more prisoners, **Ch'od** and **Raza**, jumped in to assist him. The four detainees stole a starship and escaped. As the leader of the band of fugitives calling themselves **Starjammers**, Corsair guided the team around the galaxy to plunder Shi'ar starships for booty on their quest for retribution.

As time passed, Corsair helped the **X-Men** battle the D'ken-serving **Shi'ar Imperial Guard**. After their combined forces defeated the Guard and helped depose D'ken, **Jean Grey** used her telepathic powers to examine Corsair's mind and learned he was Cyclops' father. Corsair, feeling the time wasn't right, asked her to keep the secret between themselves for the time being. Eventually, Cyclops and Havok both learned who Corsair really was.

Grateful for the Starjammers' help in defeating her brother, **Lilandra** put an unofficial end to the Shi'ar Empire's opposition to the team once she was installed as the new Majestrix. Corsair maintains a wariness of other people and planets in the Shi'ar Empire who operate counter to Lilandra's rule, and continues to lead the team's efforts in a fight against those who choose to oppress others.

POWERS/ WEAPONS

- Skilled hand-to-hand combatant
- Master swordsman

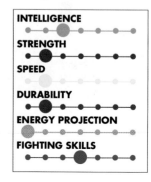

INTELLIGENCE						
STRENGTH						
SPEED						
DURABILITY						
ENERGY PROJECTION						
FIGHTING SKILLS						

Art by Carlos Pacheco

POWERS/WEAPONS

- Enhanced agility, speed, and reflexes
- Retractable claws, hyper-keen senses, night vision

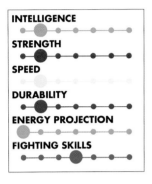

INTELLIGENCE
STRENGTH
SPEED
DURABILITY
ENERGY PROJECTION
FIGHTING SKILLS

Real Name: Unpronouncable
First Appearance: *X-Men* #107 (1977)

Height: 5'6"
Weight: 120 lbs

Hepzibah's race, the Mephitisoids, were conquered by the Shi'ar. Hatred of their oppressors led to numerous revolts, and resulted in the Mephitisoids being placed under permanent martial law. Imprisoned for her actions, Hepzibah faced cruel treatment at the hands of her jailers. When Corsair rebelled against their keepers, Hepzibah joined in and helped form the Starjammers. She soon fell in love with Corsair, and the two were bonded for life. But Hepzibah's fanaticism has put strains on their relationship—she will not rest until the Shi'ar are destroyed and her people freed.

HEPZIBAH

POWERS/WEAPONS

- Cybernetic implants that render him nearly indestructible
- Enhanced vision

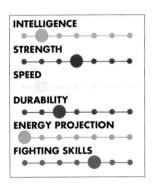

INTELLIGENCE
STRENGTH
SPEED
DURABILITY
ENERGY PROJECTION
FIGHTING SKILLS

Real Name: Raza Longknife
First Appearance: *X-Men* #107 (1977)

Height: 5'11"
Weight: 366 lbs

When the Shi'ar exterminated his entire race, the fiercely religious Raza was subjected to scientific experiments that implanted him with cybernetic devices. When Raza rebelled against his treatment, the Shi'ar had him thrown in the Slave Pits. After meeting Corsair, Ch'od, and Hepzibah, Raza and his new allies escaped and became the intergalactic pirates the Starjammers. Now cursed with an artificially prolonged life, Raza fights the Shi'ar for denying him the chance to die honorably in battle like the rest of his people.

RAZA

POWERS/WEAPONS

- Flight
- Psychic ability to mentally scan the interiors of bodies of living beings in order to assist medical diagnosis
- High empathic ability

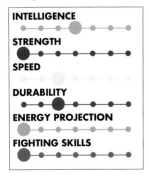

INTELLIGENCE
STRENGTH
SPEED
DURABILITY
ENERGY PROJECTION
FIGHTING SKILLS

Real Name: Unrevealed
First Appearance: *Uncanny X-Men* #156 (1982)

Length: 1'6"
Weight: 65 lbs

When lives must be saved and broken bodies must be healed, there is one powerful alien willing and able to do the job: Sikorsky. So named by Corsair after a helicopter manufacturer that makes vehicles that resemble Sikorsky's own physical appearance, this alien insectoid practices his craft as the resident physician onboard the Starjammer. A superb healer of both organic and cybernetic systems, Sikorsky, when not tending to his teammates, often helps allies in need. He once healed Colossus following a serious injury at the hands of the renegade Shi'ar Deathbird.

SIKORSKY

WEAPON X

Art by Georges Jeanty

First Appearance:
Incredible Hulk #180 (1974)

The most successful of the experimental Weapon Plus programs, Weapon X started out as a clandestine genetic-research organization sanctioned by the Canadian military. Its purpose was to transform mutants into obedient super-soldiers—with consent not necessarily a requirement. The program seemed to come to a grinding halt once one experiment in particular went very wrong: An unwilling test subject, <u>Wolverine</u>, escaped and savagely killed many of the program's scientists and guards. After this disaster, and with the program already plagued by funding issues, the Canadian government decided to pull the plug. But years later, a program official known only as the <u>**Director**</u> successfully lobbied for the relaunch of Weapon X, driven by a lust for revenge. During Wolverine's escape, the Director had been badly scarred in the rampage. Blaming his disfigurement on the scourge of mutants, the Director had a score to settle—and would go to any lengths to win his now very personal war against mutantkind.

Exacting a diabolical quid pro quo, the reinvigorated Weapon X program under the Director provides a safe haven for criminal mutants during a prescribed term of servitude. In return for money, better controlled powers, and immunity from law enforcement, the mutants who seek out Weapon X willingly embark on suicide missions or, more frequently, hunt down rogue mutants at the behest of the Director. Those mutants who are approached to join the program and choose not to participate are exterminated. Weapon X houses a host of law-breaking mutants who, unaware of the Director's desire to live in a world free of mutants, are all too willing to sell what is left of their souls to aid and abet his plans. And with the Director's construction of his concentration camp, "Neverland," he just might get his wish—much sooner than he ever thought possible.

DIRECTOR

On duty as a security guard at the original <u>Weapon X</u> complex in Canada, the Director was savagely attacked and mutilated by <u>Wolverine</u> during Wolverine's original escape from the facility. Saved from death, the Director made but one request to his doctors: do nothing to repair his horrible facial scars. The Director wanted the scars to serve as his reminder that what was done must be undone—though not by means of any plastic surgery. The wounds, it seemed, ran much deeper than the Director's skin.

Real Name:
Malcolm (full name unrevealed)
First Appearance:
Wolverine #160 (2001)

Height: 6'1"
Weight: 185 lbs
Eye Color: Brown
Hair Color: Black

Fueled by this incident, the Director returned to the original Weapon X installation and retrieved the mental implants used by the original program to control Wolverine. The Director methodically reactivated them and brought Wolverine under his control. The Director then sent Wolverine to kill Senator Drexel Walsh, who was intending to go public with knowledge of Weapon X, but the shock of committing murder disabled Wolverine's implants, freeing him of the Director's control.

But one setback did not a failure make; the Director realized that Wolverine might have been just a pet project en route to something greater. With renewed purpose, the Director went full speed ahead towards reviving the Weapon X project to fulfill his diabolical desires. In order to make Weapon X a success, the Director realized he would have to tolerate some mutants, even if only to manipulate them for use as his covert operatives. As a means to an end, the Director lured scores of on-the-run or injured mutants to his project, promising them hiding places and enhanced abilities in exchange for their services as operatives. No dummy, the Director took great care to implant devices in his wards during his enhancement processes that prevented them from rising up to harm their superiors, including the Director.

All the while, as he assembled the mutants and repaired and enhanced their bodies, the Director kept a little secret to himself. A secret that brought him much joy and invigorated his spirit: Soon, very soon, with more and more mutants under his control, a concentration camp would be built—where mutants whose skills proved useless to Weapon X would be incarcerated and eventually exterminated. He calls his camp "Neverland."

As he inches ever closer to realizing his dream—his final act of vengeance for the scars he forces himself to wear on his face—the Director may be the one who brings mutantkind to an end.

Art by Georges Jeanty

AGENT JACKSON

Real Name: Brent Jackson
First Appearance: *Wolverine* #163 (2001)

Height: 5'11"
Weight: 190 lbs

POWERS/WEAPONS

- Skilled covert operative
- Excellent marksman and hand-to-hand combatant

Working as an operative for the international law enforcement agency known as S.H.I.E.L.D., Brent Jackson was assigned to head up the manhunt for <u>Wolverine</u>. They managed to capture Wolverine and his ally <u>Beast</u>, and sent them both to the Cage, a maximum security prison for superhumans. But Agent Jackson was hardly the hero. With great craft and cunning, he had in fact infiltrated S.H.I.E.L.D. as a mole for <u>Weapon X</u> to position himself as the agent assigned to capture Wolverine, whom Weapon X had actually brainwashed into killing the judge. Fooling even the most intelligent and cynical law enforcement agents with his well-rehearsed demeanor and eager-to-please attitude, Agent Jackson secured the access codes to Wolverine's cell in the Cage. He turned the codes over to his Weapon X agent <u>Sabretooth</u>, who abducted Wolverine and took him back to Weapon X headquarters. Ultimately, Wolverine escaped their clutches. Now back in his capacity as the right-hand man of the <u>Director</u>, Jackson is responsible for maintaining the day-to-day operations of Weapon X, including coordinating strike missions, recruitment, personnel management, and other tasks critical to the group's goals.

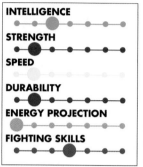

INTELLIGENCE
STRENGTH
SPEED
DURABILITY
ENERGY PROJECTION
FIGHTING SKILLS

Art by Georges Jeanty

AGENT ZERO

Real Name: Unrevealed
First Appearance: *Weapon X: The Draft— Agent Zero* #1 (2002)

Height: Unrevealed
Weight: Unrevealed

POWERS/WEAPONS

- Genetic enhancement rendering his body devoid of scent
- Ability to generate a corrosive enzyme that can melt steel and turn healing abilities deadly
- Special body armor that absorbs sound vibrations, rendering him absolutely silent, and sometimes nearly invisible, when he moves

Though his former life remains a mystery, this much is known: Agent Zero was saved from certain death by the <u>Weapon X</u> project. Desperate to survive no matter the cost, he acquiesced to his "savior's" request that, in return for saving his life, Agent Zero would serve as a field operative for Weapon X.

After healing Agent Zero, Weapon X ultimately outfitted him with everything that would make it possible to take down and kill their primary target: <u>Wolverine</u>.

But Agent Zero was an old friend of Wolverine's and could not fulfill his mission. This was not an unexpected turn of events, however. The <u>Director</u> knew Agent Zero wouldn't murder his friend, and had intended for the mission to succeed only in further corroding Agent Zero's already-fragile psyche. The Director knows that once Agent Zero is broken, he will be putty in Weapon X's hands.

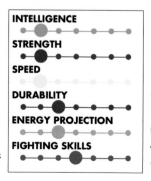

INTELLIGENCE
STRENGTH
SPEED
DURABILITY
ENERGY PROJECTION
FIGHTING SKILLS

Art by Georges Jeanty

AURORA

After her parents were killed in a car crash and her twin brother Jean-Paul (**Northstar**) was sent to live with relatives who couldn't afford to take in both of them, Jeanne-Marie Beaubier went to live at Madame DuPont's School for Girls in Quebec. Jeanne-Marie was miserable at Madame DuPont's School and, at the age of thirteen, attempted suicide by throwing herself from the roof of one of the school buildings. However, instead of falling to her death, Beaubier discovered she had the ability to fly at great speed. A deeply religious girl, Jeanne-Marie mistook her mutant act for a divine miracle. When she explained to a nun what happened, the sister condemned her as a blasphemer and severely beat her. The violence triggered Jeanne-Marie's split personality—one more extroverted and far less inhibited than her own. Under the influence of this second personality, Jeanne-Marie secretly left the school that same night. On returning three days later, she had no memory of where she had been or what she had done, and she was again disciplined. The resulting trauma was so great that Jeanne-Marie repressed her second personality for several years.

Some time later, under the influence of her extroverted personality, Jeanne-Marie traveled to Montreal and got mugged. When **Wolverine** came to her rescue, he invited Jeanne-Marie to meet **Guardian**, who was in the process of organizing **Alpha Flight**. Guardian accepted her as a recruit and reunited her with her estranged brother. But Aurora still found herself unexpectedly shifting from one personality to the other. Each of her personalities strongly disliked the other, thinking the other belonged to an entirely different person.

During an encounter with the cannibalistic sorceror named Mauvais (**Wendigo**), her already-fragile mind was further damaged and she was once again committed to a psychiatric hospital. A former lover, **Wild Child**, came to Aurora's rescue bearing good news: She could finally rid herself of her dual personalities forever by joining **Weapon X**. Aurora agreed, and the procedure was a success. Eventually, she embarked on a mission with Wild Child, but it was a trap set up by the renegade **Sabretooth**, who viciously assaulted her and scarred her face.

Real Name:
Jeanne-Marie Beaubier
First Appearance:
X-Men #120 (1979)

Height: 5'11"
Weight: 140 lbs
Eye Color: Blue
Hair Color: Black

POWERS/ WEAPONS

- Superhuman speed
- Generation of light
- Ability to accelerate the molecules of people and objects causing them to tear themselves apart

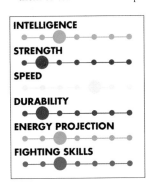

INTELLIGENCE

STRENGTH

SPEED

DURABILITY

ENERGY PROJECTION

FIGHTING SKILLS

Art by Georges Jeanty

KANE

Real Name:
Garrison Kane
First Appearance:
X-Force #2 (1991)

Height:	6'2"
Weight:	480 lbs
Eye Color:	Blue
Hair Color:	Black

Garrison Kane's life as a fighter began when he joined a mercenary group led by <u>Nathan Summers</u>. On a mission with the group, Kane lost all his limbs in a trap set by <u>Stryfe</u>. Blaming Nathan for all of his pain and suffering and for abandoning him in his limbless state, Kane was rescued by the first incarnation of the <u>Weapon X</u> project, which provided him with cybernetic limbs to replace the ones he had lost. Kane soon came face-to-face with Stryfe, the man responsible for maiming him, but he would fare no better the second time around: Stryfe destroyed Kane's bionics. This time, however, Nathan Summers took Kane back to the future time from which Nathan hailed. Kane was outfitted with advanced techno-organic technology, and he joined Nathan in the fight against <u>Apocalypse</u>.

On returning to the present, Kane sought to retire from the life of a mercenary and attempted to settle down with his lover, Copycat. Still, no matter how hard he tried, he could not run from who he was, and Kane soon found himself in the employ of international weapons dealers from Advanced Idea Mechanics, who had captured <u>Guardian</u>. <u>Alpha Flight</u> and their ally <u>Wolverine</u> rescued Guardian, and Wolverine pummeled Kane before leaving the scene.

Kane realized he needed to be stronger, better equipped, and greatly enhanced. There was one way to get the job done. After the <u>Director</u> revived the Weapon X program, Kane accepted an offer to join the organization and underwent further bionic augmentation. One of his first missions was to kill Copycat. Before Kane could slaughter Copycat, the wisecracking mercenary Deadpool saved the girl—and blew Kane to pieces in the process. It mattered little. Weapon X rebuilt Kane to near-perfection.

Kane revels in the act of pushing himself beyond his limits, obsessed with the need to better himself, no matter what the cost. He sees Weapon X as a means to that end. Now more cyborg than man, Kane has found a home in Weapon X, thanks to his unswerving allegiance and a willingness to follow orders without question.

POWERS/WEAPONS

- Bionic appendages that house various weapons
- Ability to see in the infrared portion of the light spectrum
- Ability to project holograms
- Computerized targeting system

INTELLIGENCE	
STRENGTH	
SPEED	
DURABILITY	
ENERGY PROJECTION	
FIGHTING SKILLS	

Art by Georges Jeanty

MARROW

Targeted for extinction by <u>Mr. Sinister</u>'s <u>Marauders</u>, a very young Marrow narrowly escaped the massacre in the <u>Morlocks</u>' underground home. Marrow and the other survivors were taken to a dimensional rift where time passed more quickly than it did on Earth, and she soon grew into adulthood. She was placed in charge of Gene Nation, a new faction of the Morlocks bent on gaining revenge for the massacre. In their most daring effort, Marrow and Gene Nation decided to mark the anniversary of the massacre by killing one hundred humans for every Morlock who died in the tunnels that day. After Marrow had helped kidnap a subway car filled with humans, the <u>X-Men</u> descended on her group and freed their captives.

Ultimately, <u>Callisto</u> convinced Marrow to give up her crusade against humanity, and Marrow reluctantly joined the X-Men in hopes of finding acceptance and a normal life. The mutant heroes welcomed her into their ranks, but Marrow eventually left the X-Men after the enigmatic scientist known as the <u>High Evolutionary</u> created a device that nullified all mutants' powers. Marrow then attempted to live a normal life, returning to school. Once the High Evolutionary's device was destroyed, however, her powers returned and she soon found herself reverting to her original persona. But she had grown used to her "normal" self, and she was desperate not to live the life of a superhero any longer.

Driven insane by her loss, Marrow approached the recently revived <u>Weapon X</u> project to see if they could give her a normal body again. Scientists at the project altered Marrow's genetic code, slowing her disfigurement and granting her full control of her powers. Like every other mutant who sought out Weapon X's help, Marrow had to pay a heavy price for their services. Weapon X ordered Marrow to assassinate D'Gard, her one-time ally in Gene Nation. It was too late to break her deal with the devil, and Marrow was pushed to the brink of emotional collapse by her teammates <u>Kane</u> and <u>Mesmero</u> in order to complete her mission. In the end, the best Marrow could do was to grant her old and dear friend a swift death.

Real Name:	
	Sarah (full name unrevealed)
First Appearance:	
	Cable #15 (1994)
Height:	6'
Weight:	160 lbs
Eye Color:	Blue
Hair Color:	Purple

POWERS/WEAPONS

- Hyper-accelerated metabolism that forced her bones to protrude from her skin
- Entire skeleton has enhanced durability
- Proficiency at using blade-shaped bones as throwing weapons or in hand-to-hand combat
- Razor-sharp extendable claws on each hand

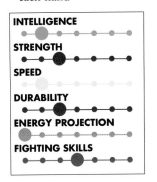

INTELLIGENCE

STRENGTH

SPEED

DURABILITY

ENERGY PROJECTION

FIGHTING SKILLS

Art by Georges Jeanty

MESMERO

Real Name:
Unrevealed
First Appearance:
X-Men #49 (1968)

Height:	5'10"
Weight:	180 lbs
Eye Color:	Red
Hair Color:	Green

Look into his eyes—deep into his eyes—relax, and breathe deeply; it won't take but a second to succumb.

Mesmero started life as a stage hypnotist and manager of a small traveling carnival. He believed good fortune was smiling on him when **Magneto** employed him to hypnotize a young Lorna Dane (**Polaris**) into thinking she was Magneto's daughter. Since Mesmero was a hypnotist and not a mentalist, he had no idea that "Magneto" was, in fact, nothing more than an android duplicate created by a master robotics engineer planned to use androids to help him accumulate a vast personal fortune. In the end, however, no one earned a dime: Mesmero dropped his control over Dane, overconfidently assuming that she would obey her supposed father no matter what happened, and his cluelessness helped ruin the engineer's plans.

While Mesmero is a powerful hypnotist, he frequently proves hapless in difficult situations. At one point, Mesmero successfully captured the **X-Men** by hypnotizing them into believing that they were circus performers. After **Beast** interfered with Mesmero's control and released his teammates, the real Magneto appeared and, rendering Mesmero unconscious, transported him to South America, where he was left stranded. Later, after another hypnotic episode had gone awry, Mesmero was defeated by **Shadowcat**'s pet dragon **Lockheed**—and a group of students from St. Searle's School for Young Ladies.

Unfazed by his defeat at the hands of small pets and girls, Mesmero continued to ply his trade, still thinking he was the greatest, most gifted hypnotist who had ever lived. He ran afoul of the X-Men once more when he hypnotized them into believing they were living in medieval times. Mesmero played the role of the evil wizard, but was knocked unconscious by Shadowcat, breaking the illusion. Believing his hypnotic abilities were in need of augmentation, the power-hungry Mesmero accepted the assistance of the **Weapon X** project, which was more than happy to accommodate his wish in exchange for service. As a result of their genetic enhancements to his powers, Mesmero may now be one of the most powerful mutants on the planet—and he knows it.

POWERS/ WEAPONS

- Ability to psionically take mental control of any sentient being who looks into his eyes

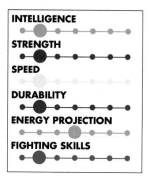

INTELLIGENCE	
STRENGTH	
SPEED	
DURABILITY	
ENERGY PROJECTION	
FIGHTING SKILLS	

Art by Georges Jeanty

SABRETOOTH

Unlike ferocious animals that kill to live, Sabretooth lives to kill. It is a way of life for which he offers no excuses and makes no apologies.

In many ways, Sabretooth resembles his archenemy <u>Wolverine</u>: Both are feral, furious fighters, both have adamantium bonded to their skeletons, both have accelerated healing factors, both have pasts they barely remember, and both served in the CIA. But there is one distinct, profound difference that sets these two mutants apart: Wolverine can keep the animal side of his psyche in check; Victor Creed cannot and will not.

Sabretooth can piece together bits and pieces of his past—but the pieces are all grim. Mostly, he remembers the brutal psychological abuse heaped upon him by his father. Forced to live in a dark, dank basement, Sabretooth survived his traumatic childhood to become the ultimate warrior. He has a psychotic need to hunt, fight, and kill. His viciousness not confined to human, Sabretooth will strike dead any mutant who stands in his way.

During his tenure with the CIA, he frequently partnered with Wolverine. Both were subjected to the <u>Weapon X</u> project, and both were implanted with false memories which would forever cloud their pasts. On a mission in Berlin, the two uneasy allies separated permanently after Sabretooth became unhinged and murdered a double agent he considered expendable. Their tenuous alliance turned into full-blown hatred, and each now views the other as his mortal enemy.

While he prefers his solitude, Sabretooth has been known to take up with dubious organizations from time to time, including: the <u>Brotherhood of Evil Mutants</u>, a genetic terrorist organization; the <u>Marauders</u>, a team of superhuman assassins; X-Factor, a government-sponsored mutant strike force; and Weapon X, the reinvigorated program now run by the man known only as the <u>Director</u>.

Brutal, ruthless, and out of control, Victor Creed roams the world as Sabretooth—a man who answers to no one and keeps no killer instinct in check.

Real Name:
Victor Creed
First Appearance:
Iron Fist #14 (1977)

Height: 6'6"
Weight: 275 lbs
Eye Color: Amber
Hair Color: Blond

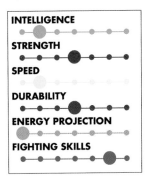

INTELLIGENCE

STRENGTH

SPEED

DURABILITY

ENERGY PROJECTION

FIGHTING SKILLS

POWERS/ WEAPONS

- Accelerated healing factor
- Superhumanly acute senses
- Indestructible adamantium skeleton and claws

Art by Georges Jeanty

SAURON

Real Name:
Karl Lykos

First Appearance:
X-Men #59 (1963)

Height: 7'
Weight: 200 lbs
Eye Color:
Brown (as Lykos),
red (as Sauron)
Hair Color:
Brown (as Lykos),
none (as Sauron)

POWERS/ WEAPONS

- Drains the life force from living beings into his body
- Hypnosis
- Projection of concussive energy blasts

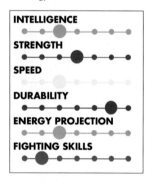

INTELLIGENCE

STRENGTH

SPEED

DURABILITY

ENERGY PROJECTION

FIGHTING SKILLS

As a young boy, Karl Lykos accompanied his father on an expedition to a Chilean island with a physician friend, Dr. Andersson, and his daughter Tanya. Attacked by a pterodactyl, Karl drove the beast away—but not before the creature wounded him, requiring Dr. Andersson to save his life. When his father died, Karl went to live with Tanya and her father. Soon after, his desire to drain the life energy from other living beings began. As Karl grew older, he fell in love with Tanya—a romance that didn't please Dr. Andersson, who saw the impoverished orphan Karl as a poor match for his daughter. Determined to prove Dr. Andersson wrong, Karl left to become a doctor himself. Once he became a successful practicing hypnotherapist, however, his urges to siphon life forces from others increased dramatically. When the **X-Men** brought an injured **Havok** to his office for treatment, Havok's energy triggered Karl's metamorphosis into a creature that retained his human intelligence and ability to speak but distorted Karl's personality into a twisted reflection of what it had been before. The transformation was transitory, however; as the power from the stolen life forces wore off, Sauron reverted back to his human form.

After siphoning off more superhuman life forces, Sauron tried to kill both the doctor and his daughter, but he was thwarted by the X-Men. Distraught, Karl made his way to the Savage Land to try and manage his desires. He subsisted on a life-force diet of only animals there, and eventually reunited with Tanya. Their love would not last. Years later, **Toad** captured Karl and Tanya, and used her life energies to transform Karl back into Sauron—this time permanently. After Tanya was killed in the process, Sauron embarked on a rampage of terror and chaos

Most recently, Sauron was recruited by the **Weapon X** project, which offered to genetically alter his abilities to allow him to rechannel the life energy he absorbs and expel it as blasts of concussive energy from his hands. In the course of the procedure to achieve these enhancements, Sauron's intelligence was reduced. With newer, more powerful abilities, Sauron believes he is using the project to serve his own ends—at least, that's what the **Director** wants him to believe.

Art by Chris Bachalo

WILD CHILD

When Wild Child's parents discovered he was a mutant and kicked him out of the house, the boy had nowhere to go. Taken in by a subversive organization, Wild Child was subjected to vile experiments by the group in their attempt to create the perfect killing machine. To achieve their goal, they injected Wild Child with an assassin's DNA, causing his bestial side to emerge and ending all hopes that he could ever live a normal life. When the assassin whose DNA had been extracted decimated the organization's base, Alpha Flight members rescued Wild Child from the ruins and took him in. But life with Alpha Flight just never seemed to work out for Wild Child. Though he wanted to do the right thing, he frequently engaged in killing sprees and berserk rages that ostracized his teammates. Wild Child desperately wanted to maintain his relationship with his lover Aurora, but his continued violent behavior made that almost impossible.

Wild Child found some reason for optimism when he was offered a place on a government-sponsored mutant strike force by Valerie Cooper, a long-time associate of Wild Child's who had attempted to treat his violent tendencies years earlier. Wild Child served with the team until his body began mutating even further. He left to explore his new mutations and find his true self.

Trying to come to terms with his out-of-control powers, Wild Child was eventually recruited by the Weapon X project, which planned to genetically alter him and perfect his superhuman abilities. Now enhanced to Weapon X's specifications, Wild Child, along with Sabretooth, attempted to recruit Sunfire into their organization on one of his first missions for the group. When Sunfire refused and set Sabretooth ablaze, Wild Child shot him. But Wild Child also insulted Sabretooth, and Sabretooth responded by slashing Wild Child's throat.

Months afterward, Weapon X sent Wild Child to rescue his former lover Aurora from a psychiatric hospital. Once Aurora's mind was healed by the Weapon X program, Wild Child sought to rekindle his romance with her, but she rejected him. Later, the two were paired together for a mission to secure the services of a teleporter for the program. The mission turned out to be a trap set by Sabretooth, who forced Wild Child to watch as he savagely attacked Aurora. Wild Child has yet to recover from the resulting trauma. Turned out and cast aside, Wild Child might have had a shot at redemption if the right organization had found him. But Wild Child must face his future with the framework built by the consequences of his past.

Real Name:
Kyle Gibney
First Appearance:
Alpha Flight #1 (1983)

Height: 5'8"
Weight: 152 lbs
Eye Color: Green-blue
Hair Color: None

POWERS/ WEAPONS

- Powerful claw-like fingernails
- Superhumanly acute hearing
- Able to see in absolute darkness

INTELLIGENCE	
STRENGTH	
SPEED	
DURABILITY	
ENERGY PROJECTION	
FIGHTING SKILLS	

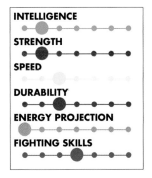

Art by Georges Jeanty

MADISON JEFFRIES

Real Name: Madison Jeffries
First Appearance: *Alpha Flight* #1 (1983)

Height: 6'1"
Weight: 195 lbs

POWERS/WEAPONS
• Psionic manipulation of machinery

He is the man who will help the **Director** build his dream—whether he wants to or not. A highly skilled mechanic and master builder—and a former member of **Alpha Flight**—Madison Jeffries became a victim of brainwashing and was being held against his will when an unlikely group of liberators arrived: **Weapon X**. Killing everyone in their path, Weapon X operatives "rescued" Madison and took him to the Director. Taking advantage of Madison's weakened mind, the Director recruited him to assist in the construction the Neverland concentration camp for mutants.

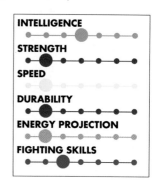

INTELLIGENCE					
STRENGTH					
SPEED					
DURABILITY					
ENERGY PROJECTION					
FIGHTING SKILLS					

WASHOUT

Real Name: John (full name unrevealed)
First Appearance: *X-Force* #129 (2002)

Height: 5'10"
Weight: 180 lbs

POWERS/WEAPONS
• Ability to transform part or all of his body into water
• Project high-pressure jets of water from his hands

As if being a chronic bed-wetter weren't bad enough, young Washout discovered that he had the mutant ability to generate a spurt of water from his body on touch. With nowhere to turn, Washout accepted the **Director**'s offer to join **Weapon X**. After undergoing a process that enhanced his mutant ability to the point where he could transform his entire body into water and create almost any shape imaginable with it, Washout was thrilled by the results. But his powers leave him dehydrated and—unknown to Washout—the more frequently he uses them, the closer he comes to killing himself.

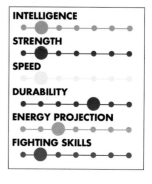

INTELLIGENCE					
STRENGTH					
SPEED					
DURABILITY					
ENERGY PROJECTION					
FIGHTING SKILLS					

DR. WINDSOR

Real Name: Charles Windsor
First Appearance: *Wolverine* #173 (2002)

Height: 5'9"
Weight: 165 lbs

In spite of personal injury, exposure, and everything that makes men quake with fear, courage and decency must prevail wherever the face of evil appears. When Dr. Windsor allowed himself to be recruited into **Weapon X**, thinking he could further expand on his already profound scientific skills, he knew nothing of the group's much more insidious and awful plans. But once he learned of the **Director**'s scheme to incarcerate mutants in the concentration camp known as "Neverland," Dr. Windsor refused to sit idly by and watch the genocide take place. Seeking to aid those trapped in the camp, Dr. Windsor risked his own life to help mutants escape the horrible fate behind the gates of Neverland.

XAVIER INSTITUTE

First Appearance:
X-Men #1 (1963)

Art by Frank Quitely

Perhaps the most important address to mutants is 1407 Graymalkin Lane in Salem Center, Westchester County, New York. It is where they learn. It is where they grow. It is the only chance they have to improve the skills that will ultimately save the world from the coming genetic war.

Built specifically to educate and train specially chosen young mutants, the Xavier Institute for Higher Learning sits on the stately grounds of **Professor X**'s ancestral mansion.

This unique secondary school helps its students to learn how to better utilize, control, and understand their mutant abilities in pursuit of peaceful coexistence between man and mutant, in addition to learning traditional academic subjects.

The Institute recruits students from all walks of mutantkind, from those exhibiting morphological to psionic abilities. Its first student was **Jean Grey**, a scared, emotionally scarred mutant just coming to terms with her ability to absorb other people's memories and feelings. Now a teacher, Jean uses her own experience to help counsel and guide those mutants, who, much like her, are confused and anxious about the special gifts they were born with.

Years of secrecy prevented the public from knowing about the existence of the Institute, but the veil was lifted when **Cassandra Nova** appeared on television and exposed the truth about the mutants and their teachers. Although there was some violent backlash at first, the surrounding towns have shown great restraint toward the school as well as its students.

At the Xavier Institute, the practice of preaching peace continues.

ANGEL

Real Name:	Angel Gonzales	**Height:**	5'1"
First Appearance:	*New X-Men* #118 (2001)	**Weight:**	105 lbs

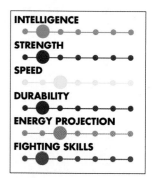

POWERS/WEAPONS

- Flight
- Vibration of her wings can create deafening ultrasonics
- Highly acidic projectile vomit

Thanks to an abusive stepfather who drove her from her home at age fourteen, Angel faces a desperate battle against her feelings of self-hatred. Plagued by neuroses, Angel initially despised the other students at the <u>Xavier Institute</u>—if only because she envied the confidence they had in themselves. Though she eventually warmed to and developed a bond with <u>Beak</u> and the <u>Stepford Cuckoos</u> during a battle against <u>Cassandra Nova</u>, her struggle to keep her attitude in check continues.

INTELLIGENCE
STRENGTH
SPEED
DURABILITY
ENERGY PROJECTION
FIGHTING SKILLS

BEAK

Real Name:	Barnell Bohusk	**Height:**	5'9"
First Appearance:	*New X-Men* #117 (2001)	**Weight:**	122 lbs

POWERS/WEAPONS

- Limited degree of flight

Even among other mutants at the <u>Xavier Institute</u>, Beak felt cursed by his inability to fly and isolated because of his appearance. Shunned by his peers, Beak found a friend in <u>Beast</u>, who knows too well what it's like to be judged on looks alone. Even under Beast's guidance, Beak could not break the spell of loneliness and despair. Fate, however, is subject to change. After <u>Angel</u> planted a passionate kiss on Beak, his life seemed to turn around. Beak was rejuvenated by a new emotion: love. Unknown to him, the kiss was nothing more than the result of a spiteful bet.

INTELLIGENCE
STRENGTH
SPEED
DURABILITY
ENERGY PROJECTION
FIGHTING SKILLS

ANNIE GHAZIKHANIAN

Real Name:	Annie Ghazikhanian	**Height:**	5'7"
First Appearance:	*Uncanny X-Men* #411 (2002)	**Weight:**	145 lbs

Registered nurse Annie Ghazikhanian had no idea she could develop such deep feelings for the mysterious man in a coma who was in her care. After all, she had more pressing things on her mind than falling in love—like coming to terms with her son, <u>Carter Ghazikhanian</u>, who had become a mutant, a species for which she had great distrust and disdain. But after a newspaper story revealed her patient's name—Alex Summers (<u>Havok</u>), a mutant himself—she had come to a crossroads. With both her son and her object of affection revealed to be mutants, Annie had to make a choice: learn to accept and understand them, or maintain her suspicions and cut her losses right now. When <u>Cyclops</u> came to the hospital to retrieve his brother, Annie made her decision. Along with Carter, she returned with Cyclops to the <u>Xavier Institute</u> to help nurse Havok back to health.

POWERS/WEAPONS

- Untapped telepathy and telekinesis

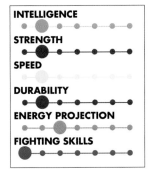

Real Name:	Carter Ghazikhanian
First Appearance:	*Uncanny X-Men* #411 (2002)
Height:	4'2"
Weight:	72 lbs

Carter doesn't understand. Why would his mother, who denied his own mutant abilities, choose to leave her hospital to live at a mansion teeming with powerful mutants? Carter only knows that when his mother, Annie Ghazikhanian, uprooted him from their home, he finally got a shot at earning newfound respect from his mom—and at actually making friends with kids who understand him. Sure enough, Carter made friends with the young mutant Squid-Boy—and his mother is slowly dissolving her ill will towards others of his kind.

CARTER GHAZIKHANIAN

POWERS/WEAPONS

- Superhuman intellect

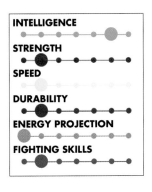

Real Name:	Quentin Quire
First Appearance:	*New X-Men* #122 (2002)
Height:	5'8"
Weight:	129 lbs

Once the top student at the Xavier Institute, Kid Omega plunged to the bottom when he began to doubt Professor X's teachings. After he learned he was adopted, Kid Omega developed a hostile view of the world and a habit for the devastating drug Kick, which increases superhuman mutant powers—and slowly drives addicts insane. Joining forces with Radian, Redneck, Glob and Tattoo, Kid Omega even went so far as to kidnap Professor X, but he was stopped by the Stepford Cuckoos and incarcerated in a statis tube.

KID OMEGA

POWERS/WEAPONS

- Suppresses the mutant abilities of others
- Telepathic communication

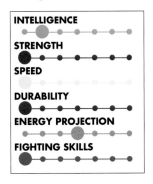

Real Name:	Martha Johansson
First Appearance:	*New X-Men* #118 (2001)
Height:	Inapplicable
Weight:	Inapplicable

Once she discovered she had mutant powers, young Martha Johansson left home. Before long, John Sublime's U-Men captured her to harvest her powers. Sublime removed Martha's brain and used drugs to control her powers, which incapacitated Cyclops and Emma Frost. After the pair broke free, Martha exacted her revenge on Sublime by telepathically forcing him to fall from his high-rise office building to his death. Martha, sans body, later enrolled as a student at the Xavier Institute, where she was granted mobility via anti-gravity floats.

MARTHA

SLICK

Real Name: Unrevealed
First Appearance: *New X-Men* #126 (2002)
Height: 2'3"
Weight: 240 lbs

POWERS/WEAPONS
- Creation of an illusory solid self-image to disguise his true appearance
- Enhanced charisma

Slick was once just a shy mutant boy. Pug-nosed, pointy-eared, diminutive, and with webbed feet, Slick could never manage to overcome his appearance—so he built an illusory one that was tall, handsome, and trim. In his new guise, Slick quickly went on to become one of the Xavier Institute's most popular students. He even managed to land a girlfriend, Tattoo. After Kid Omega revealed Slick's true nature, it didn't take long before Slick learned a lesson in image over substance. Aghast at Slick's real body, Tattoo rejected him and took up with Kid Omega's cause.

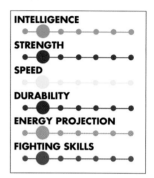

INTELLIGENCE
STRENGTH
SPEED
DURABILITY
ENERGY PROJECTION
FIGHTING SKILLS

SQUID-BOY

Real Name: Samuel Pare
First Appearance: *Uncanny X-Men* #410 (2002)
Height: 4'2"
Weight: 80 lbs

POWERS/WEAPONS
- Ability to breathe and talk underwater

With the physical attributes of a fish, Sammy Pare was a perfect target for local bullies. Intent on stopping the harassment, Sammy plotted to shoot his tormentors. A meeting with Professor X saved Sammy from a potentially deadly showdown, however, and he came to choose enrollment in the Xavier Institute over murder. On the way to his new home and school, Squid-Boy wound up rescuing Juggernaut from certain death in the ocean. His effort not only saved Juggernaut but also helped forge a meaningful friendship between the two mutants.

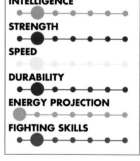

INTELLIGENCE
STRENGTH
SPEED
DURABILITY
ENERGY PROJECTION
FIGHTING SKILLS

STEPFORD CUCKOOS

Real Name: Esme, Sophie and three unnamed others
First Appearance: *New X-Men* #118 (2001)
Height: 5'3" (all)
Weight: 115 lbs (all)

POWERS/WEAPONS
- Telepathy

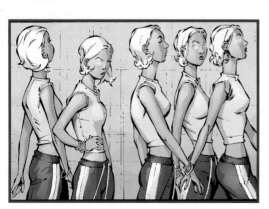

They are a testament to the power of the group versus the individual. Acting separately, their powers are minimal; as a cohesive unit, they are among the most powerful telepaths on the planet. Although the Cuckoos were instrumental in defending the mansion against attacks by John Sublime's U-Men and Cassandra Nova, disaster struck when they tried to intervene in Kid Omega's drug-fueled riots at the Xavier Institute. Sophie used Cerebra and the power-enhancing drug Kick to boost the Cuckoos' abilities. They defeated Kid Omega, but Sophie died from the strain.

INTELLIGENCE

STRENGTH

SPEED

DURABILITY

ENERGY PROJECTION

FIGHTING SKILLS

Real Name:
Unrevealed
First Appearance:
New X-Men #135 (2002)

Height:
6'5"
Weight:
220 lbs

POWERS/WEAPONS

• Ability to emit a pulse of high-frequency strobe light directly from his brain

BASILISK

INTELLIGENCE

STRENGTH

SPEED

DURABILITY

ENERGY PROJECTION

FIGHTING SKILLS

Real Name:
Unrevealed
First Appearance:
New X-Men #126 (2002)

Height:
Inapplicable
Weight:
Inapplicable

POWERS/WEAPONS

• Gaseous form

DUMMY

INTELLIGENCE

STRENGTH

SPEED

DURABILITY

ENERGY PROJECTION

FIGHTING SKILLS

Real Name:
Unrevealed
First Appearance:
New X-Men #135 (2002)

Height:
4'2"
Weight:
50 lbs

POWERS/WEAPONS

• Superhuman strength

ERNST

INTELLIGENCE

STRENGTH

SPEED

DURABILITY

ENERGY PROJECTION

FIGHTING SKILLS

Real Name: Herman (full
name unrevealed)
First Appearance:
New X-Men #117 (2001)

Height:
6'5"
Weight:
216 lbs

POWERS/WEAPONS

• Highly flammable paraffin body

GLOB HERMAN

NO-GIRL

Real Name:
Unrevealed
First Appearance:
New X-Men #135 (2002)

Height:
Unrevealed
Weight:
Unrevealed

POWERS/WEAPONS

• Unknown

INTELLIGENCE
STRENGTH
SPEED
DURABILITY
ENERGY PROJECTION
FIGHTING SKILLS

RADIAN

Real Name:
Unrevealed
First Appearance:
New X-Men #126 (2002)

Height:
5'8"
Weight:
140 lbs.

POWERS/WEAPONS

• Generation of blinding flashes of ultraviolet light

INTELLIGENCE
STRENGTH
SPEED
DURABILITY
ENERGY PROJECTION
FIGHTING SKILLS

REDNECK

Real Name:
Unrevealed
First Appearance:
New X-Men #126 (2002)

Height:
6'1"
Weight:
190 lbs

POWERS/WEAPONS

• Generation of intense heat from his hands

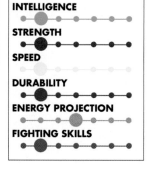

INTELLIGENCE
STRENGTH
SPEED
DURABILITY
ENERGY PROJECTION
FIGHTING SKILLS

TATTOO

Real Name:
Unrevealed
First Appearance:
New X-Men #126 (2002)

Height:
5'7"
Weight:
130 lbs

POWERS/WEAPONS

• Intangibility that allows physical attacks to pass through her without harm
• Chameleon skin

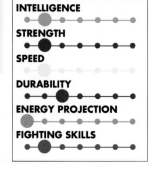

INTELLIGENCE
STRENGTH
SPEED
DURABILITY
ENERGY PROJECTION
FIGHTING SKILLS

XAVIER MANSION

The base of operations for the <u>X-Men</u> and home to the <u>Xavier Institute</u>, the Xavier Mansion is located at 1407 Graymalkin Lane in the town of Salem Center in New York State's Westchester County. The mansion belongs to the team's founder, <u>Professor X</u>, and has been in his family's possession for ten generations. A Dutch seafaring ancestor of Xavier's built it of local stone in the 1700s on the edge of Breakstone Lake.

Through the years, the mansion has been electrified, refurbished and modernized. Many of the renovations have involved the installation and construction of facilities for use by the X-Men— including the addition of subterranean hangar buildings, the Danger Room and its support equipment, and high-speed transport tunnels. Rebuilt and expanded several times during the last few years with an eye toward personal comfort, space and security, the mansion incorporates advanced alien technology provided by <u>Lilandra</u> of the <u>Shi'ar</u>.

Xavier's estate covers an extensive area between Graymalkin Lane and Breakstone Lake. There is an Olympic-size swimming pool directly to the rear of the mansion. Elsewhere on the property are stables and a boathouse. Hangars and a takeoff pad for the X-Men's Blackbird jet are located in areas of the estate far from public view. These facilities may be reached from the mansion by means of high-speed magnetic rail cars that travel through an underground tunnel.

XAVIER MANSION

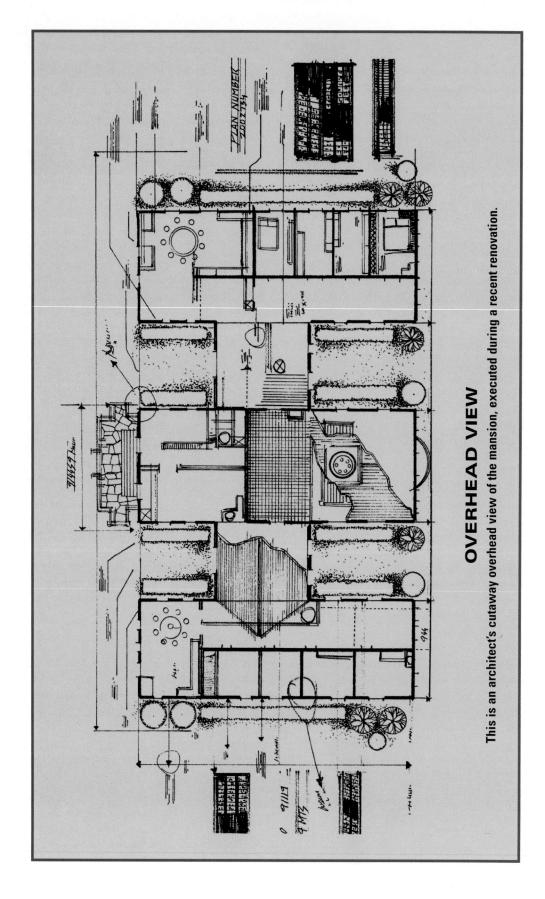

OVERHEAD VIEW

This is an architect's cutaway overhead view of the mansion, executed during a recent renovation.

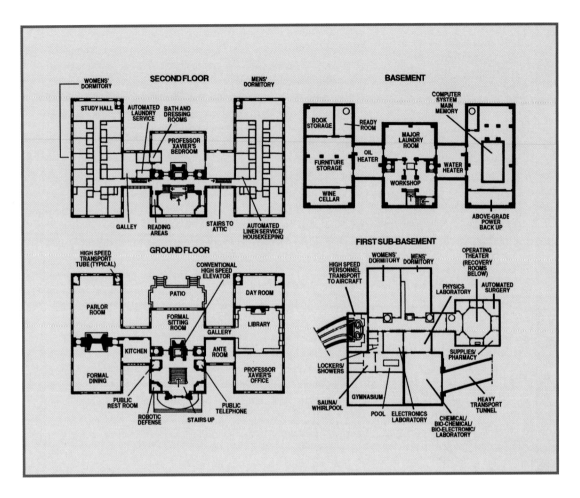

SECOND FLOOR

WOMENS' DORMITORY
STUDY HALL
AUTOMATED LAUNDRY SERVICE
BATH AND DRESSING ROOMS
MENS' DORMITORY
PROFESSOR XAVIER'S BEDROOM
GALLEY
READING AREAS
STAIRS TO ATTIC
AUTOMATED LINEN SERVICE/ HOUSEKEEPING

BASEMENT

COMPUTER SYSTEM MAIN MEMORY
BOOK STORAGE
READY ROOM
MAJOR LAUNDRY ROOM
FURNITURE STORAGE
OIL HEATER
WORKSHOP
WATER HEATER
WINE CELLAR
ABOVE-GRADE POWER BACK UP

GROUND FLOOR

HIGH SPEED TRANSPORT TUBE (TYPICAL)
CONVENTIONAL HIGH SPEED ELEVATOR
PATIO
DAY ROOM
PARLOR ROOM
FORMAL SITTING ROOM
LIBRARY
GALLERY
KITCHEN
ANTE ROOM
FORMAL DINING
PROFESSOR XAVIER'S OFFICE
PUBLIC REST ROOM
ROBOTIC DEFENSE
STAIRS UP
PUBLIC TELEPHONE

FIRST SUB-BASEMENT

HIGH SPEED PERSONNEL TRANSPORT TO AIRCRAFT
WOMENS' DORMITORY
MENS' DORMITORY
OPERATING THEATER (RECOVERY ROOMS BELOW)
PHYSICS LABORATORY
AUTOMATED SURGERY
LOCKERS/ SHOWERS
SUPPLIES/ PHARMACY
SAUNA/ WHIRLPOOL
GYMNASIUM
POOL
ELECTRONICS LABORATORY
HEAVY TRANSPORT TUNNEL
CHEMICAL/ BIO-CHEMICAL/ BIO-ELECTRONIC/ LABORATORY

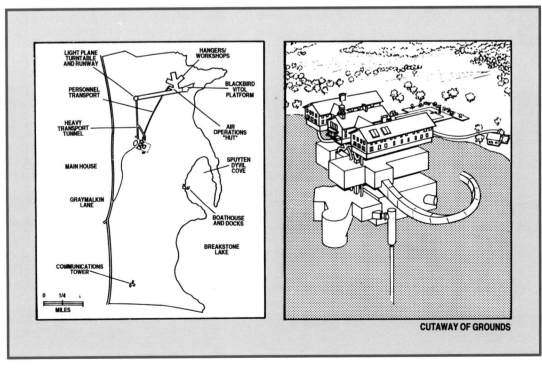

LIGHT PLANE TURNTABLE AND RUNWAY
HANGERS/ WORKSHOPS
PERSONNEL TRANSPORT
BLACKBIRD V/TOL PLATFORM
HEAVY TRANSPORT TUNNEL
AIR OPERATIONS "HUT"
MAIN HOUSE
SPUYTEN DYVIL COVE
GRAYMALKIN LANE
BOATHOUSE AND DOCKS
BREAKSTONE LAKE
COMMUNICATIONS TOWER
0 1/4
MILES

CUTAWAY OF GROUNDS

XAVIER MANSION

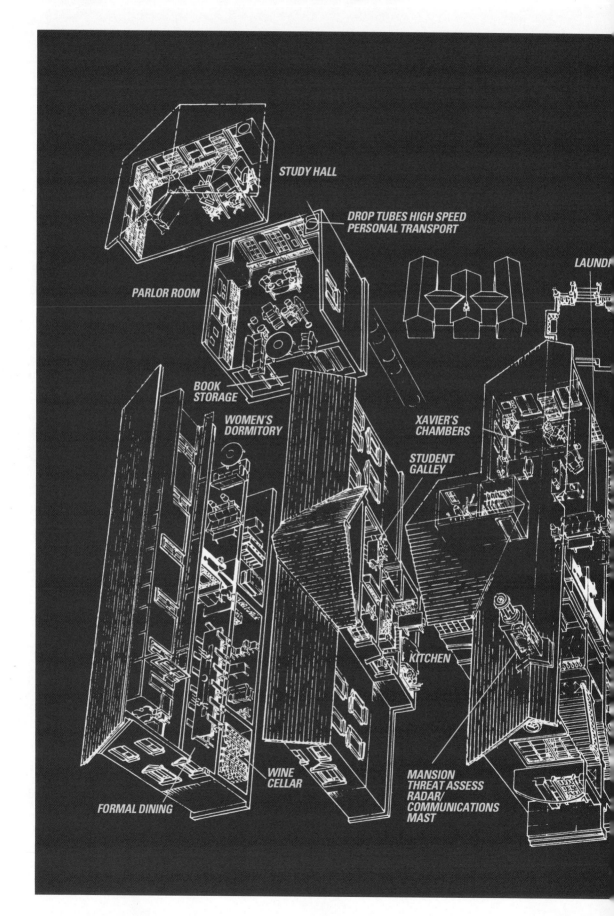

STUDY HALL

DROP TUBES HIGH SPEED
PERSONAL TRANSPORT

PARLOR ROOM

LAUNDR

BOOK
STORAGE

WOMEN'S
DORMITORY

XAVIER'S
CHAMBERS

STUDENT
GALLEY

KITCHEN

WINE
CELLAR

FORMAL DINING

MANSION
THREAT ASSESS
RADAR/
COMMUNICATIONS
MAST

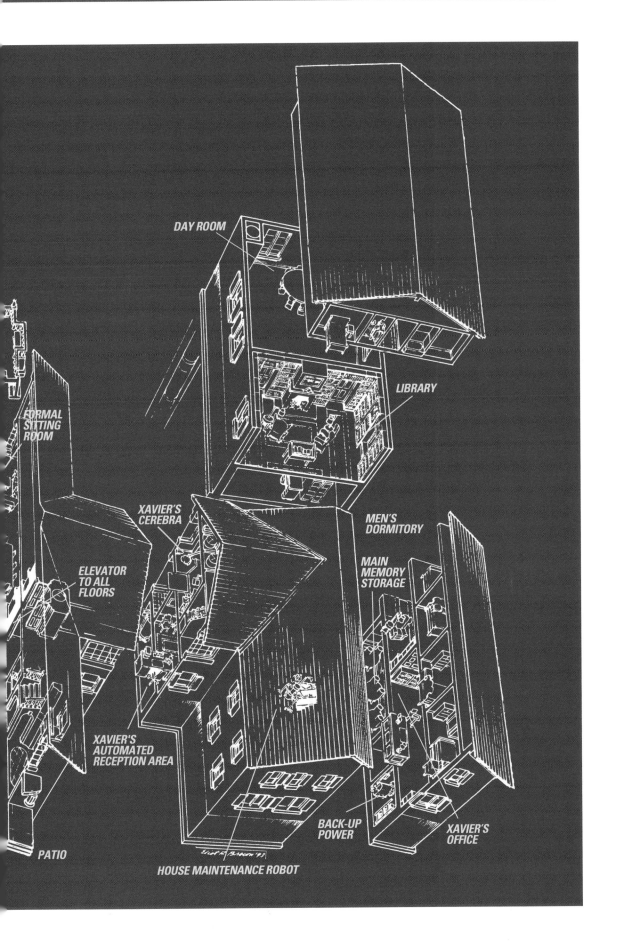

DAY ROOM

LIBRARY

FORMAL
SITTING
ROOM

XAVIER'S
CEREBRA

MEN'S
DORMITORY

ELEVATOR
TO ALL
FLOORS

MAIN
MEMORY
STORAGE

XAVIER'S
AUTOMATED
RECEPTION AREA

BACK-UP
POWER

XAVIER'S
OFFICE

PATIO

HOUSE MAINTENANCE ROBOT

XAVIER MANSION

Art by John Byrne

DANGER ROOM MASTER CONTROL

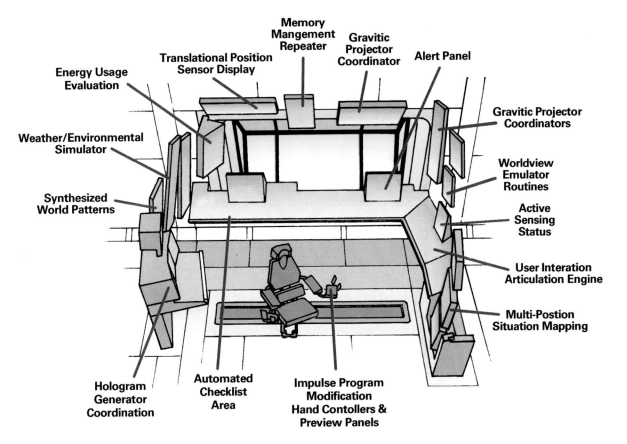

Energy Usage Evaluation

Translational Position Sensor Display

Memory Mangement Repeater

Gravitic Projector Coordinator

Alert Panel

Gravitic Projector Coordinators

Weather/Environmental Simulator

Worldview Emulator Routines

Synthesized World Patterns

Active Sensing Status

User Interation Articulation Engine

Multi-Postion Situation Mapping

Hologram Generator Coordination

Automated Checklist Area

Impulse Program Modification Hand Contollers & Preview Panels

To the untrained eye, it is a featureless room. To anyone who enters and engages its systems, however, it is clear the Danger Room is the ultimate battle simulator. Behind unassuming gray paneled walls exist a multitude of exercise and combat paraphernalia designed to put even the most well-trained mutant through his paces. The Danger Room can assume a three-dimensional, interactive environment conducive to the constant refinement of teamwork vital to the X-Men's daily operations.

The original Danger Room was located on the mansion's first floor and employed advanced technology designed on Earth, including robots. The current Danger Room, located on Sub-Basement Level Two, instead employs Shi'ar technology—including laser cannons, omnium spring vises, pyrotechnic extension lances, sensory-deprivation cocoons and extraordinarily sophisticated holographic projectors. X-Men training there may be pitted against formidable opponents that are actually either holograms or highly advanced robots, both created by Shi'ar means. Solid surfaces with thoroughly realistic appearances are achieved with accurate surface-texture modeling laid on polygonal surfaces of overlapping gravity fields; "projectiles" are composed of rapidly moving, tightly focused force fields.

The Danger Room World-View Model Library includes digital models of more than 50 million objects and their attributes. There are more than 120 levels of increasing difficulty in the Danger Room's computers.

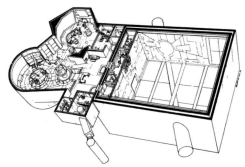

XAVIER MANSION

Art by Frank Quitely

The technological "big sister" to Cerebro, Cerebra is a machine used primarily by **Professor X** for the purpose of locating mutants. A sort of global positioning system, it detects aberrations in electromagnetic brain-wave activity most often attributed to biological mutations, allowing users to observe the distinctive signature of the X-gene that grants mutants their special gifts. The computer system in Cerebra can roughly measure the amount of superhuman power possessed by the mutant, determine the mutant's geographical location and even specify the identity of the mutant if given sufficient data.

Although anyone can be taught to use it, Cerebra acts most effectively when linked to the mind of Professor X or a being with similar telepathic abilities. By wearing a special headset connected to Cerebra, Xavier is able to increase Cerebra's ability to detect mutant brain waves. Cerebra magnifies his psionic senses to the tenth power, boosting his mutant-locating abilities to global range. Individual members of the **X-Men** have sometimes carried smaller versions of Cerebro and Cerebra with them. A portable Cerebro or Cerebra, in telemetric contact with the main computer console, can detect the presence of a mutant at short range.

Professor X began work on Cerebro before he founded the X-Men. He used an early version of the device, Cyberno, to locate Scott Summers (**Cyclops**), his first recruit. Xavier completed his first true Cerebro machine shortly after the fifth X-Man, **Jean Grey**, joined the team. He named Cerebro after the human cerebrum, the largest section of the human brain and the part responsible for transmitting psionic waves. The **Beast** developed Cerebra just prior to the emergence of **Cassandra Nova**.

XAVIER MANSION

BLACKBIRD

The **X-Men** Blackbird—intended to act as a trans-sonic transportation device—is equipped to fly long-duration, high-altitude reconnaissance missions and shorter trips to any climate. A mission-specific add-on pod can be equipped for several preplanned or exotic mission scenarios.

The Blackbird is based on a projected design by Clarence "Kelly" Johnson, former head of the Lockheed Aircraft Corporation's Advanced Development Projects Group (the "Skunk Works") prior to his retirement. The Skunk Works were responsible for the design and fabrication of the 1960s and 1970s record-holding, high-performance strategic/reconnaissance craft the SR-71, and its offensive version, the YF-12A. These craft are two-seaters, while the X-Men Blackbird (projected designation: RS-150) accommodates a flight crew of three with four passengers (projected by escape gear; more "loose" passengers are possible).

The RS-150 was never realized as part of the U.S. reconnaissance program—but in the early '70s, the international law-enforcement agency S.H.I.E.L.D. acquired its design and exotic tooling experience from Lockheed and produced an unspecified number of these highly classified aircraft. Only one survives today: the X-Men Blackbird, since rebuilt using ultra-advanced Shi'ar technology and further modified by Forge.

Art by Kia Asamiya

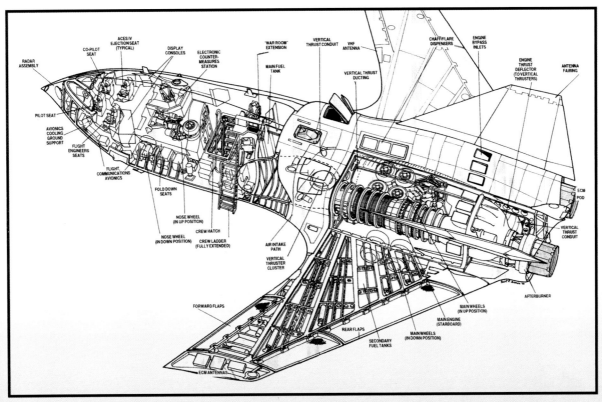

RADAR ASSEMBLY

PILOT SEAT

AVIONICS COOLING GROUND SUPPORT

FLIGHT ENGINEERS SEATS

FLIGHT, COMMUNICATIONS AVIONICS

FOLD DOWN SEATS

NOSE WHEEL (IN UP POSITION)

NOSE WHEEL (IN DOWN POSITION)

CREW HATCH

CREW LADDER (FULLY EXTENDED)

CO-PILOT SEAT

ACES IV EJECTION SEAT (TYPICAL)

DISPLAY CONSOLES

ELECTRONIC COUNTER-MEASURES STATION

"WAR ROOM" EXTENSION

MAIN FUEL TANK

VERTICAL THRUST CONDUIT

VHF ANTENNA

VERTICAL THRUST DUCTING

CHAFF/FLARE DISPENSERS

ENGINE BYPASS INLETS

ENGINE THRUST DEFLECTOR (TO VERTICAL THRUSTERS)

ANTENNA FAIRING

ECM POD

VERTICAL THRUST CONDUIT

AIR INTAKE PATH

VERTICAL THRUSTER CLUSTER

FORWARD FLAPS

REAR FLAPS

SECONDARY FUEL TANKS

MAIN WHEELS (IN DOWN POSITION)

MAIN ENGINE (STARBOARD)

MAIN WHEELS (IN UP POSITION)

AFTERBURNER

ECM ANTENNAS

X-CORPORATION

Mutants are not indigenous to North America. They are everywhere. In every corner of the globe. In every continent. In the largest of cities to the smallest of villages. And that only means one thing: that mutants are being subjugated on a global scale. They need help. They need rescue. They need the X-Corporation.

Rising from the ashes of **Banshee**'s paramilitary X-Corps, the X-Corporation maintains headquarters in Hong Kong, Amsterdam, Mumbai, Melbourne, and Paris. From these exotic global locales, the X-Corporation fulfills their mandate to monitor mutant rights violations across the globe. Staffed by superhumanly-powered members of the various teams borne of the vision of its founder, **Professor X**, all mutants in peril need do is simply think of the emergency "X" and they will register on the X-Corporation's Cerebra units, devices used to detect mutants. Trained X-Men will then be dispatched to assist no matter what the situation, no matter how grave the danger. Persecution and extermination of mutants is not an isolated American problem. It has gone international. It is growing in epic proportions. And it must be stopped. The X-Corporation intends to do just that.

First Appearance:
New X-Men Annual (2001)

Art by Igor Kordey

ABYSS

Real Name:	Nils Styger	**Height:**	Variable
First Appearance:	*Cable* #40 (1997)	**Weight:**	Variable

After he was cured of the Legacy Virus, Abyss went to Berlin as a member of the **X-Corporation** to battle the fire-wielding **Fever Pitch**. But both mutants were captured by members of the **Banshee**-led mutant militia group, X-Corps. Following the revelation that **Mystique** had infiltrated the X-Corps in an attempt to seize its assets for her own use, a wounded Banshee freed Abyss from his confinement, allowing the young mutant to confront Mystique and suck her into the void within his body.

POWERS/WEAPONS

- Possesses a shadowy form that acts as a portal into an energy source of pure darkness

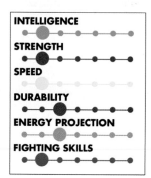

INTELLIGENCE

STRENGTH

SPEED

DURABILITY

ENERGY PROJECTION

FIGHTING SKILLS

POWERS/WEAPONS

- Ability to manipulate an energy source of pure to create mentally-controlled solid objects such as pincers, rings, columns, and spheres

INTELLIGENCE

STRENGTH

SPEED

DURABILITY

ENERGY PROJECTION

FIGHTING SKILLS

Real Name: Laynia Sergeievna Petrovna (Krylova)
First Appearance: *Champions* #7 (1976)

Height: 5'6"
Weight: 125 lbs

Darkstar was taken from her widower father to be raised in a Soviet school for mutants, where she studied to become a government agent. When the academy was shut down, Darkstar became a Soviet Super Soldier, fighting on behalf of her country's citizenry. But she soon became disillusioned with the Soviet Union and defected to the United States. Eventually she joined the Paris arm of the X-Corporation; on her first mission, she became possessed by a bacterial consciousness. She was killed by Fantomex to prevent the spread of the bacteria.

DARKSTAR

POWERS/WEAPONS

- Enhanced strength, speed and agility
- Superhumanly acute sight, hearing and smell

INTELLIGENCE

STRENGTH

SPEED

DURABILITY

ENERGY PROJECTION

FIGHTING SKILLS

Real Name: Maria Callasantos
First Appearance: *New Mutants* #98 (1991)

Height: 5'9"
Weight: 132 lbs

When her mother's drug-addicted boyfriend tried to rape her sister Thornn, Feral killed him. Enraged over her boyfriend's death, Feral's mother killed the girl's pet pigeons—and Feral killed her mother in return. The two frightened sisters went underground and joined the Morlocks. When Masque assumed control of the group, Feral left. Forced to serve prison time for her crimes, Feral escaped and eventually came to serve in the X-Corporation along with Thornn. Though the two are now teammates, their mutual antagonism has yet to abate.

FERAL

POWERS/WEAPONS

- Projection of blasts of intense heat and flame from his hands
- Flight

INTELLIGENCE

STRENGTH

SPEED

DURABILITY

ENERGY PROJECTION

FIGHTING SKILLS

Real Name: Unrevealed
First Appearance: *Generation X* #50 (1999)

Height: 5'9"
Weight: Unrevealed

Fever Pitch was a member of Gene Nation, a re-formation of the embattled Morlocks. After Gene Nation was defeated, he wound up fleeing to Germany, where he briefly fought Abyss before being captured by the paramilitary group X-Corps and telepathically coerced to do their bidding. After he was freed from his brainwashing, Fever Pitch went on a rampage in Paris, hell-bent on setting the famous Louvre ablaze. But before Fever Pitch could ruin centuries of artwork, Iceman cooled the fiery mutant's jets. Frozen solid, Fever Pitch was taken into police custody.

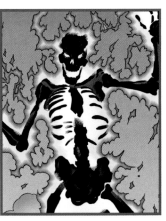

FEVER PITCH

M

Real Name: Monet St. Croix
First Appearance: *Generation X* #1 (1994)

Height: 5'7"
Weight: 125 lbs

POWERS/WEAPONS
• Enhanced strength
• Flight
• Virtual invulnerability
• Low-level telepathy

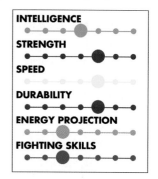

Raised by an ambassador father in Monaco, M is accustomed to the finest things money can buy. Despite her predisposition for Prada shoes and exotic vacations, she is also a vicious fighter, having honed her mutant skills as a member of Generation X amid the sometimes-acrimonious atmosphere of <u>Emma Frost</u>'s Massachusetts Academy. M knows all too well that no matter how much money she was born into, her mutant status still makes her a pariah—not just in high society, but at all levels of society. M now serves as a member of the Paris, France branch of the <u>X-Corporation</u>.

| INTELLIGENCE |
| STRENGTH |
| SPEED |
| DURABILITY |
| ENERGY PROJECTION |
| FIGHTING SKILLS |

MULTIPLE MAN

Real Name: James Arthur Madrox
First Appearance: *Giant-Size Fantastic Four* #4 (1975)

Height: 5'11"
Weight: 168 lbs.

POWERS/WEAPONS
• Ability to create exact living duplicates of himself upon any physical impact and later absorb the copy back into himself

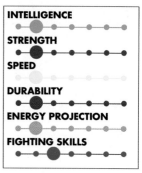

On the day he was born, Jamie Madrox created an exact duplicate of himself when the doctor slapped him on the rear. Weeks later, at <u>Professor X</u>'s urging, Jamie's father moved the family to an isolated farm. Jamie was given a special suit that neutralized his ability. In time, Professor X invited Jamie to join the <u>X-Men</u>. Jamie declined, opting instead to take a position as laboratory assistant to Dr. <u>Moira MacTaggert</u> at her genetic research station on Muir Island. Multiple Man now serves as a member of the Paris, France branch of the <u>X-Corporation</u>.

| INTELLIGENCE |
| STRENGTH |
| SPEED |
| DURABILITY |
| ENERGY PROJECTION |
| FIGHTING SKILLS |

RADIUS

Real Name: Jared Corbo
First Appearance: *Alpha Flight: In the Beginning...* #-1 (1997)

Height: 6'
Weight: 190 lbs

POWERS/WEAPONS
• Permanently surrounded by a personal force-field

The son of <u>Unus</u> the Untouchable, Jared and his half-brother Adrian (<u>Flex</u>) lived as wards of Hull House, an orphanage in Ontario. Department H eventually recruited both men to join <u>Alpha Flight</u>. Relegated to second-tier status, he joined the paramilitary strike force X-Corps. When the X-Corps were betrayed from within by <u>Mystique</u>, Radius clashed with some of the group's rogue members. During the fight, <u>Avalanche</u> opened up a chasm in the earth beneath Radius and then sealed it above him, trapping him within the earth. It remains unclear whether Radius survived.

| INTELLIGENCE |
| STRENGTH |
| SPEED |
| DURABILITY |
| ENERGY PROJECTION |
| FIGHTING SKILLS |

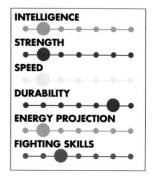

POWERS/WEAPONS

- Generation of powerful vibratory waves

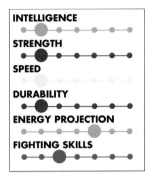

Real Name: Julio Esteban Richter
First Appearance: *X-Factor* #17 (1987)

Height: 5'9"
Weight: 162 lbs

Now a member of the X-Corporation, Julio Richter is the son of Louis Richter, Mexico's most notorious black market arms dealer. Young Julio left home after witnessing Stryfe murder his father over an arms deal gone wrong. Rictor's quest to find his father's killer took up most of his young life. During the course of one battle, he came face to face with Nathan Summers, and Rictor thought he had finally found his father's killer. Only years later would Rictor find out that Stryfe was nothing more than a monstrous clone of Nathan.

RICTOR

POWERS/WEAPONS

- Superhuman strength, speed, reflexes, endurance and durability
- Ability to bestow half her strength to another

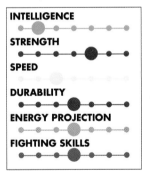

Real Name: Ruth Bat-Seraph
First Appearance: *Incredible Hulk* #256 (1981)

Height: 5'11"
Weight: 150 lbs

A native Israeli, Ruth Bat-Seraph became the first member of the "Super-Agent" program formed by the Israeli secret service, the Mossad. After her first-born son was killed by Palestinian terrorists, Sabra brought the terrorists to justice, despite government admonitions not to get involved. Sabra has recently joined the X-Corporation and accompanied the X-Men to survey the ruins of the destroyed mutant island nation of Genosha. Despite her international dabblings, Sabra remains a staunch defender of Israel; any who dare threaten it will feel her wrath.

SABRA

POWERS/WEAPONS

- Superhuman vocal cords, throat, and lungs that allow her to create powerful sonic waves with her voice
- Flight

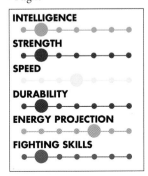

Real Name: Theresa Rourke (Cassidy)
First Appearance: *Spider-Woman* #37 (1982)

Height: 5'7"
Weight: 130 lbs

Unknown to her father Banshee, the infant Siryn survived a bomb blast that killed her mother. Secretly taken in by her uncle, Black Tom Cassidy, Siryn eventually developed her father's sonic powers, which Black Tom exploited. After one crime spree, Black Tom was temporarily incarcerated; while in custody, Tom exonerated Siryn of responsibility for her crimes and wrote a letter to Banshee explaining who she was. The X-Men brought Siryn back to their headquarters, where she was reunited with her father. Today, Siryn serves the X-Corporation.

SIRYN

SUNPYRE

| **Real Name:** | Leyu Yoshida | **Height:** | 5'7" |
| **First Appearance:** | *Uncanny X-Men* #392 (2001) | **Weight:** | 125 lbs |

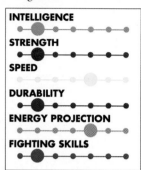

Sister of <u>Sunfire</u>, Sunpyre came to the <u>X-Men</u> after she answered a telepathic call for help from <u>Jean Grey</u>, who needed assistance in defeating <u>Magneto</u> after he had kidnapped <u>Professor X</u>. Sunpyre left the X-Men after Magneto's defeat and soon came to join the paramilitary organization X-Corps after her brother rejected a similar offer. When conducting scientific research on <u>Abyss</u>, Sunpyre was killed by <u>Mystique</u>, who had infiltrated the X-Corps to usurp its assets.

POWERS/WEAPONS
- Ionization of matter into a fiery plasma state, capable of reaching 1,000,000 degrees Fahrenheit
- Flight

INTELLIGENCE
STRENGTH
SPEED
DURABILITY
ENERGY PROJECTION
FIGHTING SKILLS

THORNN

| **Real Name:** | Lucia Callasantos | **Height:** | 5'10" |
| **First Appearance:** | *X-Force* #6 (1992) | **Weight:** | 137 lbs |

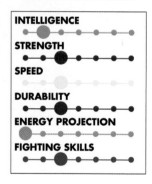

Thornn escaped her mother's boyfriend's attempted rape only because her sister <u>Feral</u> killed the man and then their mother too. The sisters fled for the safety of the <u>Morlocks</u>. When <u>Masque</u> took over control of the Morlocks from <u>Callisto</u>, Thornn had no problem with the change in leadership—but Feral did and left. Feeling betrayed, Thornn tried to lure her sister back and failed. Angry over her abandonment, Thornn turned Feral in to the police, telling them about the double murder. After Feral escaped, she and Thornn found themselves together again in the <u>X-Corporation</u>.

POWERS/WEAPONS
- Enhanced strength, speed, and agility
- Superhumanly acute senses
- Can see in total darkness

INTELLIGENCE
STRENGTH
SPEED
DURABILITY
ENERGY PROJECTION
FIGHTING SKILLS

WARPATH

| **Real Name:** | James Proudstar | **Height:** | 7'2" |
| **First Appearance:** | *New Mutants* #16 (1984) | **Weight:** | 350 lbs |

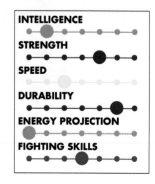

After his brother <u>Thunderbird</u> was killed serving as a member of the <u>X-Men</u>, James became bitter towards <u>Professor X</u>, whom he blamed for his brother's untimely demise. James was so angered that he accepted an offer from <u>Emma Frost</u> to join the <u>Hellions</u>. Warpath eventually sought out Professor X, though, and made peace with him after a confrontation, finally realizing that Xavier was not to blame for Thunderbird's death. He now serves the <u>X-Corporation</u> in Mumbai, India.

POWERS/WEAPONS
- Superhuman strength, speed, stamina, durability, agility, and reflexes
- Flight

INTELLIGENCE
STRENGTH
SPEED
DURABILITY
ENERGY PROJECTION
FIGHTING SKILLS

X-STATIX

Art by Mike Allred

First Appearance:
X-Force #116 (2001)

Employing savvy marketing skills and glomming all the glory and riches they can get, the X-Statix are more than happy to enjoy the spoils a media-crazed world provides. This team of mutants-for-hire consciously chose celebrity status over <u>Professor X</u>'s dream of peaceful coexistence between man and mutant.

The enterprising X-Statix burst onto the 21st century scene eager to exploit and capitalize on society's obsession with the sensational. Their merchandising rights and media manipulation have fattened their wallets accordingly. And while most mutants are feared and discriminated against, this crew is widely embraced and adored—thanks in large part to the team of high-priced public relations people who report and spin their every move.

Unlike the <u>X-Men</u>, who don't fight for profit, these daring, flashbulb-friendly mutants offer their services for high-profile missions at a very high price. The X-Statix have a high turnover rate—caused not by disillusionment, but by death. Over and over again, members gamble with their lives in their efforts to become celebrities (and to fight evil).

While some members believe their pay more than makes up for the discrimination their kind as a group suffers, others question whether any amount of money can ever compensate for one's loss of pride, self, identity, and, as is often the case, life. Dealing with these dilemmas in their own individual way is X-Statix's ever-changing line-up of colorfully named mutant celebrities who are sometimes willing to trade in their lives for fame and money.

ANARCHIST

Real Name:
Tike Alicar
First Appearance:
X-Force #116 (2001)

Height:	6'3"
Weight:	225 lbs
Eye Color:	Brown
Hair Color:	Black with orange streaks

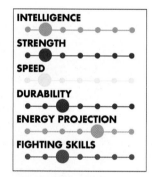

INTELLIGENCE

STRENGTH

SPEED

DURABILITY

ENERGY PROJECTION

FIGHTING SKILLS

POWERS/ WEAPONS

• Toxic sweat

Paranoid. Neurotic. Hypersensitive. While it seems all these character traits make him better suited to an analyst's couch than fighting villains for fortune and fame, the Anarchist manages to set his issues aside when there are lives (and money) on the line.

Recruited into <u>X-Statix</u> after the untimely death of <u>Sluk</u>, the Anarchist had a difficult time ignoring his increasing sense of paranoia. Convinced he was destined to become nothing more than a stereotype, the Anarchist developed a chip on his shoulder, at one point stating, "I'm a black mutant, and in this country, that's like being black with a little black added!"

The Anarchist's festering resentments of course did little to stop the bitter infighting within the team. If anything, he only fanned the flames and made the situation worse. More concerned with his public appearance and the X-Statix's popularity ratings than with being a team player, the Anarchist's attitude has caused much of the internal strife that has plagued the team.

When new candidates were nominated for membership on the team, the Anarchist vetoed the black mutant the <u>Spike</u>, fearing that the team would accept only one black member. Instead, the Anarchist voted for the time-stopping <u>Lacuna</u>, who was indeed selected as the new member but turned X-Statix down in favor of hosting her own television talk show. Against the Anarchist's self-serving arguments, the Spike was recruited after all and challenged the Anarchist on national television, calling him "'Captain Coconut'—black on the outside, but white on the inside."

The Spike wasn't far from the truth: White foster parents in Alaska had raised the Anarchist, and despite his grandstanding about his race, he continues to rub even members of the black community the wrong way. To this day, the Anarchist engages in his childhood obsessive-compulsive disorder, and tries to turn his skin white by washing his hands dozens of times each day.

The Anarchist managed to deal with his various neuroses and developed an attraction to his teammate <u>Dead Girl</u>. Together the pair left the X-Statix for a time to tour as "The Death & Anarchy Roadshow," performing live in front of large crowds. They both eventually had a change of heart and rejoined the X-Statix in time to help the <u>Orphan</u> battle the powerful mutant Arnie Lundberg (<u>Mysterious Fan Boy</u>).

Art by Mike Allred

DEAD GIRL

She remembers when she wasn't dead. When she was warm. When she bled, breathed, lived, and loved. She remembers coming to New York City, alive in the alivest city in the world. She wanted to act. She needed to act. She wanted a stage. How did the end happen? She remembers: a man. An actor. A killer.

She remembers waking up in the dark. The dark, damp smell. The sound of the worms and the fidgeting of the living city all around. Somehow, she remembers what happened. He must have thought he was so clever, burying her body there. Who would look for a missing person among the dead in a graveyard? But he didn't know that life teemed through the sinews of the dead. The dead, the real dead, maybe taking pity on her long weeks of wailing, found her killer rehearsing lines in his small room. They whispered new lines into his living ear and summoned him to the burial grounds—just to make sure she was still there. She remembers lying in the darkness and hearing his noises above her—and then the first crack of light that revealed his face when she dug herself out of her grave and proceeded to make a mattress out of his bones.

Perhaps the best part of being dead is the ability to die over and over again. Knowing she has an infinite life cycle allows Dead Girl to throw herself into the line of deadly fire so her less immortal teammates can live.

Time and again, she has saved the **Anarchist** from certain doom, and even ran off with him to star in their "Death & Anarchy Roadshow" after the **X-Statix** declined to give her the "sexy" superhero status once afforded to the really dead **U-Go Girl**. But duty (and perhaps ego) snapped her back to reality and, with the Anarchist in tow, she rejoined the X-Statix to help the **Orphan** battle the threat posed by Arnie Lundberg (**Mysterious Fan Boy**).

Real Name:
Unrevealed
First Appearance:
X-Force #125 (2002)

Height: 5'7"
Weight: 130 lbs
Eye Color: Red
Hair Color: Grayish-green

INTELLIGENCE	
STRENGTH	
SPEED	
DURABILITY	
ENERGY PROJECTION	
FIGHTING SKILLS	

POWERS/ WEAPONS

- Ability to communicate with the cells, bacteria, and disintegrating tissue of corpses to learn what happened to the deceased
- Can rebuild her body's molecular structure after suffering even the most severe injuries
- Can animate and control parts of her body even after they have been severed

Art by Mike Allred

ORPHAN

Real Name:
Guy Smith
First Appearance:
X-Force #117

Height:	6'1"
Weight:	185 lbs
Eye Color:	Purple
Hair Color:	White

When Guy Smith was born an obvious mutant, his anti-mutant parents tried to murder him by setting fire to their home, but baby Guy survived. His parents were sent to jail and Guy was raised as an orphan with no knowledge of his parents or their murderous inclinations. Following the manifestation of his abilities, Guy's senses were heightened to extreme levels, and he attempted everything from drugs to studying martial arts and mental disciplines to control the acuteness of his senses, but nothing helped.

Years later, Guy learned that his parents were still alive—and that they had deliberately started the fire in an attempt to kill him. It was this revelation that caused Guy to develop suicidal tendencies, playing Russian roulette with a loaded revolver at the end of every day. When Guy eventually came to the attention of **Professor X**, the mutant mentor designed a special suit that empowered Guy to temper and control his undiluted senses, allowing him to cope with everyday life and ascend to the coveted role as team leader of the X-Statix.

Before long, though, **Spike Freeman** had had it with the Orphan's leadership style and ordered the **Coach** to arrange the Orphan's death. Using **U-Go Girl**'s enmity towards Guy, the Coach tricked her into loading every chamber of the Orphan's gun. Thanks to his heightened senses, the Orphan easily detected the change in weight of the revolver and confronted the Coach. In the ensuing fight, U-Go Girl shot and killed the Coach after experiencing a change of heart. The Orphan's relationship with U-Go Girl helped him finally give up playing Russian roulette—at least for a time.

After U-Go Girl was killed in battle, the Orphan became despondent and turned once more to the safety and comfort of his deadly Russian roulette ritual. Despite all the wealth and fame he enjoyed as part of the X-Statix, the pain of losing teammates and loved ones caused Guy to quit the team following the revelation of the Orphan's role in the death of the powerful young mutant Arnie Lundberg (**Mysterious Fan Boy**).

POWERS/ WEAPONS

- Superhumanly enhanced senses of touch, taste, smell, sight, and hearing
- Can sense vulnerability, whether emotional or physical
- Antennae that grant him an innate radar-like detection ability

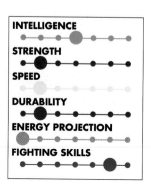

INTELLIGENCE	
STRENGTH	
SPEED	
DURABILITY	
ENERGY PROJECTION	
FIGHTING SKILLS	

PHAT

He's all "down wit' it"—dissin' and dismissin' villains and keepin' it real with his "homies." And it's all a sham.

This is William Robert "Billy Bob" Reilly, who is living his life as a first-rate poseur. His rather banal upbringing in a middle-class Jacksonville, Florida family certainly wouldn't catch the attention of X-Statix, and his agent knew it. In an effort to get Billy Bob recruited to join the team, his crafty agent created a whole new and much more interesting take on the young man's life: a gangsta rapper persona with a dysfunctional family. Not only were they dysfunctional, but his mother and father were "alcoholics" who turned young Billy Bob out into the streets not far from the "trailer park" where they lived.

Sleazy? Sure. Deceitful? Of course. Did it work? Like a charm.

After he and several others were recruited to replace X-Statix members killed in a mission gone awry, Phat didn't necessarily live up to the high-flying, high-profile lifestyle of the typical X-Statix. Expected to be out in front, glomming all the media spotlight he could get, Phat instead hung back, content to speak his affected grammar and reap the piles of cash instead.

But Spike Freeman put the kibosh on Phat's media-shy ways and forced him to get his face out there. So Phat and another media-shunning member, Vivisector, planned to steal some of the spotlight away from their teammates. Their initial plan was pretty pedestrian: show up loaded and act like bratty two-year-olds at U-Go Girl's television premiere. It seemed to have some effect, but they needed to improve their juvenile efforts somehow.

So they cooked up another scheme and decided to pretend to be gay. Trouble was, it turns out neither one was doing much pretending. Though they soon discovered they were in love, Phat had zero comfort with being so "out." When he reverted back to his churlish behavior, Vivisector had little choice but to dump him.

Even though he wears his best "bling bling" and does his best to keep in character, Phat drops his developed persona to step up to the plate for the X-Statix whenever he is needed. No matter how deep he goes to disguise his outward appearance, Phat is still a mutant willing to fight the good fight against those who would do his team harm.

Real Name:
William Robert Reilly
First Appearance:
X-Force #117 (2001)

Height: 5'9"
Weight: 155 lbs
Eye Color: Blue
Hair Color: Blond

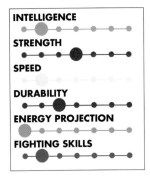

INTELLIGENCE
STRENGTH
SPEED
DURABILITY
ENERGY PROJECTION
FIGHTING SKILLS

POWERS/ WEAPONS

• Ability to increase the mass of different parts of his body by manipulating the fat underneath his skin, causing the fat to stretch

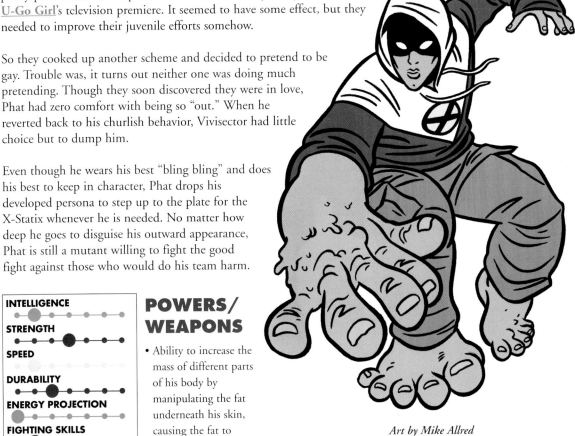

Art by Mike Allred

U-GO GIRL

Real Name:
"Edie" Constance Sawyer
First Appearance:
X-Force #116 (2001)

Height:	5'7"
Weight:	125 lbs
Eye Color:	Green
Hair Color:	Red

Growing up in a Ma-and-Pa-Kettle house with Ma-and-Pa-Kettle parents wasn't easy. Edie Sawyer's father always gave her the feeling she didn't belong. It didn't help that Edie often found herself waking up in bizarre places, a malady her doctors diagnosed as sleepwalking. To soothe herself, Edie bought a cheap television set and taught herself to talk like the actors and actresses she saw, dreaming all the while that their scripted dialogues and interesting locales would take her away to places much less dreary than her own home.

When Edie was 15, she slept with a handsome young San Franciscan passing through town and wound up pregnant. Scared and confused, Edie hid her growing belly until it was too obvious to conceal. Confessing to her mother, Edie learned she was just repeating family history. The man she knew as her father wasn't her biological father, who had in fact been another stranger "passing through town."

Entrusting her daughter Katie to her mother to be raised as her own, Edie left to pursue her dreams in California as a member of the **X-Statix**.

She eventually fell in love with the **Orphan**, despite having hated him at first when he was chosen over her to lead the team. It was the Orphan who convinced U-Go Girl to confront her past before they could pursue a future together. Together they went back to the farm where she grew up, but U-Go Girl's mother cautioned her not to reveal to the child she was her mother, if only to spare the girl grief should she witness U-Go Girl's death on television. U-Go Girl complied and, like any good big sister, took the girl on a whirlwind teleportation tour before returning home.

Shortly after the trip, U-Go Girl, well aware that part of the high price that comes with serving with X-Statix is death, knew the time had come to pay her ultimate due. Wounded by a spike through her stomach, she died in her lover's arms.

Art by Mike Allred

POWERS/ WEAPONS

• Teleportation

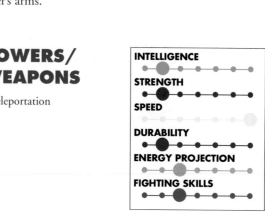

INTELLIGENCE	
STRENGTH	
SPEED	
DURABILITY	
ENERGY PROJECTION	
FIGHTING SKILLS	

VENUS DEE MILO

At age 11, while on a family visit to her grandparents' home, Dee Milo's superpowers manifested and she transformed into a being of pure energy. The resulting explosion killed Venus's family, leaving her an orphan. After Professor X found Venus, he built the girl a containment suit that allowed her to assume a human appearance; otherwise, she was now nothing more than a living ball of energy. The suit hardly guaranteed her an easier life, however; it just made it a little easier to look good as she walked through her troubled existence—eight years of therapy, four suicide attempts, a manic-depressive and self-loathing personality, and the need to take drugs to stave off nightmares about her family's death.

Things started looking up for Venus when the X-Statix tapped her to replace dead member U-Go Girl as the "sexy" member of the team. She had everything the X-Statix needed: spunk, charm, and sex appeal. There was just one little thing standing in the way: an ironclad contract binding her to mutant talent agent Solomon O'Sullivan that prevented her from plying her trade for anyone other than his made-for-TV O-Force crew. Flying in the face of the contract, Venus joined up with the X-Statix anyway and accompanied them on a mission to dispose of a dirty bomb. For her efforts, she received the respect of the team—and a restraining order slapped against her by Solomon's cutthroat attorney, Sharon Ginsburg.

Fortunately, Spike Freeman knows a clever way of dealing with restraining orders and contracts: an endless supply of money. Solomon O'Sullivan was only too happy to take several million of Spike's dollars off his hands, and cut Venus Dee Milo loose of her obligations to him. But as an X-Statix member, Venus may have gotten more than she bargained for—namely, a seemingly insurmountable public relations debacle, since the public sees her as nothing more than an opportunist trying to fill the shoes of a martyred dead hero. However, with some help from her teammates and her continued prowess in battle, Venus Dee Milo hopes to turn the tide of public opinion to her favor.

Real Name:
Dee Milo
First Appearance:
X-Statix #1 (2002)

Height: 5'6"
Weight: Indeterminate
Eye Color: Yellow
Hair Color: Black

Art by Mike Allred

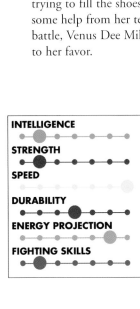

INTELLIGENCE

STRENGTH

SPEED

DURABILITY

ENERGY PROJECTION

FIGHTING SKILLS

POWERS/ WEAPONS

- Body consists of a pure energy form
- Teleportation
- Projection of energy blasts

VIVISECTOR

Real Name:
Myles Alfred
First Appearance:
X-Force #117 (2001)

Height: 5'6"
Weight: 125 lbs
Eye Color: Brown
Hair Color: Brown

Son of an esteemed academic father and a renowned ethnomusicologist mother, Myles Alfred was a brilliant student at Harvard and the author of a critically acclaimed pamphlet on the famous poet Walt Whitman. When he was bullied by his Ivy League peers, Myles discovered that he was a superhuman mutant able to transform into a werewolf-like creature during times of anger or fear. Myles learned to control his transformations over time.

Though he went into it with great trepidation, Myles was one of several new recruits who joined the X-Statix to replace members who had been killed on a mission gone horribly wrong. Vivisector eventually grew used to his new life and found some comfort level with the team. But then Vivisector and his teammate Phat were both told by owner Spike Freeman that they were not doing enough to share in the fame afforded to the other team members: the Anarchist, U-Go Girl and the Orphan. Egged on by Spike, the two sought to steal more of the spotlight, showing up drunk to the television debut of U-Go Girl and acting like loud

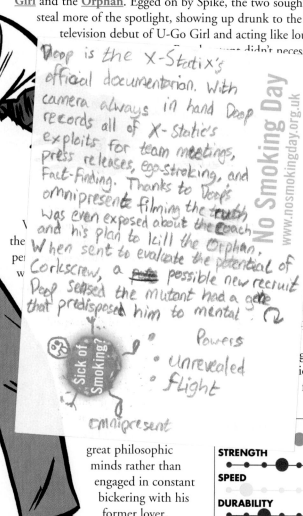

Deep is the X-Statix's official documentarian. With camera always in hand Deep records all of X-Statix's exploits for team meetings, press releases, ego-stroking, and fact-finding. Thanks to Deep's omnipresent filming the truth was even exposed about the Coach and his plan to kill the Orphan. When sent to evaluate the potential of Corkscrew, a ~~poss~~ possible new recruit, Deep sensed the mutant had a gene that predisposed him to mental.

Powers
• Unrevealed
• Flight

omnipresent

great philosophic minds rather than engaged in constant bickering with his former lover.

POWERS/ WEAPONS

• Lycanthropic shape-shifting

STRENGTH						
SPEED						
DURABILITY						
ENERGY PROJECTION						
FIGHTING SKILLS						

Art by Mike Allred

COACH

POWERS/WEAPONS

- Mutant powers derived from his missing arm

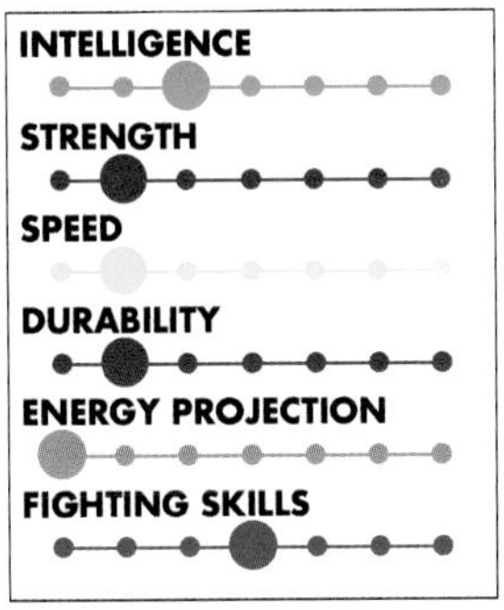
INTELLIGENCE
STRENGTH
SPEED
DURABILITY
ENERGY PROJECTION
FIGHTING SKILLS

Real Name: Unrevealed
First Appearance: *X-Force* #116 (2001)
Height: 5'11"
Weight: 180 lbs

Once known as "The Arm," the Coach was responsible for organizing the X-Statix's missions, recruiting new members and ensuring the ongoing profitable merchandising of the team. With sales down, Coach decided that killing off team members could potentially cause the market for the X-Statix merchandise to explode, and he decided the Orphan was the right mutant to go. But the Coach's plan backfired when U-Go Girl shot and killed him to save the Orphan's life.

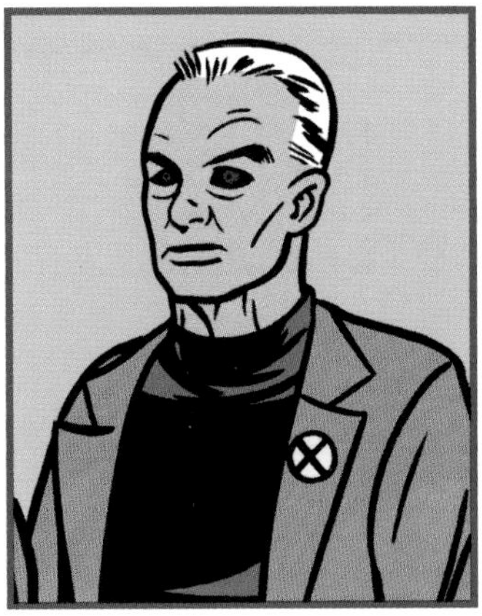

DOOP

POWERS/WEAPONS

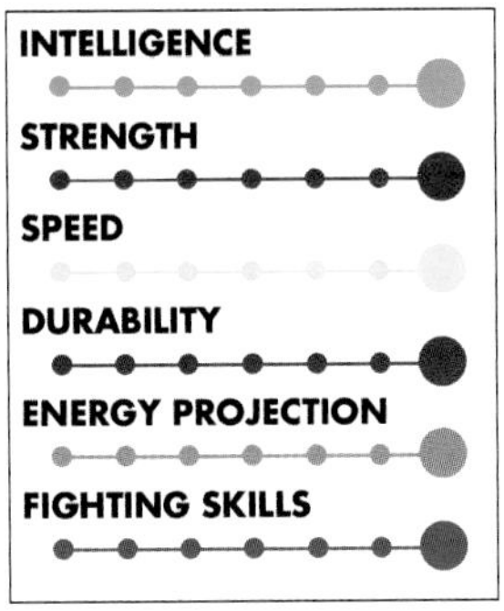
INTELLIGENCE
STRENGTH
SPEED
DURABILITY
ENERGY PROJECTION
FIGHTING SKILLS

Real Name: Doop
First Appearance: *X-Force* #116 (2001)
Height: 3'5"
Weight: Unrevealed

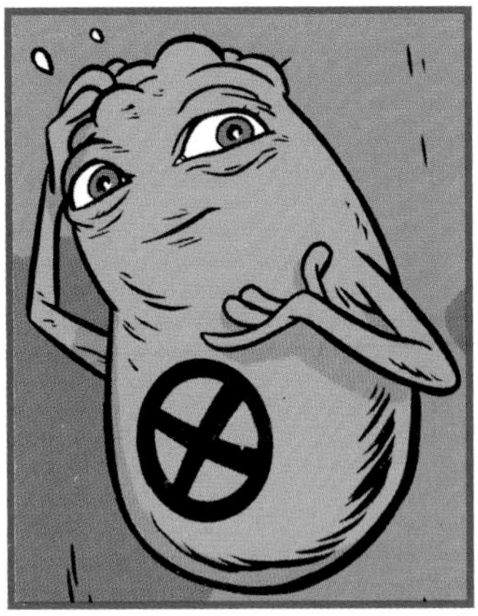

SPIKE FREEMAN

Real Name: Spike Freeman
First Appearance: *X-Force* #120 (2001)
Height: 5'10"
Weight: 150 lbs

Spike Freeman made trillions as a software developer. In the hope of adding to his coffers, Spike bankrolled the X-Statix and, like any savvy businessman, went after the real source of money: licensing. Exploiting the X-Statix's fame and celebrity for all that it was worth, Spike successfully licensed the team's name for every product under the sun. Spike also incited Phat and Vivisector to attempt to steal some of the media spotlight afforded to the team's more popular members: the Orphan, the Anarchist, and U-Go Girl. Showing some sign of contrition, Spike recently learned the error of his greedy ways and has become more of a team player, putting his masterful management, marketing, and business skills to work for the betterment of the X-Statix. He even came to respect the Orphan's leadership skills, and began to trust his judgment in various matters affecting the team.

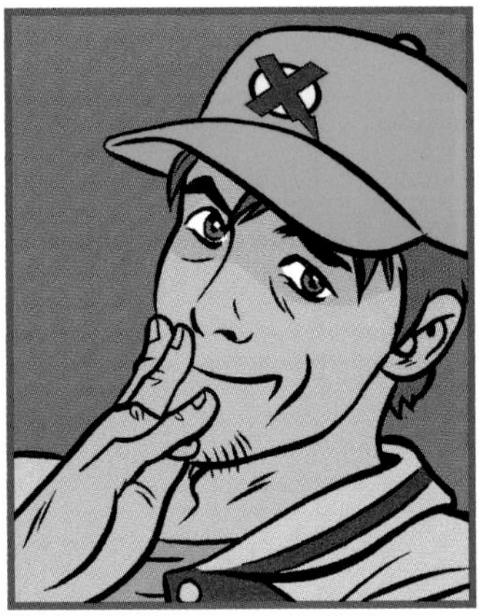

LACUNA

Real Name: Woodstock (full name unrevealed)
First Appearance: *X-Force* #121 (2001)

Height: 5'5"
Weight: 118 lbs

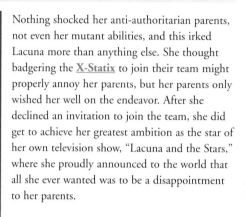

Nothing shocked her anti-authoritarian parents, not even her mutant abilities, and this irked Lacuna more than anything else. She thought badgering the X-Statix to join their team might properly annoy her parents, but her parents only wished her well on the endeavor. After she declined an invitation to join the team, she did get to achieve her greatest ambition as the star of her own television show, "Lacuna and the Stars," where she proudly announced to the world that all she ever wanted was to be a disappointment to her parents.

POWERS/WEAPONS

• Creation of a temporary ripple in the timestream, allowing her to "freeze" time

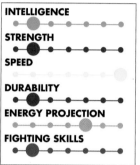

INTELLIGENCE
STRENGTH
SPEED
DURABILITY
ENERGY PROJECTION
FIGHTING SKILLS

MYSTERIOUS FAN BOY

Real Name: Arthur K. Lundberg
First Appearance: *X-Statix* #1 (2002)

Height: 5'7"
Weight: 120 lbs

After bullies beat Arnie into a coma, he clung to life only thanks to the sound of U-Go Girl's voice. But once he recovered, Arnie learned she had died. Arnie blamed the Orphan and began to use his powers to terrorize his hometown in revenge. The Orphan confronted Arnie to convince him to use his powers for good, but Arnie blackmailed him into letting him join the X-Statix. To permanently end the threat that Arnie posed, the Orphan recruited Lacuna to use her powers to inject him with a lethal cocktail that affected the arrhythmia in the left ventricle of his heart.

POWERS/WEAPONS

• Alters and restores the physiology of other living beings
• Raises and animates corpses

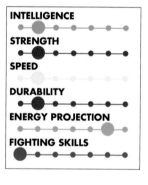

INTELLIGENCE
STRENGTH
SPEED
DURABILITY
ENERGY PROJECTION
FIGHTING SKILLS

O-FORCE

First Appearance: *X-Statix* #1 (2002)

America, meet your hand-picked team of superheroes: the O-Force! Overkill! Ocean! Obituary! Ocelot! Orbit! Ooze! Capitalizing on America's love affair with "reality" shows, mutant talent agent Solomon O'Sullivan decided to create his personal imitation of life by having various mutants compete for America's love and affection. Though a ratings bonanza, the team proved anything but combat worthy when they weren't fighting other actors. During a battle against Arnie Lundberg (Mysterious Fan Boy), O-Force was decimated by a band of zombies. Solomon was subsequently mobbed by angry fans who blamed him for O-Force's defeat, many believing that the contestants who became O-Force weren't truly mutants and that their so-called powers were actually no more than special effects.

POWERS/WEAPONS

- Ability to cure most known ailments and afflictions
- Low-level telekinesis

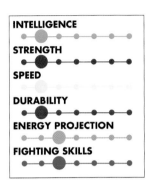

INTELLIGENCE	
STRENGTH	
SPEED	
DURABILITY	
ENERGY PROJECTION	
FIGHTING SKILLS	

Real Name: Anna (full name unrevealed)
First Appearance: X-Force #117 (2001)
Height: 5'6"
Weight: 126 lbs

An object of worship in Ireland following the emergence of her mutant abilities, Anna was killed during her first mission with the X-Statix. Dying, Anna made the Orphan promise to find the father she never knew; when he agreed, she crumbled into dust, which the Orphan then inhaled. Once the Orphan had tracked down Anna's father, he sneezed, covering the man in Anna's dust. Somehow, Anna's father experienced her memories and personality from the dust, and he thanked the Orphan for letting him get to know his daughter.

SAINT ANNA

POWERS/WEAPONS

- Generation of razor sharp bone spikes, which he can launch at high speeds

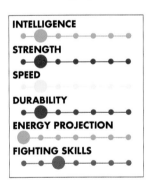

Real Name: Unrevealed
First Appearance: X-Force #121 (2001)
Height: 6'1"
Weight: 170 lbs

Brought on board by Spike Freeman to bring more racial diversity to the team, the cocky Spike took an immediate dislike to teammate and fellow African-American Anarchist, calling the seasoned, if paranoid, team veteran "'Captain Coconut'—black on the outside, white on the inside" at a press conference. Thus began the constant power struggle between the Spike and the Anarchist over who was the more worthy of the two. The Spike's brawn ultimately imploded under the weight of his bombast when he was killed in a battle against the villainous Bush Rangers.

THE SPIKE

POWERS/WEAPONS

- Production of a gelatinous, corrosive, acid-like substance that can completely dissolve solid matter

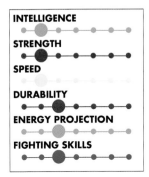

Real Name: Axel Cluney
First Appearance: X-Force #116 (2001)
Height: 6'2"
Weight: 225 lbs

When Zeitgeist's powers manifested, they nearly burned the face off his girlfriend. Zeitgeist's guilt over the incident still plagued him years later, even though he had joined X-Statix and tried to bury his nagging feelings underneath the fame and fortune that had come his way. Perhaps blinded by his relentless self-absorption, Zeitgeist became a pawn in one of Coach's plans to increase the team's popularity, and was killed in an explosion during a deliberately botched attempt to rescue popular music act Boyz R Us from the hands of a terrorist group.

ZEITGEIST

BATTERING RAM

Real Name:
Unrevealed
First Appearance:
X-Force #116 (2001)

Height:
7'4"
Weight:
515 lbs

POWERS/WEAPONS

• Superhuman strength, stamina, and a high degree of resistance to physical injury

INTELLIGENCE
STRENGTH
SPEED
DURABILITY
ENERGY PROJECTION
FIGHTING SKILLS

BLOKE

Real Name:
Michael Tork
First Appearance:
X-Force #117 (2001)

Height:
6'9"
Weight:
380 lbs

POWERS/WEAPONS

• Chameleon-like ability to blend into any environment

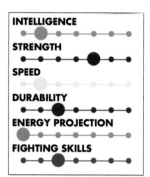

INTELLIGENCE
STRENGTH
SPEED
DURABILITY
ENERGY PROJECTION
FIGHTING SKILLS

GIN GENIE

Real Name:
Beckah Parker
First Appearance:
X-Force #116 (2001)

Height:
5'7"
Weight:
130 lbs

POWERS/WEAPONS

• Alcohol-fueled shockwave generation

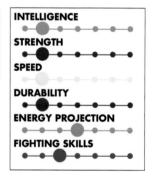

INTELLIGENCE
STRENGTH
SPEED
DURABILITY
ENERGY PROJECTION
FIGHTING SKILLS

LA NUIT

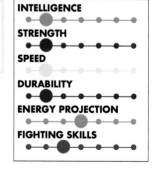

Real Name:
Pierre Truffaut
First Appearance:
X-Force #116 (2001)

Height:
6'3"
Weight:
172 lbs

POWERS/WEAPONS

• Projection of a dark, cloak-like aura used primarily for stealth purposes

INTELLIGENCE
STRENGTH
SPEED
DURABILITY
ENERGY PROJECTION
FIGHTING SKILLS

INTELLIGENCE

STRENGTH

SPEED

DURABILITY

ENERGY PROJECTION

FIGHTING SKILLS

Real Name:
Unrevealed
First Appearance:
X-Force #116 (2001)

Height:
Variable
Weight:
Indeterminate

POWERS/WEAPONS

- Protoplasmic body
- Projection of destructive beams from his hands
- Flight

PLAZM

INTELLIGENCE

STRENGTH

SPEED

DURABILITY

ENERGY PROJECTION

FIGHTING SKILLS

Real Name:
Byron Spencer
First Appearance:
X-Force #116 (2001)

Height:
5'9"
Weight:
140 lbs

POWERS/WEAPONS

- Facial tentacles exude a neurotoxin that causes paralysis in other beings

SLUK

INTELLIGENCE

STRENGTH

SPEED

DURABILITY

ENERGY PROJECTION

FIGHTING SKILLS

Real Name:
Unrevealed
First Appearance:
X-Force #119 (2001)

Height:
Variable
Weight:
Indeterminate

POWERS/WEAPONS

- Smoke-like form

SMOKE

INTELLIGENCE

STRENGTH

SPEED

DURABILITY

ENERGY PROJECTION

FIGHTING SKILLS

Real Name:
Unrevealed
First Appearance:
X-Force #119 (2001)

Height:
5'7"
Weight:
125 lbs

POWERS/WEAPONS

- Razor-sharp teeth and claws

SUCCUBUS

CEREBRA FILES

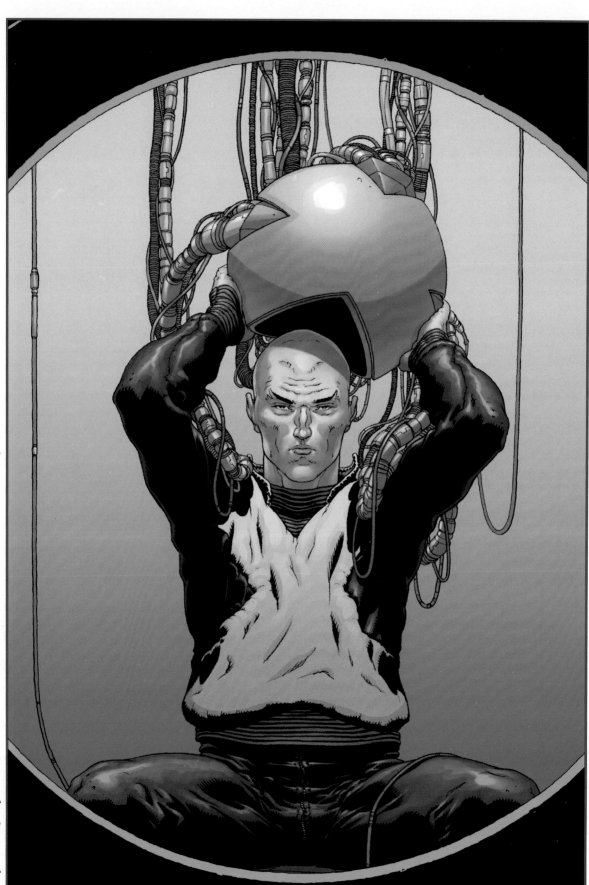

APOCALYPSE

Born nearly five thousand years ago in Egypt, Apocalypse inspired fear even as an infant. Ugly and malformed, he was abandoned by his own tribe to die in the harsh desert sun. Wandering the Earth, Apocalypse found himself in China, where he stumbled upon an alien ship that had crashed into a mountain long ago. He stayed in the ship for thousands of years, learning the secrets of the alien technology and devising a suit of bio-armor for himself. This bio-armor granted Apocalypse the ability to change form, as well as allowing his body to become extremely malleable. Using the alien technology to artificially prolong his life, Apocalypse became more powerful over time.

Real Name:
En Sabah Nur
First Appearance:
X-Factor #5 (1986)

Height: Variable
Weight: Variable
Eye Color: Blue
Hair Color: None

In the late 19th century, Apocalypse surfaced in London, where he plotted to slay the royal family of the time. He found an assistant in Dr. Nathaniel Essex, whose own desire for scientific knowledge led him to foresee the mutants that would be abundant in these modern times. Apocalypse earned the allegiance of Essex and transformed him into <u>Mr. Sinister</u>. In the 20th century, Apocalypse created his Four Horsemen to do his bidding—but his efforts were always thwarted by the <u>X-Men</u> and their allies. Apocalypse is infamous for infecting the baby <u>Nathan Summers</u> with the techno-organic virus that caused him to be taken 2,000 years into an alternate future, where he matured into Apocalypse's mortal enemy. Though Nathan survived, the virus was meant to ensure he would never be able to access his full power and thus be a true threat to Apocalypse.

After centuries of plotting, planning, and waiting, Apocalypse put his master plan into action when he gathered together twelve mutants who had long been destined to usher in a new golden era for mutantkind. Apocalypse intended to use them to boost his powers and alter reality to his liking. But his plans went awry when the Twelve broke free, and Apocalypse attempted to use <u>X-Man</u> as a new host body to replace his own, which he had nearly burnt out. <u>Cyclops</u> intervened and appeared to sacrifice himself, merging with Apocalypse in an attempt to defeat the ages-old mutant. Cyclops eventually managed to assume control of his physical form, but continually struggled to keep Apocalypse's will from dominating him. In a climactic encounter, <u>Jean Grey</u> tore Apocalypse's spirit from Cyclops' body, and Nathan Summers fulfilled his destiny by destroying the eternal mutant once and for all.

POWERS/ WEAPONS

- Superhuman strength
- Ability to alter the atomic structure of his body at will to change form
- Ability to increase size by taking on additional mass from an extra-dimensional source

INTELLIGENCE

STRENGTH

SPEED

DURABILITY

ENERGY PROJECTION

FIGHTING SKILLS

Art by Tom Raney

APOCALYPSE'S HORSEMEN

First Appearance:
X-Factor #15 (1987)

Famine. War. Pestilence. Death. The Four Horsemen of this Apocalypse were servants handpicked to usher in the beginning of the reign of <u>Apocalypse</u> himself. Skillfully preying on the vulnerability of sick or injured mutants, Apocalypse offered the chosen few the physical redemption they so desperately sought in return for their servitude as his Horsemen.

Apocalypse's first recruit was the <u>Morlock</u> named <u>Plague</u>, whom he rescued from being slaughtered by the <u>Marauders</u>. Apocalypse genetically altered Plague to become Pestilence. Next was Abraham Lincoln Kieros, a mutant whose severe injuries incurred as a soldier during the Vietnam War resulted in paralysis and continual confinement in an iron lung in a Veterans Administration hospital. Apocalypse restored the man to health and genetically altered him to become War. Apocalypse then recruited the young anorexic mutant Autumn Rolfson and genetically altered her into Famine. And then there was Death. The X-Man <u>Archangel</u>, despondent after losing his wings, attempted to commit suicide by crashing his plane. But Apocalypse rescued him from his doomed mission and offered to restore his wings if he would join the Horsemen and do Apocalypse's bidding. It was an offer Archangel could not turn away, no matter how loathsome the idea was.

After a number of defections and defeats at the hands of the <u>X-Men</u> and their allies, Apocalypse returned his remaining Horsemen to their original states. But he did not abandon the idea of the group entirely.

Eventually, Apocalypse revived the concept with four new Horsemen: <u>Wolverine</u> became Death; <u>Deathbird</u> became War; <u>Caliban</u> became Pestilence; and Rory Campbell, the man one day destined to become <u>Ahab</u>, became Famine. Wolverine ultimately overcame Apocalypse's programming and rejoined the X-Men. Following the death of Apocalypse, the three remaining Horsemen reverted to their former selves.

Art by Walter Simonson

ARCADE

The assassin-for-hire known only as Arcade has given numerous (and vastly different) accounts of his past life with no evidence to substantiate any of them. In fact, there is nothing to prove or disprove that Arcade is, according to at least one version of his story, the spoiled and lazy son of a millionaire living in Beverly Hills, California. Arcade claimed his father cut off his allowance when he turned 21, saying Arcade didn't deserve it. In retaliation, Arcade killed his father in an explosion, and inherited his father's vast wealth as a result. In killing his father, Arcade discovered that he had both a talent and a liking for murder, and set out to become an assassin-for-hire. Within a year, he felt confident enough to boast he had become the best assassin in the United States. But Arcade became bored with killing by ordinary means, and so he used his inheritance to construct his first Murderworld, a hidden complex of high-tech death traps designed to resemble an amusement park. There are no height requirements inside Murderworld. No ride fees. No lines. But any visitor can expect a wait—to die.

Whatever the truth may be about his life up to that point, the story of his life after he began using Murderworld is clear: Arcade now kills victims for large sums of money by trapping them inside Murderworld. He designs and constructs special traps for individual victims after studying their strengths and weaknesses. Arcade's customary fee is one million dollars per victim—a token amount, as his expenses often exceed that sum. To Arcade, the game itself is more important than the cost.

Seeking new challenges, Arcade set his sights on various superhuman beings and decided to kill them. His first encounter with costumed adventurers was the capture of Spider-Man and **Captain Britain**. Since then, Arcade has attempted to kill off the **X-Men** and their allies on numerous occasions with his Murderworlds. Arcade originally employed two assistants, known only as Miss Locke and Mr. Chambers, but Arcade killed Miss Locke after she horribly scarred his face. Seeking to frame **Wolverine** for the murder, Arcade was defeated instead by Wolverine, **Gambit** and his own former ally, **Mastermind II**, who left Arcade in a temporary state of delusion.

Real Name:
Unrevealed
First Appearance:
Marvel Team-Up #65
(1978)

Height: 5'6"
Weight: 140 lbs
Eye Color: Blue
Hair Color: Red

INTELLIGENCE
STRENGTH
SPEED
DURABILITY
ENERGY PROJECTION
FIGHTING SKILLS

POWERS/ WEAPONS

- Natural aptitude for mechanics, architecture and applied technology

Art by Bryan Hitch

BASTION

Real Name:	Inapplicable	Height:	6'3"
First Appearance:	*X-Men* #52 (1996)	Weight:	375 lbs

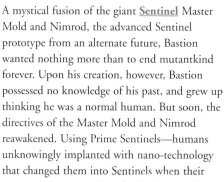

POWERS/WEAPONS

- Enhanced strength
- Flight via boot jets

INTELLIGENCE

STRENGTH

SPEED

DURABILITY

ENERGY PROJECTION

FIGHTING SKILLS

A mystical fusion of the giant <u>Sentinel</u> Master Mold and Nimrod, the advanced Sentinel prototype from an alternate future, Bastion wanted nothing more than to end mutantkind forever. Upon his creation, however, Bastion possessed no knowledge of his past, and grew up thinking he was a normal human. But soon, the directives of the Master Mold and Nimrod reawakened. Using Prime Sentinels—humans unknowingly implanted with nano-technology that changed them into Sentinels when their programming was activated—Bastion sought to eradicate the mutant menace. His Prime Sentinels, part of his anti-mutant strike force, Operation: Zero Tolerance, brutally attacked and captured the <u>X-Men</u>, taking over the <u>Xavier Institute</u> to access <u>Professor X</u>'s files. After the X-Men escaped, <u>Senator Robert Kelly</u> and <u>Henry Gyrich</u> convinced the President and the international law-enforcement agency S.H.I.E.L.D., who had previously turned a blind eye to Bastion's activities, to intervene and close down Operation: Zero Tolerance. Some time later, Bastion escaped government custody and attempted to once again rise to power. He was seemingly destroyed following the intervention of <u>Nathan Summers</u>, but his robotic remains were taken into government custody.

BELASCO

Real Name:	Belasco	Height:	6'4"
First Appearance:	*Ka-Zar the Savage* #11 (1982)	Weight:	250 lbs

POWERS/WEAPONS

- One of the most powerful of all Earthborn sorcerers
- Ability to hurl bolts of mystical force, mesmerize victims, transform people into animals, and raise the dead under certain circumstances

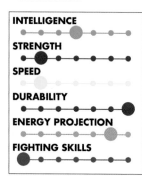

INTELLIGENCE

STRENGTH

SPEED

DURABILITY

ENERGY PROJECTION

FIGHTING SKILLS

The powerful sorcerer Belasco inhabited Limbo, an other dimensional plane where years can pass in the same time that moments elapse on Earth. When Belasco brought the <u>X-Men</u> to Limbo, he seized Illyana Rasputin (<u>Magik</u>), the then-seven-year old sister of <u>Colossus</u>. Belasco then granted her great potential mystic power. Illyana became Belasco's apprentice, and he intended to use Illyana to bring the Elder Gods to Earth once she reached adulthood. After turning thirteen, however, Illyana defeated Belasco in battle and drove him from Limbo. She became the realm's new mistress, and eventually used her powers to return to Earth. She found only seconds had passed since the X-Men had returned. After Illyana's death from the Legacy Virus, Belasco re-established himself as ruler of Limbo. He kidnapped whom he believed to be the sorceress <u>Margali Szardos</u>, but she had actually switched places with her daughter Amanda Sefton (<u>Magik II</u>). With <u>Nightcrawler</u>'s help, the mother and daughter sorceresses managed to switch their bodies back and defeat Belasco. Feeling his power ebbing, Belasco fled. Sefton was subsequently left in charge of Limbo.

BLACK TOM CASSIDY

As the heir to the family fortune and the estate of Cassidy Keep in Ireland, Thomas Cassidy literally threw it all away when he wagered both the fortune and the estate on a throw of dice. After losing everything to his younger cousin Sean Cassidy (<u>Banshee</u>), Tom's losses continued to mount. When he and Sean competed for the love of Maeve Rourke, Tom came up the loser once again. With hate in his heart for Sean, Tom set off to make his own way in life but had no intention of regaining his wealth or status through hard work. Rather, Tom turned to crime as a way of seeking thrills and money. Not every venture was a success, and Tom later wound up in a Third World jail, where he met imprisoned mercenary Cain Marko (<u>Juggernaut</u>). Cassidy and Marko struck up a friendship, and Cassidy used his own mutant power to enable both of them to escape.

Real Name:
Thomas Samuel Eamon Cassidy
First Appearance:
X-Men #99 (1976)

Height:	6'
Weight:	200 lbs
Eye Color:	Blue
Hair Color:	Black

Eventually, Black Tom made his way to Northern Ireland. After a bomb set off by the Irish Republican Army killed Sean's wife Maeve, Black Tom made off with her infant daughter. Theresa (<u>Siryn</u>), whom Sean never even knew existed. Black Tom decided to secretly raise the girl as his own. As Theresa grew into adolescence, she developed superhuman powers akin to her father's. Eager to exploit the girl's abilities to help him ply his criminal trade, Black Tom forced Theresa to help him commit crimes. But Theresa's heart was never in a life of crime. While briefly in the custody of legal authorities, Black Tom exonerated Theresa of responsibility for her crimes and wrote a letter to Banshee explaining who Theresa was. He then escaped while Banshee and Theresa enjoyed their first meeting.

Years later, Black Tom, wounded by a gunshot, was taken to a genetic engineering facility to cure him of his life-threatening injuries. His injured body parts were replaced with a wood-like substance through which he could now focus and project his mutant powers, and Black Tom felt like a new man. He could never imagine what kind of new man he was about to become. The genetic experimentation had infected him with a virus that proceeded to transform an increasing amount of Black Tom's body into the wood-like substance, which, while nearly killing him, ultimately mutated him into a sentient plant-like being with vast new superhuman powers.

INTELLIGENCE

STRENGTH

SPEED

DURABILITY

ENERGY PROJECTION

FIGHTING SKILLS

POWERS/ WEAPONS

- Generation of blasts of concussive force or heat
- Ability to grow to immense size
- Degree of superhuman strength
- Ability to create simulacra of human beings from plant matter and mentally control their actions

Art by Dave Johnson

BROOD

First Appearance:
Uncanny X-Men #155
(1982)

Length:	8'
Weight:	Yellow or red
Eye Color:	Blue
Hair Color:	None

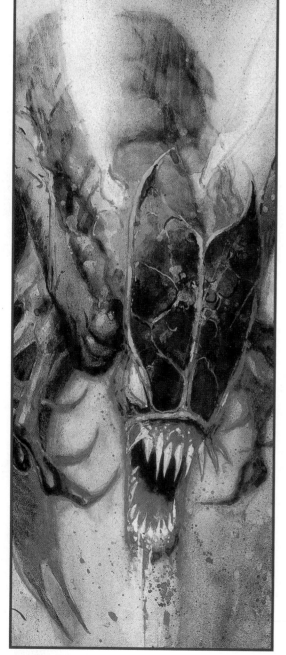

Art by Bill Sienkiewicz

They need bodies—not just any bodies, but bodies of superior life forms. Bodies they can use to incubate their eggs—eggs that will copy their host's powers, and eggs that will eventually hatch to become the forces their race needs to rise up to conquer the Earth. They are the Brood, a savage insectoid alien race who travel through space in ships created from the living bodies of the passive alien race known as the Acanti. To further their race and reproduce themselves, the Brood must implant eggs into other living beings, wherein the embryo metamorphoses its host's body until it hatches. Upon hatching, the newborn fully consumes its host and converts it into a member of the Brood. As a result of the afterbirth feast, the new Brood gains any powers and abilities the host possessed.

Nature, of course, dictates that the greater the power of the host, the greater the power of the offspring. With that always in mind, the Brood seek out the strongest, most powerful forces in the universe to achieve the greatest breeding—forces such as the <u>X-Men</u>. The mutant heroes' destruction of the Brood Queen resulted in primal stresses being inflicted upon Broodworld itself, which exploded.

Bearing a fierce hatred of the X-Men for their destruction of the Brood home planet, the Brood still have yet to win a battle against their mortal enemies and perfect breeding hosts. Losing battle after battle to the X-Men in their attempts to conquer Earth, the Brood have been just as unsuccessful at their attempts to implant their eggs in members of the mighty team.

With hope running out for implanting the X-Men, the Brood implanted eggs into latent mutants during one breeding mission, hoping to create a force of Brood with superhuman abilities that could at least rival those of the X-Men. Realizing that it was too late to save the hosts, and seeking to prevent the Brood from implanting any more people, the X-Men slew the mutant Brood in a feverish battle.

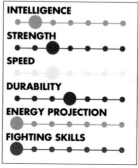

INTELLIGENCE

STRENGTH

SPEED

DURABILITY

ENERGY PROJECTION

FIGHTING SKILLS

POWERS/ WEAPONS

- Firstborn Brood possess the ability to teleport and are fierce warriors in battle
- Newborn Brood gain any powers and abilities their host possessed

CAPTAIN BRITAIN

Shortly after his parents were killed in an explosion, graduate student Brian Braddock nearly lost his life as well. Fleeing a breach at the nuclear research facility where he worked, Brian took off on his motorcycle and accidentally ran the speeding vehicle off a cliff. As he lay near death, the spirits of the god-wizard Merlin and Roma, Goddess of the Northern Skies, appeared to him and granted him superhuman strength and stamina. The patron spirits decreed that Brian would be Britain's champion, and gifted him with a mystical star-scepter to enhance his fighting skills.

Captain Britain later learned the truth about his family's extra-dimensional origins and his metaphysical connection to the land and people of Otherworld—a glorious kingdom positioned at the nexus of reality where science and sorcery exist as one. Thanks to these revelations, Captain Britain achieved a kind of spiritual peace most human beings never reach in a lifetime.

But Captain Britain's services were still required, and Brian fought to save an alternate reality from the world-warping madness that was Sir James Jaspers. Brian failed and was killed—but even in death there was no escaping his destiny. Merlin resurrected the fallen hero, who came to join Meggan, Shadowcat, Lockheed, Nightcrawler and Rachel Summers in forming Excalibur, England's premier super-hero team.

Though he remained a member of Excalibur, Captain Britain tried to quit the superhero life again, this time to concentrate on science—and his marriage to Meggan. After the couple had wed in a ceremony on Otherworld, they retired to live a normal life in England, and Captain Britain returned to work at the nuclear research facility he had left so many years earlier. However, the Braddocks' peace was shattered when Captain Britain learned that a seemingly insane Roma had decimated Otherworld in a quest to dominate all reality. Finally fulfilling his destiny as the true monarch of Otherworld, Captain Britain helped rescue Roma from the thrall of a sentient super-computer.

Real Name:
Brian Braddock
First Appearance:
Captain Britain #1
(1976)

Height: 5'11"
Weight: 214 lbs
Eye Color: Blue
Hair Color: Blond

Art by Alan Davis

INTELLIGENCE	
STRENGTH	
SPEED	
DURABILITY	
ENERGY PROJECTION	
FIGHTING SKILLS	

POWERS/ WEAPONS

- Superhuman strength, stamina, and reflexes
- Flight
- Mystical force field

DOMINO

Real Name:
Neena Thurman
First Appearance:
X-Force #8 (1992)

Height: 5'8"
Weight: 120 lbs
Eye Color: Blue
Hair Color: Black

POWERS/ WEAPONS

• Possesses the ability to generate a psionic aura around herself that affects probability, thus causing events and situations to "fall into place" for her benefit

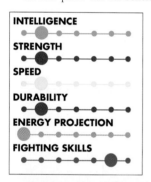

INTELLIGENCE

STRENGTH

SPEED

DURABILITY

ENERGY PROJECTION

FIGHTING SKILLS

After a long and distinguished career in many fields of covert activity, Domino took an undercover position as a bodyguard for Milo Thurman, a genius prodigy in predicting world events and shifts in the balance of power between governments.

Over time, Milo found an interest of his own: Domino. The two eventually married, but their relationship ended after a subversive organization's raid on the government facility where Milo was being housed. The act drove Domino into even deeper cover, and Milo's government superiors told him that Domino was dead.

Domino subsequently joined a team of mercenaries led by Nathan Summers, marking the beginning of a long and intimate friendship with the soldier from the future. Years later, Milo Thurman was taken hostage by Donald Pierce and his Reavers. Domino defeated Pierce and the Reavers, but was unable to save her husband.

After returning for a time to her lone, mercenary ways, Domino eventually signed on as a member of the Hong Kong branch of the X-Corporation. Domino investigated the activities of John Sublime, leader of the Third Species Movement, who had just acquired a Chinese prison where the mutant Xorn was being held captive. Domino had to seek the aid of the X-Men to defeat the Sublime's U-Men, a group of humans who sought to harvest mutant body parts to graft onto themselves. Together, the heroes defeated the U-Men and freed Xorn.

Art by Leinil Francis Yu

SENATOR ROBERT KELLY

As a United States senator from Boston, Massachusetts, Robert Kelly had long regarded mutants as a threat to national security. To cope with this supposed danger, he promoted such legislation as the Mutant Registration Act. If passed, the law would have required genetically empowered individuals to disclose their abilities to the government.

An assassination attempt on Kelly by the <u>Brotherhood of Evil Mutants</u> was foiled by the <u>X-Men</u>, but it fueled the Senator's resolve to pass the Registration Act. He cultivated a partnership with <u>Sebastian Shaw</u>, who oversaw the construction of <u>Sentinels</u> on behalf of the government and supported Kelly's efforts. Unknown to the Senator, Shaw himself was a mutant and the Black King of the <u>Hellfire Club</u>. Following a meeting with Shaw in New York, the Senator's limousine was demolished by debris from a fight involving the X-Men. Kelly survived, but his wife Sharon died in the wreckage. Kelly's grief strengthened his belief that mutants were too dangerous to be allowed to run rampant, and he pushed for the production of additional Sentinels that would hunt down and kill every mutant alive.

Along with <u>Henry Gyrich</u>, the Senator supported Operation: Zero Tolerance, a government-sponsored initiative intended to rid the world of mutants. Only after the Senator discovered that <u>Bastion</u> was using the program as a cover to convert innocent humans into Sentinels and trample on the rights of U.S. citizens did Kelly withdraw his support. Fearing for his life, he turned to the X-Men to help stop Bastion. Despite once again being saved by the X-Men, the Senator turned his back on their cause when he announced his candidacy for president, running on an anti-mutant platform.

On a campaign stop in Boston, the Brotherhood struck again, more determined than ever to kill the mutant-hating Senator. Only saved from certain death by the dying <u>Pyro</u>, the Senator had no choice but to reevaluate his stance on mutants. After all this time, he had turned a corner. Finally, mutants would have someone on the otherside in their corner who was willing to work through the political system to ensure their rights as citizens and their safety at the hands of a mutant-fearing populace. But it was all too good to be true. At a college rally, an anti-mutant activist named Alan Lewis, believing the Senator had betrayed his human brothers by toning down his rhetoric, did what the Brotherhood had failed to do in the past: He assassinated Robert Kelly.

Real Name:
Robert Edward Kelly
First Appearance:
X-Men #135 (1980)

Height: 5'10"
Weight: 175 lbs
Eye Color: Brown
Hair Color: Brown
with graying temples

Art by Salvador Larroca

MOIRA MACTAGGERT

Real Name:
Moira Ann Kinross
MacTaggert
First Appearance:
X-Men #96 (1976)

Height:	5'7"
Weight:	135 lbs
Eye Color:	Blue
Hair Color:	Brown

The daughter of a powerful Scottish nobleman, Moira Kinross was a brilliant student of the biological sciences and selected genetics as her specialty. She later married Joseph MacTaggert, a thuggish, abusive Royal Marine commando with political ambitions, but the marriage was disastrous and the couple eventually separated.

While in school, Moira met Charles Xavier (**Professor X**), who was working toward a doctorate at Oxford University. The two fell in love immediately. Eventually, they became engaged, pending the annulment of Moira's marriage to Joe. After Charles was drafted into military service, Moira promised to wait for him. But without explanation Moira sent him a letter breaking off their engagement and stating that she was returning home to Scotland. Moira intended to reconcile with Joe, but he proved to be just as brutal as before. The last straw came when Moira and Joe visited New York City, where Joe beat and sexually assaulted Moira, causing her to be hospitalized for a week and leaving her pregnant. From then on, Moira lived apart from her husband, who refused to grant her a divorce, and she kept the fact that he had a son secret from him for twenty years.

Moira enjoyed a brilliant career as one of the world's leading geneticists, earning a Nobel Prize for her work, and she founded a Mutant Research Center on Muir Island, off the coast of Scotland. She eventually renewed contact with Professor X during a period he spent in England working on a degree in psychiatry. The two discussed the possibility of establishing a school for training mutants in the use of their powers, and Moira became the Professor's silent partner in founding the **Xavier Institute**.

No amount of training could help Moira cure her son Kevin (**Proteus**), who had developed destructive mutant powers. Proteus attacked and possessed Joe's body, killing him and using it in an attempt to kill his mother. Before Proteus could carry out his threat, **Colossus** destroyed the raging young man. Subsequently, Moira came to take as her ward the young orphaned Scottish girl Rahne Sinclair (**Wolfsbane**), whom Moira had delivered as a baby, after Sinclair manifested a lycanthropic mutant power and was attacked by an angry mob.

Years after working through the torment of her past, Moira devoted her energies to finding a cure for the deadly Legacy Virus ravaging the world's mutant population. Just as she discovered the cure, Muir Island came under attack by **Mystique** and her **Brotherhood of Evil Mutants**. Mortally wounded in the explosion that destroyed her research center, Moira clung to life just long enough for Professor X to make telepathic contact and obtain the formula for the cure. **Beast** was able to extrapolate a working antidote from Moira's formula, released when Colossus sacrificed himself to disperse it into the atmosphere.

Art by Brandon Peterson

CASSANDRA NOVA

A bitter and broken Cassandra Nova began her lifelong mission of revenge from the moment of her doomed birth. As the in-utero twin of **Professor X**, Cassandra attempted to strangle Charles in the womb, but he fought back with his exceptional telepathic abilities. As a result of the psychic struggle, Cassandra was stillborn, but her psyche managed to live on. It took forty long, hard years clinging to a sewer wall underneath the hospital, but Cassandra used her own telepathic and telekinetic powers to copy Charles's cells and slowly build her own body.

For every ounce of compassion her brother has, Cassandra has only hatred. And unlike Charles, who only wants peace between man and mutant, Cassandra's main mission and driving ambition is to see the extermination of her brother Charles—along with the extermination of other mutants. Summoning all of her cunning and mutant ability, Cassandra unleashed a fleet of **Sentinels** on the island of Genosha, annihilating the mutant population of 16 million, including **Magneto**. No one, not even Charles, could stop her. They could only stand back in horror and watch it all happen.

After the Genosha massacre, Cassandra allowed herself to be captured by her brother and the **X-Men** in a calculated move. She then attacked her captors at the **Xavier Institute** and, during the struggle, unknown to the X-Men, exchanged bodies with her brother while permitting her own to be severely damaged. Cloaked in her brother's body, she announced to the world via television the secret Charles had long kept hidden: He was a mutant like his trained X-Men. While the public did turn its scrutiny on Charles, the move backfired on Cassandra; rather than allowing the truth to ruin him, the revelation made Charles stronger. Once he had resumed possession of his body, he was grateful she had taken a step that he could not take himself. After Cassandra attempted to usurp control of the **Shi'ar** empire and use the **Shi'ar Imperial Guard** to attack the X-Men, she ultimately fell into a trap set by **Jean Grey** that virtually destroyed her brain and, along with it, her powers. Now, with her psyche entrenched in the synthetic brain of a morphogenic alien, the X-Men and Charles hope they can teach Cassandra to become human.

Real Name:
Cassandra Nova
First Appearance:
New X-Men #114 (2001)

Height: 5'4"
Weight: 115 lbs
Eye Color: Blue
Hair Color: None

POWERS/ WEAPONS

- Telekinesis
- Telepathy

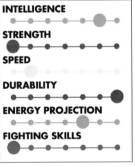

INTELLIGENCE

STRENGTH

SPEED

DURABILITY

ENERGY PROJECTION

FIGHTING SKILLS

Art by Frank Quitely

ONSLAUGHT

Real Name:	Inapplicable	**Height:**	10'
First Appearance:	*X-Man* #15 (1996)	**Weight:**	900 lbs

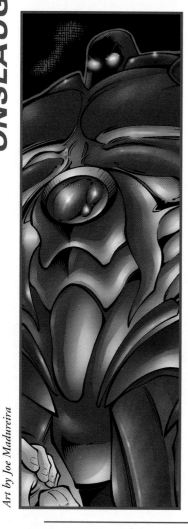

Art by Joe Madureira

POWERS/WEAPONS

• Possessed the mutant abilities of Professor X and Magneto, making him one of the most powerful psionic beings ever to have existed

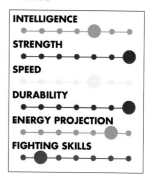

INTELLIGENCE
STRENGTH
SPEED
DURABILITY
ENERGY PROJECTION
FIGHTING SKILLS

To the world at large, <u>Professor X</u> is a man of peace. But his calm exterior belies a torrent of subconscious doubts, fears, and anxieties. During a battle between the <u>X-Men</u> and the <u>Acolytes</u>, Professor X used his telepathic powers to shut down <u>Magneto</u>'s mind in a moment of foolish arrogance. During the psionic contact, Magneto's anger, grief, and lust for vengeance entered Professor X's consciousness. His terrible thought patterns combined with every long-suppressed negative emotion that Professor X had endured, and something awful was born. Its name was Onslaught. Festering like a psychic wound in Xavier's mind, Onslaught soon began to manifest himself to others. Over time, Onslaught became so powerful that he was able to free himself from Professor X's mind and take control of the powerful telepath's body. Wreaking havoc the likes of which the universe had never seen, Onslaught was on course to dominate all mutants and mankind; it seemed no one, not even the most powerful superheroes on Earth, could stop him. One by one, they fell to defeat at Onslaught's hands. Even Xavier's physical separation from Onslaught proved futile; once Onslaught was no longer tethered to his original host, he became a being of pure psionic energy and more unstoppable than before.

Knowing it might be the last chance to stop the threat forever, the non-mutant heroes—including members of the Avengers and the Fantastic Four—flew into the torrent of psionic energy, disrupting Onslaught's form. Onslaught was destroyed—along with the heroes. The mutant members of the assembled teams, including the X-Men, were unable to help. If Onslaught came to possess a mutant host, he would become invincible. Later, it was revealed that the Avengers and the Fantastic Four did not die after all. Rather, the heroes were reborn in a pocket universe. They returned to their rightful home months later.

PHALANX

First Appearance:	*Uncanny X-Men* #305 (1993)	**Height:**	Variable
		Weight:	Variable

POWERS/WEAPONS

• Highly intelligent
• Ability to assimilate inorganic matter to increase their mass

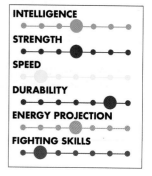

INTELLIGENCE
STRENGTH
SPEED
DURABILITY
ENERGY PROJECTION
FIGHTING SKILLS

The Phalanx are an offshoot of the alien Technarchy, a race of techno-organic beings from deep space bent on galactic conquest. The Phalanx first manifested on Earth when members of the anti-mutant group the Friends of Humanity voluntarily infected themselves with <u>Warlock</u>'s transmode virus, transforming themselves into techno-organic beings better able to wage war against mutantkind. They soon found themselves taken over by the virus's basic operating program: assimilate other beings into the Phalanx collective by infecting them with the virus. The Phalanx planned to conquer the galaxy—but, with the help of Warlock, the <u>X-Men</u> were able to defeat them.

SENTINELS

They seek. They hunt. They destroy. They will not stop until there is no mutant left alive.

First Appearance:
X-Men #14 (1965)

Even though his two children, Tanya and Larry, were mutants themselves, Dr. Boliver Trask could not shake his dread of *Homo superior* and feared that one day, mutants would rule *Homo sapiens*. Unwilling to accept this fate, Dr. Trask decided to create Sentinels: immense, 30-foot-tall robots designed specifically to hunt down and kill mutants.

Trask created a prototype called the Master Mold and manufactured the first wave of robots, Mark I Sentinels, from it. But the logic he had instilled in the Sentinels led them to decide they could best protect humanity by taking control of it. They summarily rebelled against Trask and held him prisoner along with the X-Men. Trask, realizing he had made a grave mistake by creating this terrible threat to humanity, sacrificed his life by triggering an explosion that destroyed not just the Sentinels but the Master Mold as well.

Deciding to blame the X-Men for his father's death, Larry rebuilt a new fleet of Sentinels. These Mark II Sentinels could now analyze any threat and determine how best to counter it, making them nearly indestructible. But sensing Larry's mutant nature, the Mark II Sentinels turned on him, killing him and destroying their own kind in the ensuing battle. The Sentinel program, however, did not die with the Mark II, and countless sanctioned, covert Sentinel bases still exist around the world—operated by both mutant-hunting humans and Sentinels themselves. Using Trask's original designs, Steven Lang, Sebastian Shaw, and even the U.S. government have all created Sentinels to serve their own purposes.

The latest model of Sentinels are the product of a shadow-ops program, assimilating raw materials from automobile and aircraft components, machine parts, and building materials to keep pace with genetic mutation. These wild Sentinels appear in many shapes and sizes, including microscopic nano-Sentinels. Now super-adaptive, these creations mimic the abilities and maneuvers of their targets. Perhaps even more deadly than their forebears, the latest incarnation of Sentinels saw the greatest and most vicious proof of their power when they methodically annihilated 16 million citizens of the mutant enclave Genosha—including its leader, Magneto.

Art by Frank Quitely

WILLIAM STRYKER

Real Name:
William Stryker

First Appearance:
Marvel Graphic Novel #5 (1982)

Height:	5'11"
Weight:	170 lbs
Eye Color:	Brown
Hair Color:	White

A master sergeant in the U.S. Army Rangers, William Stryker and his pregnant wife Marcy had a car accident in the Nevada desert, causing Marcy to go into labor. Stryker delivered his son and was shocked to see the baby was born an abomination. He immediately killed the child. When his wife asked for her baby, Stryker broke her neck. Seeking to disguise the cold-blooded murder of his family—and hoping to kill himself in the process—Stryker loaded their bodies in the wreck of their car, got inside with them and lit a match that ignited the leaking gas. The explosion blew Stryker clear of the wreckage, however, and he survived. His wife and child were burned beyond recognition, leaving no one to know of his crime but himself. Try as he might, Stryker could not forget the events of that day, and he turned to alcohol for solace. Soon after, Stryker read a magazine article featuring **Professor X** and the growing mutant population. After months of torment, Stryker finally found the first clue as to what his child had been: a mutant. It was at that moment Stryker turned to religion, believing his wife had been the vessel through which God had revealed Satan's most insidious plot against humanity—to corrupt them through their children while they were still in the womb. From that misguided beginning came his ministry, the Stryker Crusade. For years, Stryker labored to amass a power base with which to strike out against mutantkind.

Stryker learned of the **X-Men** from a devoted member of his crusade who was a senior officer of the FBI. Stryker became convinced Xavier was the Antichrist, the supposed friend of mankind that would ultimately lead them to destruction. Stryker commanded his soldiers to capture Xavier and intended to brainwash him into becoming a weapon to use against his own kind. Xavier was strapped into a machine that would amplify his psionic sensitivity, enabling him to detect the unique brainwave patterns of both active and latent mutants and then destroy their minds. At a sermon in Madison Square Garden, Stryker preached to the masses as the psionic device was activated. **Magneto** confronted Stryker while the X-Men, with whom Magneto had temporarily allied himself, managed to free Professor X and destroy Stryker's machine. When Stryker was later arraigned on charges arising out of the activities of his soldiers, he denounced the indictment as religious persecution and predicted the eventual vindication of himself and his crusade.

Art by Brent Eric Anderson

JOHN SUBLIME

John Sublime was a 30-year-old pharmaceutical company owner who secretly longed to be a superhuman mutant. He believed that humans should be able to advance themselves in the same way that genetics had allowed mutants to improve. Using his pharmaceutical company as a front for an illegal mutant organ harvesting operation, Sublime and others with the same desire dissected mutants and grafted the mutant body parts onto and into themselves. Sublime then formed the U-Men, a group of humans implanted with mutant organs who did his bidding.

Real Name:
John Sublime
First Appearance:
New X-Men Annual
(2001)

Height: 5'8"
Weight: 162 lbs
Eye Color: Blue
Hair Color: Black
(toupee)

Sublime believed in his theory of genetic perfection so much that he invested his fortune into founding the Third Species Movement, and even wrote a best-selling book titled *The Third Species* that outlined his philosophy. Following Sublime's public announcement of the formation of the Third Species Movement, he bought an old prison near Hong Kong where the mutant Xorn was being held prisoner. His efforts to make the Chinese prison into a mutant organ farm were thwarted when the X-Men were alerted to his activities by the Hong Kong branch of the X-Corporation, and the team swiftly defeated Sublime's U-Men, destroyed the prison, and freed Xorn. This setback did nothing to destroy Sublime's dreams, for he continued to secretly fund his Augmen project, which had successfully performed mutant organ grafts on children. Unfortunately for Sublime, Iceman shut down the operation after he was lured to the company under false pretenses in an attempt to use him as a living superconductor.

Sublime, in a supreme act of hubris, later met Cyclops and Emma Frost in private in his posh office. He showed them Martha Johansson, a runaway mutant the U-Men had captured whose living brain had been put in a container. Sublime used Martha's superhuman telepathic abilities to subdue Cyclops and Emma Frost; as they were taken away for harvesting, he ordered his U-Men to attack the Xavier Institute and claim it as an organ farm.

While Jean Grey defeated the U-Men who sought to invade her home, Cyclops and Emma broke free of Martha's control. Dangling Sublime out of an open window, Emma threatened to drop him if he didn't stop his illegal organ thefts. Though Emma may not have really wanted to kill Sublime, just shake a little sense into him, someone else meant to do him greater harm: Martha. Martha's mutant brain telepathically forced Sublime to free himself from Frost's grip and caused the mutant wannabe to plummet to his death.

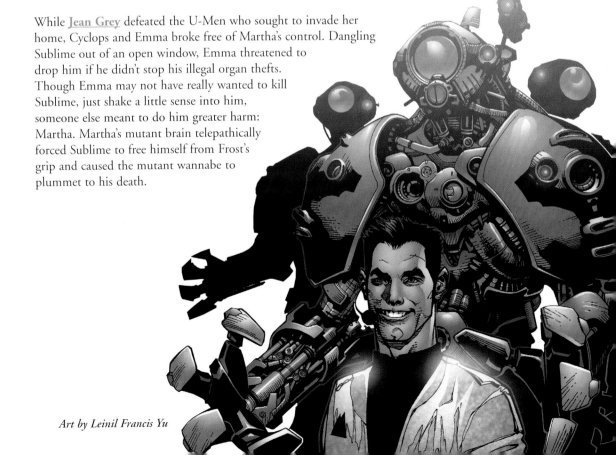

Art by Leinil Francis Yu

WENDIGO

Real Name:
Various
First Appearance:
Incredible Hulk #162
(1973)

Height:	9'7"
Weight:	1,800 lbs
Eye Color:	Red
Hair Color:	White

POWERS/
WEAPONS

- Razor-sharp claws and teeth
- Accelerated healing factor
- Immunity to all forms of disease

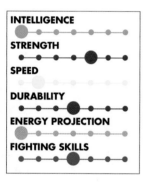

INTELLIGENCE	
STRENGTH	
SPEED	
DURABILITY	
ENERGY PROJECTION	
FIGHTING SKILLS	

The Wendigo is the result of an ancient curse laid down by the Elder Gods of Canadian folklore that transforms any person who eats the flesh of another human being in the Canadian wilderness into a massive, fur-covered humanoid beast.

In the first modern documented case of the Wendigo, three Canadians—Paul Cartier, Georges Baptiste and Henri Cluzot—were hunting in the Canadian North Woods when wolves attacked them. Cluzot was mortally wounded, and his friends took him inside a cave for shelter. As the men began to starve, Cluzot died. Cartier, on the verge of insanity, resorted to eating the dead man's flesh. In doing so, he fell victim to the curse that transformed him into the Wendigo. Ultimately, Baptiste and Cartier's sister Marie attempted to transfer the curse to the Hulk, with whom Cartier had clashed several times as the Wendigo. Marie tranquilized the Hulk, then summoned the Wendigo. But before she could begin the necessary ritual, the Hulk awoke and attacked the Wendigo. In the midst of their battle, they were confronted by <u>Wolverine</u>, who had been sent by the Canadian government to subdue the Hulk. Wolverine and the Hulk together took down the Wendigo, but fought each other as Marie prepared the Wendigo for the transferral process. She then gassed the two combatants, reverting the Hulk to his human form of Dr. Bruce Banner. Seeing Banner, Baptiste lost all resolve to help Marie transfer the curse to the Hulk. Marie tried to move Banner, but he reverted back to the Hulk and renewed his fight with Wolverine. Unseen, Baptiste snuck into the cave in which the Wendigo lay and completed the ritual, which transferred the curse from Cartier to himself, transforming him into the Wendigo.

The Wendigo was next seen attacking campers around Hudson Bay. Aided by Wolverine and <u>Nightcrawler</u>, <u>Alpha Flight</u> narrowly defeated the Wendigo. <u>Shaman</u> cast a spell that removed the curse, freeing Baptiste. In its most recent incarnation, the Wendigo attacked Wolverine and the medieval French cannibal Mauvais as the pair did battle in Canada. After feasting on the Wendigo's heart, Mauvais transferred the curse onto himself. He was confronted by Wolverine and Alpha Flight, and ultimately defeated by the Elder Gods of the North, who trapped him in the dimension of the ancient Great Beasts.

Art by Leinil Francis Yu

POWERS/WEAPONS

- Powerful mystical entity, not mutant by nature

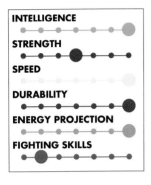

INTELLIGENCE

STRENGTH

SPEED

DURABILITY

ENERGY PROJECTION

FIGHTING SKILLS

Real Name: Inapplicable
First Appearance: *Uncanny X-Men* #188 (1984)

Height: 12'
Weight: Inapplicable

The Adversary is an ancient mystical entity, possibly demonic in nature, who seeks to destroy the present universe and create a new one in its place. The Cheyenne Indians refer to the Adversary as the "The Great Trickster." The Cheyenne's shaman, <u>Forge</u>, was trained from birth to combat the Adversary, and the <u>X-Men</u> willingly agreed to sacrifice their lives so Forge could cast the spell needed to defeat the Adversary. But <u>Roma</u> was able to use her great powers to return the X-Men to life.

ADVERSARY

POWERS/WEAPONS

- Superhuman healing factor
- Above-average strength, speed, and dexterity
- Proficient in the use of virtually any weapon

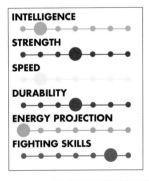

INTELLIGENCE

STRENGTH

SPEED

DURABILITY

ENERGY PROJECTION

FIGHTING SKILLS

Real Name: Alex Hayden
First Appearance: *Agent X* #1 (2002)

Height: 6'
Weight: 215 lbs

Though he has no memory of his past, he has a clear vision for his future: become the world's greatest mercenary—or die trying. Agent X's first conscious memory consists of pain—awaking to find himself seriously injured with an "X" carved into his face, he dubbed himself Alex Hayden and obtained the help of receptionist Sandi Brandenberg and her mercenary boyfriend, Taskmaster. Now, armed with the innate abilities Taskmaster unwittingly unleashed, Alex operates Agency X—his own no-questions-asked mercenary service.

AGENT X

POWERS/WEAPONS

- Creation of spears of psionic energy
- Enhanced strength, speed and stamina

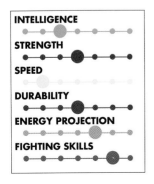

INTELLIGENCE

STRENGTH

SPEED

DURABILITY

ENERGY PROJECTION

FIGHTING SKILLS

Real Name: Roderick Campbell
First Appearance: *Fantastic Four Annual* #23 (1990)

Height: 6'1"
Weight: 166 lbs

At the request of <u>Professor X</u>, psychologist Rory Campbell accepted an offer from <u>Moira MacTaggert</u> to work at her Mutant Research Center on Muir Island, where he discovered an alternate reality in which he became the mutant-hunting Ahab. While in this alternate reality, Ahab captured <u>Rachel Summers</u>, who then fled his control after hurling him into a bank of computers; his body was horribly mangled in the ensuing explosion. Ahab's injuries rendered him a paraplegic, but, he walked again after being transformed into a cyborg.

AHAB

AMIKO

Real Name: Amiko (full name unrevealed)
First Appearance: *Uncanny X-Men* #181 (1984)

Height: 4'10"
Weight: 100 lbs

She thrived thanks to <u>Wolverine</u>'s devotion—and nearly died from it, too. Wolverine adopted Amiko when he encountered the little girl's dying mother in Japan, and he left her in the care of his beloved, <u>Mariko Yashida</u>. After Mariko's death, Wolverine entrusted Amiko to <u>Yukio</u>, who cared for the sometimes troublesome teenager as if she were her own, even going so far as to train her in the martial arts. But when <u>Lady Deathstrike</u> crippled Yukio, <u>Sabretooth</u> kidnapped Amiko. Taunting Wolverine, Sabretooth nearly killed Amiko moments after the X-Man arrived. The <u>Weapon X</u> program subsequently brought Amiko back to full health and returned her to Wolverine as a calculated show of "good faith."

BEDLAM

Real Name: Jesse Aaronson
First Appearance: *X-Force* #82 (1998)

Height: 6'
Weight: 195 lbs

Orphaned at age 5, Jesse Aaronson was separated from his older brother Christopher after both were placed in foster care. Jesse was rescued by <u>Professor X</u>, who taught him to use his powers. But his brother was the only family he had left, and when Bedlam had grown into a young man, he finally located him. When he learned that Christopher, using his mutant ability to scramble minds, had killed their parents so long ago, Bedlam fought against his brother as part of the mutant strike force founded by <u>Nathan Summers</u>, remaining a member until his apparent death in battle.

POWERS/WEAPONS
- Generation of a bioelectric field that disrupts the normal function of mechanical and electrical systems

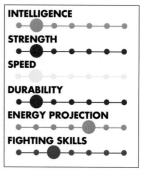

INTELLIGENCE						
STRENGTH						
SPEED						
DURABILITY						
ENERGY PROJECTION						
FIGHTING SKILLS						

BELLADONNA

Real Name: Belladonna Boudreaux
First Appearance: *X-Men* #8 (1992)

Height: 6'
Weight: 150 lbs

Belladonna Boudreaux was born to the leaders of the New Orleans Assassin's Guild. She knew nothing of the family's conflict with the Thieves' Guild, in which her best friend Remy LeBeau (<u>Gambit</u>) had been raised. The warring Guilds saw their relationship as a way to forge peace, and the two were betrothed by their respective guardians. But before the marriage was consummated, Remy left Belladonna to escape Guild life. Though she was understandably bitter towards her runaway husband, Belladonna finally made peace with Gambit and now serves as Viceroy of the Unified Guilds of New Orleans.

POWERS/WEAPONS
- Generation of blasts of plasma from her hands
- Ability to wield magic

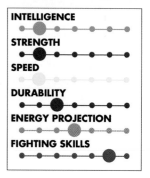

INTELLIGENCE						
STRENGTH						
SPEED						
DURABILITY						
ENERGY PROJECTION						
FIGHTING SKILLS						

POWERS/WEAPONS

- High-order telepath and telekinetic
- Limited ability to time travel
- Mechanical genius

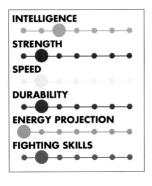

INTELLIGENCE

STRENGTH

SPEED

DURABILITY

ENERGY PROJECTION

FIGHTING SKILLS

Real Name: Unrevealed
First Appearance: *X-Men: Prime* (1995)

Height: 5'3"
Weight: 105 lbs

Born into a post-apocalyptic alternate future, Blaquesmith became the first male ever to learn the ways of the Askani Sisterhood, a group of warrior women who opposed the tyrannical rule of **Apocalypse**. Blaquesmith willingly twisted and corrupted his mortal form because he understood it was necessary to perform the task with which he had been charged: mentoring the Chosen One of the Askani, **Nathan Summers**. Blaquesmith remains steadfast in his devotion Nathan, always willing to risk his life to train the young man in the ways of the Askani.

BLAQUESMITH

POWERS/WEAPONS

- Teleportation

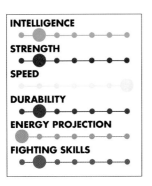

INTELLIGENCE

STRENGTH

SPEED

DURABILITY

ENERGY PROJECTION

FIGHTING SKILLS

Real Name: Lila Cheney
First Appearance: *New Mutants Annual* #1 (1984)

Height: 5'10"
Weight: 143 lbs

After escaping a life of cosmic slavery, dabbling for a time as an intergalactic thief, Lila Cheney became an interstellar star as a member of the band Cat's Laughing. Blaming Earth as a whole for her early slavery, she later tried to sell the planet to an alien race. Her failed attempt led to an encounter with the **New Mutants**, and then a long and favorable acquaintance with the young heroes and a brief romance with **Cannonball**. Years later, Cat's Laughing would have the profound honor of playing at the weddings of **Cyclops** to **Jean Grey** and **Captain Britain** to **Meggan**.

LILA CHENEY

Real Name: Valerie Cooper
First Appearance: *Uncanny X-Men* #176 (1983)

Height: 5'7"
Weight: 132 lbs

Dr. Val Cooper is a political figure who rose to become Special Assistant to the President's National Security Advisor out of her driving concern over the danger that she believed superhuman activity posed to the United States. Val fervently believed the U.S. government should be able to protect itself against superhuman mutants and, if necessary, strike back against them. Though her stance has softened somewhat over time, even allowing her to use her position to surreptitiously help the **X-Men**, Val remains very much entrenched in the bureaucracy of anti-mutant politics.

VALERIE COOPER

GRAYDON CREED

Real Name: Graydon Creed
First Appearance: *Uncanny X-Men #299* (1993)

Height: 6'
Weight: 181 lbs

Graydon Creed hated everything he had been born into. As the child of <u>Sabretooth</u> and <u>Mystique</u>, Graydon grew up to become a rabid anti-mutant lobbyist and founded the Friends of Humanity, a grassroots campaign dedicated to eradicating the mutant menace. After his campaign turned into a national movement, Creed capitalized on his notoriety and ran for president on an anti-mutant platform. But on Election Day eve, an unknown assassin disintegrated Graydon with a plasma beam. It was only later revealed that the blast was fired by a future version of Mystique who been sent back in time to ensure her son's death.

CYBER

Real Name: Silas Burr
First Appearance: *Marvel Comics Presents #85* (1991)

Height: 6'2"
Weight: 300 lbs

<u>Wolverine</u> once admired the mutant mercenary Cyber, but the pair had a falling out over a woman. Employed years later as an enforcer for a powerful drug cartel, Cyber again encountered Wolverine. Twice defeated by the X-Man, Cyber was abducted by <u>Genesis</u>, who released a swarm of flesh-eating mutant beetles that devoured the mercenary's flesh and bone, leaving only his adamantium skin intact. The adamantium was forged into a new skeleton for the true object of Genesis's recruitment: Wolverine, whose own admanatium had been stripped from his body.

POWERS/WEAPONS
- Adamantium-laced skin
- Retractable adamantium claws—one laced with a hallucinogenic, the other, a deadly neurotoxin

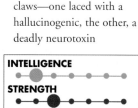

INTELLIGENCE
STRENGTH
SPEED
DURABILITY
ENERGY PROJECTION
FIGHTING SKILLS

EMPLATE

Real Name: Marius St. Croix
First Appearance: *Generation X #1* (1994)

Height: 6'3"
Weight: Unrevealed

The Algerian-born Marius St. Croix is the brother of <u>M</u>. After Marius turned to the study of dark magicks in the hope of gaining enough power to one day rule the world, his siblings banished him to another dimension. During his long years of imprisonment, Emplate learned he was a mutant when his powers manifested themselves in the form of a need to feed on the bone marrow of other mutants to live. Taken to terrorizing his sister and her friends for fresh food, Emplate has escaped to his previous pocket dimension to continue his quasi-vampiric lifestyle.

POWERS/WEAPONS
- Feeds on the bone marrow of mutants to remain in this physical plane
- Can transform others into a creature like himself

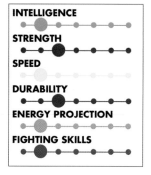

INTELLIGENCE
STRENGTH
SPEED
DURABILITY
ENERGY PROJECTION
FIGHTING SKILLS

POWERS/WEAPONS

- Misdirection
- Teleportation
- Superhuman strength, reflexes, durability and stamina

INTELLIGENCE

STRENGTH

SPEED

DURABILITY

ENERGY PROJECTION

FIGHTING SKILLS

Real Name: Jean-Phillipe (full name unrevealed)

First Appearance: *New X-Men* #128 (2002)

Height: 5'9"
Weight: 174 lbs

He is a living weapon created by the enigmatic Weapon Plus program. Infused with nano-<u>Sentinel</u> technology and artificially evolved through a thousand generations in the space of a year, Fantomex was dubbed Weapon XIII. Injured when a train carrying himself and Weapon XII crashed in the Chunnel, Fantomex sought sanctuary at the Paris headquarters of the <u>X-Corporation</u>. Leading <u>Professor X</u> and <u>Jean Grey</u> back to the Chunnel to help him stop the threat posed by Weapon XII, Fantomex activated a remote detonator and killed Weapon XII instantly.

FANTOMEX

POWERS/WEAPONS

- Ability to drain the life force of other organic beings to open portals that cross both time and space

INTELLIGENCE

STRENGTH

SPEED

DURABILITY

ENERGY PROJECTION

FIGHTING SKILLS

Real Name: Trevor Fitzroy
First Appearance: *Uncanny X-Men* #281 (1991)

Height: 6'2"
Weight: 170 lbs

A native of the same war-torn future as <u>Bishop</u>, Trevor Fitzroy was imprisoned after using his powers to embark on a life of crime. He escaped with nearly one hundred convicts, who followed him back in time to our present, where they were all tracked down and executed by Bishop; only Trevor escaped. While on the loose, he slew the <u>Hellions</u>. The <u>X-Men</u>'s intervention prevented him from killing <u>Emma Frost</u> as well. Years later, Trevor met up with Bishop one last time. Attempting to escape, he was held fast by Bishop; as his portal collapsed, Trevor was severed in two.

TREVOR FITZROY

POWERS/WEAPONS

- Superhuman telepath
- Possesses the ability to manipulate the thoughts and actions of others

INTELLIGENCE

STRENGTH

SPEED

DURABILITY

ENERGY PROJECTION

FIGHTING SKILLS

Real Name: Unrevealed
First Appearance: *Uncanny X-Men* #283 (1991)

Height: 5'9"
Weight: 157 lbs

The Gamesmaster's mutant ability to read the minds of every sentient being on the planet emerged at an early age, profoundly affecting his sanity. At some point, the Gamesmaster was contacted by the immortal sorceress <u>Selene</u>, then Black Queen of the <u>Hellfire Club</u>, to join the Upstarts, a group of wealthy and powerful individuals banded together for the sole purpose of killing mutants to earn points in a twisted game. He agreed, if only to provide a distraction from the constant chatter of the billion-plus voices in his mind.

GAMESMASTER

GENESIS

Real Name: Tyler Dayspring
First Appearance: *Cable #18 (1994)*

Height: 6'1"
Weight: 225 lbs

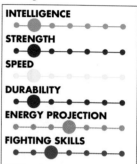

The son of <u>Nathan Summers</u> in a far-flung alternate future in which <u>Apocalypse</u> had succeeded in taking over the world, Genesis traveled back to our present following the death of Apocalypse and set out to usurp the mutant warlord's power for himself. Deciding to enlist <u>Wolverine</u>, Genesis captured the X-Man, whose adamantium had been forcibly removed from his body by <u>Magneto</u>. Genesis attempted to re-outfit Wolverine with the adamantium he had stripped from <u>Cyber</u>'s flesh, but Wolverine rejected the bonding process and killed Genesis in a feral rage.

POWERS/WEAPONS
- Ability to forge a psionic link with another consciousness and project its memories as psi-plasmic holograms

INTELLIGENCE
STRENGTH
SPEED
DURABILITY
ENERGY PROJECTION
FIGHTING SKILLS

GOBLIN QUEEN

Real Name: Madelyne Jennifer Pryor-Summers
First Appearance: *Uncanny X-Men #168 (1983)*

Height: 5'8"
Weight: 143 lbs

<u>Mr. Sinister</u> created Madelyne Pryor, the clone of <u>Jean Grey</u>, to seduce <u>Cyclops</u> and bear a child who would possess the genetic potential of both Jean and Cyclops—something Mr. Sinister had long sought for his own personal gain. Though Sinister's plans came to pass, Madelyne grew too insane to control and tried to kill herself and her child, <u>Nathan Summers</u>, to take revenge on Cyclops, who had left her to reunite with Jean. Joining <u>N'astirh</u> in his demon invasion of New York, Madelyne died fighting the <u>X-Men</u>.

POWERS/WEAPONS
- Telepathy
- Telekinesis
- Flight

INTELLIGENCE
STRENGTH
SPEED
DURABILITY
ENERGY PROJECTION
FIGHTING SKILLS

HENRY GYRICH

Real Name: Henry Peter Gyrich
First Appearance: *Avengers #165 (1977)*

Height: 6'8"
Weight: 225 lbs.

Federal Agent Henry Gyrich has devoted his career to cracking down on the national and international threats presented by the rise of mutants. In one of his first high-profile acts, the mutant-hating agent was appointed by the National Security Council to investigate unofficial reports of irregularities in the operations of the Avengers, Earth's mightiest heroes. He later went on to consult on Project Wideawake, a covert government commission created to deal with the problems posed by the growing number of mutants in America. Next, Gyrich was a key player in <u>Bastion</u>'s anti-mutant strike force Operation: Zero Tolerance—until he became a target of the <u>Sentinels</u> himself and ordered the corrupt operation closed down.

POWERS/WEAPONS

- Mother and fetus allow individuals to undergo destruction and subsequent rebirth that results in either healing or death

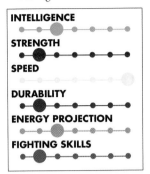

INTELLIGENCE

STRENGTH

SPEED

DURABILITY

ENERGY PROJECTION

FIGHTING SKILLS

Real Name: Radha Dastoor
First Appearance: *X-Factor* #96 (1993)

Height: 6'
Weight: 151 lbs

Convinced the mutant fetus growing inside her signaled the coming of a golden age that would see humans and mutants evolve into one race, Radha Dastoor set out to initiate the Great Destruction foretold in her best-selling books. Haven used her supporters to fan the flames of political unrest by inciting riots and wars in an alarming number of countries. Her actions caught the attention of the **Adversary**, who possessed Haven's fetus and caused it to grow to term. Haven died in childbirth, unleashing the threat of the Adversary into the world once more.

HAVEN

POWERS/WEAPONS

- Protective suit of crystallized-hafnium armor
- Highly evolved brain advanced to the upper limit of human potential

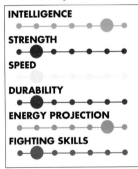

INTELLIGENCE

STRENGTH

SPEED

DURABILITY

ENERGY PROJECTION

FIGHTING SKILLS

Real Name: Herbert Edgar Wyndham
First Appearance: *Thor* #134 (1966)

Height: 6'2"
Weight: 200 lbs

Beginning life as Herbert Wyndham, an Oxford University student in the 1930s, the High Evolutionary first built a machine capable of accelerating the genetic evolution of living organisms thanks to information provided by **Mr. Sinister**. When his experiments provoked anger and hostility in his peers, Wyndham built his own research facility on Wundagore Mountain in Transia. He continues to master the art of changing the structure of living things to suit his whims, as well as engaging in engineering projects to create his tools of mutation.

HIGH EVOLUTIONARY

POWERS/WEAPONS

- Enhanced strength
- Flight via boot jets

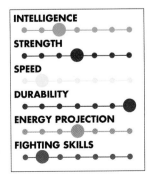

INTELLIGENCE

STRENGTH

SPEED

DURABILITY

ENERGY PROJECTION

FIGHTING SKILLS

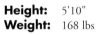

Real Name: Cameron Hodge
First Appearance: *X-Factor* #1 (1986)

Height: 5'10"
Weight: 168 lbs

Insanely jealous of overprivileged college roommate Warren Worthington III (**Archangel**), Cameron Hodge came to believe mutants were a threat to humanity. Hodge secretly plotted against Worthington, arranging to have his damaged wings amputated. When Hodge killed Archangel's fiancée, the hero beheaded him in a blind rage. Thanks to a deal he had struck with **N'astirh**, Hodge survived. He resurfaced as a head attached to a mechanical, spider-like body, and convinced others to join him in the **Phalanx**. Hodge was killed when the Phalanx's base self-destructed.

CAMERON HODGE

STEVIE HUNTER

| **Real Name:** | Stevie Hunter | **Height:** | 5'9" |
| **First Appearance:** | *X-Men* #139 (1980) | **Weight:** | 121 lbs. |

Once a talented ballet dancer, Stevie Hunter saw her career cut short by an unfortunate accident that badly injured her knee. Stevie eventually established Ms. Hunter's Dance Academy in Salem Center, New York. After <u>Shadowcat</u> began taking lessons at the school, she and Stevie became close friends. Although initially frightened by the dangerous life Shadowcat's <u>X-Men</u> friends led, Stevie stuck by Shadowcat and came to join the staff of the <u>Xavier Institute</u> as the physical trainer and therapist for both the X-Men and the <u>New Mutants</u>. Eventually, Stevie returned to her true passion and resumed teaching dance at her studio in Salem Center.

CHARLOTTE JONES

| **Real Name:** | Charlotte Jones | **Height:** | 5'7" |
| **First Appearance:** | *X-Factor* #51 (1990) | **Weight:** | 129 lbs |

Once a trauma nurse at a Brooklyn hospital and the wife of a police officer, Charlotte Jones became a police officer herself after a stray bullet killed her husband and paralyzed her son, Tommy. Charlotte, who was eventually promoted to detective, remains a steadfast ally and supporter of the <u>X-Men</u>, whom she first encountered when <u>Archangel</u> saved her life. For a time, the two were also romantically involved. When <u>Sentinels</u> from <u>Bastion</u>'s government-sponsored anti-mutant strike force Operation: Zero Tolerance abducted her son to force her to betray <u>Iceman</u> and <u>Cecilia Reyes</u>, Charlotte had no choice but to give up the pair. Fortunately, members of the X-Men rescued Tommy shortly before OZT was shut down. More recently, Charlotte called in the X-Men to help investigate the murders perpetrated by <u>Maximus Lobo</u>.

KA-ZAR

| **Real Name:** | Kevin Plunder | **Height:** | 6'2" |
| **First Appearance:** | *X-Men* #10 (1965) | **Weight:** | 215 lbs |

The second son of a British nobleman and scientist, Ka-Zar has called the Savage Land home for most of his life. After his father's murder, Ka-Zar was raised by Zabu, the last survivor of a species of saber-toothed tiger hunted to near extinction, and learned the ways of the flora and fauna of the entire hidden jungle; he came to think and act like a savage. He later regained his knowledge of his British upbringing, and met and married American explorer Shanna O'Hara. Ka-Zar and Shanna have often aided the <u>X-Men</u> in their exploits in the Savage Land.

POWERS/WEAPONS

• Natural athletic, hunting, foraging, survival, and combative abilities that have been honed to the peak of human perfection

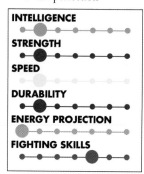

INTELLIGENCE
STRENGTH
SPEED
DURABILITY
ENERGY PROJECTION
FIGHTING SKILLS

POWERS/WEAPONS

- Master strategist
- Highly skilled in many forms of armed and unarmed combat

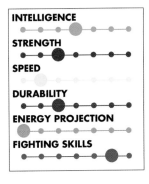

INTELLIGENCE

STRENGTH

SPEED

DURABILITY

ENERGY PROJECTION

FIGHTING SKILLS

Real Name: Unrevealed
First Appearance: *X-Treme X-Men* #10 (2002)

Height: 6'1"
Weight: 352 lbs

Khan rules a vast empire that has mercilessly conquered alternate Earths in multiple dimensions. When Khan led an assault team to the Earth inhabited by the X-Men as part of his invasion force, the powerful mutants captured him. During his captivity, Khan became infatuated with Storm. After his lieutenant rescued him, Khan kidnapped the object of his desire, swearing to make her his queen. Storm rejected him and escaped. To stave off the invasion, the X-Men focused their powers in an attack on Khan's ship, destroying it and the portal that gave Khan's armies access to Earth.

KHAN

POWERS/WEAPONS

- Ability to siphon off other mutants' energies

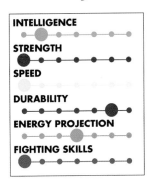

INTELLIGENCE

STRENGTH

SPEED

DURABILITY

ENERGY PROJECTION

FIGHTING SKILLS

Real Name: Krakoa
First Appearance: *Giant-Size X-Men* #1 (1975)

Height: Variable
Weight: Variable

Following the test detonation of an atomic bomb in the South Pacific, the irradiated components of the tropical island Krakoa became linked into a collective consciousness. The X-Men learned of Krakoa's existence but did not realize the island itself was the mutant when they arrived to investigate. Krakoa captured them and siphoned off their energies. Krakoa's end finally came when Polaris directed a magnetic bolt to the center of the Earth, severing the planet's primary lines of magnetic force. Krakoa was flung into space, where it apparently died.

KRAKOA

POWERS/WEAPONS

- Psionic ability to cast illusions, causing people to see, hear, touch, smell, or taste things which do not actually exist

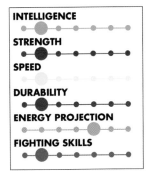

INTELLIGENCE

STRENGTH

SPEED

DURABILITY

ENERGY PROJECTION

FIGHTING SKILLS

Real Name: Regan Wyngarde
First Appearance: *X-Treme X-Men* #6 (2001)

Height: 5'10"
Weight: 147 lbs

The daughter of the powerful mutant Mastermind, Lady Mastermind took employ with Sebastian Shaw, agreeing to help him exact revenge on Sage for her years of betrayal. Lady Mastermind trapped Sage in a series of illusions designed to bind her mentally and emotionally to Shaw once again. But Sage managed to summon Lifeguard, who diverted Lady Mastermind long enough for Sage to exact her own revenge. Turning Lady Mastermind's powers against her, Sage shattered her psyche.

LADY MASTERMIND

LEGION

Real Name: David Charles Haller
First Appearance: *New Mutants* #25 (1985)

Height: 5'9"
Weight: 130 lbs

By the time **Professor X** learned of his son with Gabrielle Haller, the teenage boy had been overtaken by multiple personalities. Though the **New Mutants** were able to stabilize Legion's psyche, his mind was that of a 10-year-old boy. Naively thinking he was helping his father, Legion traveled back in time to kill **Magneto**. Legion ended up killing his father instead when Professor X selflessly dove in front of Magneto to save his life. **Bishop** traveled back in time to prevent the murder, and Legion died as a result of the energies unleashed during the encounter.

POWERS/WEAPONS
- Telepathy
- Ability to absorb the consciousness of others
- Telekinesis
- Psionic ability to start fires

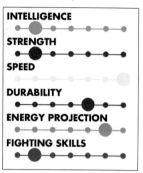

LIVING MONOLITH

Real Name: Ahmet Abdol
First Appearance: *X-Men* #54 (1969)

Height: 5'11"
Weight: 184 lbs

After determining the abilities of Alex Summers (**Havok**) canceled out his own, archaeology professor Ahmet Abdol kidnapped him and blocked cosmic rays from reaching his body. Now able to absorb more radiation than usual, Abdol grew into a 33-foot-tall giant with vast power. After the **X-Men** freed Havok, the Living Monolith reverted to normal and escaped. Through the years, Abdol continued to alternate between forms until **Apocalypse** tried to make him a conduit for absorbing the powers of other mutants. The Monolith went on a rampage that was stopped only through the efforts of **Bishop**.

POWERS/WEAPONS
- Ability to absorb cosmic radiation to increase his size, mass, strength, and resistance to physical injury

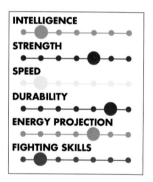

MAXIMUS LOBO

Real Name: Maximus Lobo
First Appearance: *Uncanny X-Men* #417 (2003)

Height: 6'4"
Weight: 240 lbs

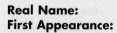

Maximus Lobo headed Lobo Technologies, a division of Worthington Enterprises owned by **Archangel**. Lobo decided he would no longer wait patiently for mankind to become extinct and led other mutants like himself to slaughter a group of humans. Called in by **Charlotte Jones** to help investigate the murders, the **X-Men** tracked the attacker's scent to Lobo Tech. While attempting to escape, Lobo set fire to the fuel tanks in the Lobo Tech warehouse, which destroyed the facility in a massive explosion. The X-Men survived, but Lobo's fate is unknown.

POWERS/WEAPONS
- Ability to transform himself into a humanoid wolf-like form

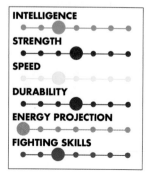

POWERS/WEAPONS

- Sorceress
- Teleportation via stepping discs

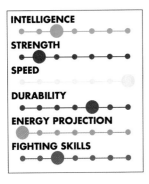

INTELLIGENCE

STRENGTH

SPEED

DURABILITY

ENERGY PROJECTION

FIGHTING SKILLS

Real Name: Jimaine Szardos; Amanda Sefton (alias)

First Appearance: *X-Men* #98 (1976)

Height: 5'6"
Weight: 125 lbs

Daughter of the Gypsy sorceress <u>Margali Szardos</u>, Jimaine Szardos grew up alongside <u>Nightcrawler</u>, whom her sympathetic mother had adopted. The two fell in love, only to be separated once Nightcrawler joined the <u>X-Men</u>. Jimaine rekindled her relationship with Nightcrawler after she helped convince Margali of Kurt's innocence in the death of her brother Stefan, but the two ultimately parted as just friends. After continuing her study of sorcery, Jimaine became the Mistress of Limbo, taking on the name Magik in honor of Illyana Rasputin (<u>Magik</u>).

MAGIK II

POWERS/WEAPONS

- Psionic ability to cast illusions, causing people to see, hear, touch, smell, or taste things which do not actually exist

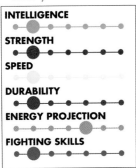

INTELLIGENCE

STRENGTH

SPEED

DURABILITY

ENERGY PROJECTION

FIGHTING SKILLS

Real Name: Martinique Jason
First Appearance: *Wolverine/Gambit: Victims* #2 (1995)

Height: 5'10"
Weight: 143 lbs

Martinique Jason is the daughter of the original mutant <u>Mastermind</u>. During her stint with the <u>Brotherhood of Evil Mutants</u>, Martinique was rendered comatose in a struggle with the <u>X-Men</u>. Later liberated by <u>Multiple Man</u>, she remained in a coma while <u>Banshee</u> used her powers to control the minds of former villains serving in his paramilitary X-Corps. But Martinique awakened, and conspired with <u>Mystique</u> to seize control of X-Corps' assets and unleash chaos across Europe. When Mystique was defeated by <u>Abyss</u>, Martinique fled.

MASTERMIND II

POWERS/WEAPONS

- Ability to absorb kinetic energy
- Weapon X augmentation that greatly retarded his aging process

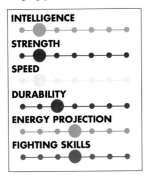

INTELLIGENCE

STRENGTH

SPEED

DURABILITY

ENERGY PROJECTION

FIGHTING SKILLS

Real Name: Christoph Nord
First Appearance: *X-Men* #5 (1992)

Height: 6'3"
Weight: 230 lbs

Born in East Germany, Maverick opposed the Communist regime and became a freedom fighter for the West Germans. So devout were his beliefs that Maverick killed his own brother, who had sworn allegiance to the East Germans, in battle. He later joined the <u>Weapon X</u> program, serving alongside <u>Sabretooth</u>, <u>Wolverine</u>, and <u>John Wraith</u>. Weapon X eventually decided Maverick had outlived his usefulness, and he was seemingly killed by Sabretooth after rejecting an offer to rejoin the program.

MAVERICK

MEGGAN

| Real Name: | Meggan Braddock | Height: | 5'7" |
| First Appearance: | *Mighty World of Marvel* #7 (1983) | Weight: | 128 lbs |

POWERS/WEAPONS
- Shapeshifting
- Flight

Manifesting her powers at birth, Meggan instinctively sprouted fur as a response to the cold. She later began reacting subconsciously to the suspicions and fears of those around her, growing wings, fangs, and talons. Rescued by **Captain Britain**, Meggan began to develop feelings for the hero, but they went unrequited. Realizing that she was an empathic metamorph, Megan synchronized herself with Captain Britain's desires and transformed herself into a stunning young woman. After years as members of Britain's premier super-team, Excalibur, the two eventually retired and were wed.

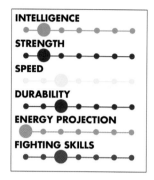

INTELLIGENCE

STRENGTH

SPEED

DURABILITY

ENERGY PROJECTION

FIGHTING SKILLS

IRENE MERRYWEATHER

| Real Name: | Irene Merryweather | Height: | 5'10" |
| First Appearance: | *Cable* #48 (1997) | Weight: | 146 lbs |

Journalist Irene Merryweather wanted more from life than the drudgery of reporting for the tabloid *The Inquiring Eye*—especially with the reputable *Daily Bugle* newspaper right next door. Irene decided to take charge of her career and report on something that really mattered: an exposé of **Sebastian Shaw**. After she got too close to revealing Shaw's true identity and actions, **Nathan Summers** rescued Irene from Shaw's clutches, and their ongoing friendship began. Her tenacity and hard work paid off when the Bugle took notice and hired Irene as a staff writer.

MOJO

| Real Name: | Mojo | Height: | 6'9" |
| First Appearance: | *Longshot* #2 (1985) | Weight: | 512 lbs |

Absolute ruler of the other dimensional Mojoworld, Mojo uses television as a means to dominate the populace. In his quest to create over-the-top programming for his entertainment-addicted citizens, he has often captured unwitting **X-Men** and forced them to serve as actors in his bizarre productions. Operating on the lunatic fringe of the creative spirit, Mojo places no boundaries on his imagination or the lengths to which he'll go to achieve his vision.

POWERS/WEAPONS
- Superhuman strength
- "Anti-lifeforce" which causes death and decay to whatever or whomever he touches

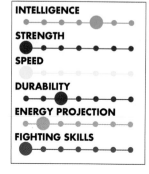

INTELLIGENCE

STRENGTH

SPEED

DURABILITY

ENERGY PROJECTION

FIGHTING SKILLS

POWERS/WEAPONS

- Flight
- Ability to shape change
- Can transform human beings into demonic creatures with his touch

INTELLIGENCE

STRENGTH

SPEED

DURABILITY

ENERGY PROJECTION

FIGHTING SKILLS

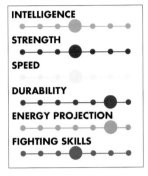

Real Name: N'astirh
First Appearance: *X-Factor* #32 (1988)

Height: Variable
Weight: Variable

N'astirh is a demon from the extra-dimensional realm of Limbo. N'astirh wanted to study sorcery under **Belasco**, ruler of Limbo, but was passed over in favor **Magik**. As a result, N'astirh stole Belasco's book of spells and fled Limbo to teach himself. After **S'ym** rose to power in Limbo, N'astirh returned to aid him in a demonic invasion of New York, intending to betray S'ym and take control of the Earth himself. Having unleashed Madelyn Pryor's full potential as the **Goblin Queen**, N'astirh fell afoul of the **X-Men**, whose combined attack caused him to explode.

N'ASTIRH

POWERS/WEAPONS

- Master ninja and martial artist possessing mystical abilities

INTELLIGENCE

STRENGTH

SPEED

DURABILITY

ENERGY PROJECTION

FIGHTING SKILLS

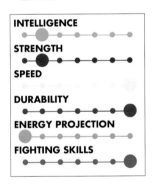

Real Name: Ogun (full name unrevealed)
First Appearance: *Kitty Pryde & Wolverine* #2 (1984)

Height: 5'9"
Weight: 146 lbs

Once **Wolverine**'s teacher, Ogun kidnapped and hypnotized **Shadowcat**, trained her in the martial arts and sent her to kill his former pupil; only the shock of the battle snapped her out of the spell. Wolverine then slew Ogun, who later returned in spirit form by possessing others' bodies, determined to kill Wolverine. After ultimately possessing **Viper**, Ogun tried to jump into Wolverine, but the X-Man's mind was too bestial and fragmented, and Ogun was driven back into Viper. Only by severely wounding Viper was Wolverine able to exorcise Ogun.

OGUN

POWERS/WEAPONS

- Secretes a lethal airborne toxin
- Arms are implanted with carbonadium tentacles

INTELLIGENCE

STRENGTH

SPEED

DURABILITY

ENERGY PROJECTION

FIGHTING SKILLS

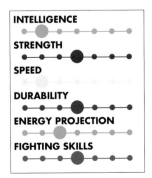

Real Name: Arkady Rossovich
First Appearance: *X-Men* #4 (1992)

Height: 6'11"
Weight: 425 lbs

Serial killer Arkady Rossovich was transformed into a state-of-the-art super-soldier by the KGB, but Omega Red could not control his abilities and was placed into suspended animation. Recovered by agents of the ninja clan known as the Hand, Omega Red clashed repeatedly with the **X-Men** and **Wolverine**. Later, he was recruited by **Sabretooth** to attack the friends and family of Wolverine alongside **Lady Deathstrike**. The two crippled **Yukio** before being abandoned by Sabretooth.

OMEGA RED

PENANCE

| **Real Name:** | Various |
| **First Appearance:** | *Generation X* #1 (1994) |

| **Height:** | 5'5" |
| **Weight:** | 130 lbs |

POWERS/WEAPONS
- Super-dense molecular structure that renders every edge of her body sharp enough to cut through stone

Penance is a spirit form of magical origin that acts as a physical and mental prison for other sentient beings. After Monet St. Croix (**M**) angered her brother, **Emplate**, he used sorcery to trap her in the form of Penance. Monet eventually escaped, and Penance took hold of Monet's twin sisters, Claudette and Nicole, merging them into one entity. Ultimately, the twins were freed, and Penance was believed to be nothing more than an empty shell. However, it appears a third victim has since been trapped in the form of Penance—possibly Marius St. Croix.

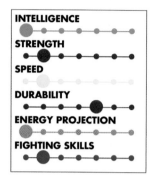

INTELLIGENCE

STRENGTH

SPEED

DURABILITY

ENERGY PROJECTION

FIGHTING SKILLS

PROTEUS

| **Real Name:** | Kevin MacTaggert |
| **First Appearance:** | *X-Men* #104 (1977) |

| **Height:** | Variable |
| **Weight:** | Variable |

POWERS/WEAPONS
- Psionic ability to manipulate and alter reality
- Telepathy

Proteus, son of **Moira MacTaggert**, manifested his dangerous mutant powers as a young boy. Moira was forced to imprison him in a specially designed cell while she worked to find a cure. Years later, he broke free. Forced to possess others to sustain himself, he made his way to Edinburgh to take possession of his father, Joseph MacTaggert. Proteus fought the **X-Men** while distorting reality throughout the city, and his tremendous outpouring of energy destroyed his father's body. When **Colossus** smashed his fists into Proteus' energy form, the resulting explosion temporarily dispersed his energies.

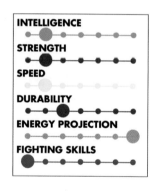

INTELLIGENCE

STRENGTH

SPEED

DURABILITY

ENERGY PROJECTION

FIGHTING SKILLS

ROMA

| **Real Name:** | Roma |
| **First Appearance:** | *Captain Britain* #1 (1976) |

| **Height:** | 6'3" |
| **Weight:** | 175 lbs |

POWERS/WEAPONS
- Master sorceress

Roma and her immortal father Merlin decreed that Brian Braddock should be Britain's champion, empowering him to become **Captain Britain**. Roma and Merlin together served as Captain Britain's patrons and advisors until years later, when Merlin seemingly died after waging an intense mystical struggle against evil forces. Roma succeeded him as the guardian of Otherworld. When a sentient computer captured Roma and tried to lay waste to Otherworld, Captain Britain helped her defeat the aggressor.

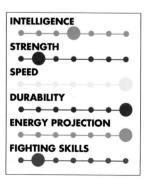

INTELLIGENCE

STRENGTH

SPEED

DURABILITY

ENERGY PROJECTION

FIGHTING SKILLS

POWERS/WEAPONS

- Strong telepathic powers
- Manipulation of the astral plane

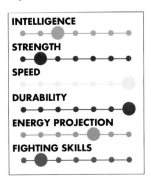

INTELLIGENCE

STRENGTH

SPEED

DURABILITY

ENERGY PROJECTION

FIGHTING SKILLS

Real Name: Amahl Farouk
First Appearance: *X-Men* #117 (1979)

Height: Variable
Weight: Inapplicable

After a meeting in a Cairo bar with <u>Professor X</u> turned into a battle between their astral forms, Amahl Farouk was defeated by a bolt of psychic force and collapsed dead at the table. Though his body died that day, the Shadow King retained his astral spirit, allowing his consciousness to survive by taking forceful possession of a physical host. From <u>Karma</u> to Professor X's son <u>Legion</u>, whom Farouk used to kill <u>Destiny</u>, the Shadow King has possessed them all, fully aware that a malignant mind is much harder to kill than a warm body.

SHADOW KING

POWERS/WEAPONS

- Genetically engineered to be the perfect warrior

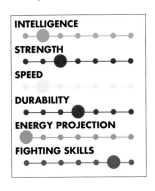

INTELLIGENCE

STRENGTH

SPEED

DURABILITY

ENERGY PROJECTION

FIGHTING SKILLS

Real Name: Gaveedra Seven
First Appearance: *New Mutants* #99 (1991)

Height: 6'3"
Weight: 195 lbs

A bio-engineered being living in the future of the alternate dimension known as the Mojoverse, Shatterstar was created to be a warrior in Mojoworld's televised gladiatorial games. Eventually managing to escape his subjugators and travel back in time, Shatterstar sought help in annihilating his world's leader, <u>Mojo</u>. Although the defeat has yet to come to pass, Shatterstar has proven to be a valuable ally of Earth's mightiest mutant teams. Shatterstar maintains his hope that one day Mojo will be no more.

SHATTERSTAR

POWERS/WEAPONS

- Ability to generate an extremely powerful tachyon energy field, typically focused through his katana sword

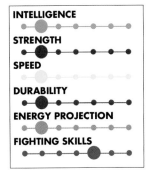

INTELLIGENCE

STRENGTH

SPEED

DURABILITY

ENERGY PROJECTION

FIGHTING SKILLS

Real Name: Keniuchio Harada
First Appearance: *Daredevil* #111 (1974)

Height: 6'6"
Weight: 250 lbs

At an early age, Keniuchio Harada began studying the fighting methods and code of honor of the medieval Japanese samurai. He bound himself to <u>Viper</u>, serving as her bodyguard. The Silver Samurai later struck an uneasy alliance with <u>Wolverine</u> to free private investigator Jessica Drew from the influence of the mystical Black Blade. After the death of his half-sister <u>Mariko Yashida</u>, Harada took over as head of Clan Yashida's business holdings with the aim of ridding it of all criminal ties.

SILVER SAMURAI

SKIDS

| **Real Name:** | Sally Blevins | **Height:** | 5'5" |
| **First Appearance:** | *X-Factor* #7 (1986) | **Weight:** | 115 lbs |

Abused by her stepfather, Skids hit the streets to find a safer life and eventually came to join the Morlocks in their underground tunnels in New York City. It was through the <u>Morlocks</u> that Skids began a close friendship with <u>Rusty Collins</u> and came under the protection of the original team of <u>X-Men</u> (including <u>Cyclops</u> and <u>Jean Grey</u>). But the pair were kidnapped and brainwashed by mutant criminals, eventually joining the <u>Acolytes</u>, in whose service Rusty was killed by Holocaust. Determined to live a normal life after Rusty's death, Skids enrolled in college to study biology.

POWERS/WEAPONS
- Ability to create a force field around her body

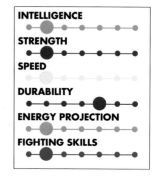

INTELLIGENCE
STRENGTH
SPEED
DURABILITY
ENERGY PROJECTION
FIGHTING SKILLS

SKIN

| **Real Name:** | Angelo Espinosa | **Height:** | 5'7" |
| **First Appearance:** | *Uncanny X-Men* #317 (1994) | **Weight:** | 110 lbs |

This former L.A. gang member faked his own death to leave his ugly past behind. Kidnapped by the <u>Phalanx</u> in an attempt to assimilate him into their collective, Skin was rescued by the <u>X-Men</u> and then invited to join the new Massachusetts Academy branch of the <u>Xavier Institute</u> to train with other young mutants. During this time, Skin was targeted by an armored vigilante who believed Skin to be responsible for the death of Angelo Espinosa, not knowing that the two were one and the same. When the Academy closed, Skin returned to Los Angeles.

POWERS/WEAPONS
- Possesses between four and six feet of extra skin on his body which he can stretch, deform, expand or compress

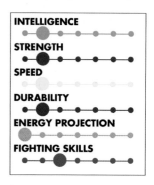

INTELLIGENCE
STRENGTH
SPEED
DURABILITY
ENERGY PROJECTION
FIGHTING SKILLS

SPIRAL

| **Real Name:** | Rita (full name unrevealed) | **Height:** | 5'10" |
| **First Appearance:** | *Longshot* #1 (1985) | **Weight:** | 162 lbs |

Captured by <u>Mojo</u>, stuntwoman Ricochet Rita was transformed by genetic engineering into Spiral, a six-armed, spell-weaving slave. Under Mojo's command, Spiral manipulated the <u>X-Men</u> into participating in TV performances designed to capture huge ratings for Mojo's television-obsessed society. While on assignment on Earth, Spiral created the Body Shoppe, where she used genetics and magic to transform people into cyborgs, including <u>Cole, Macon & Reese</u> and <u>Lady Deathstrike</u>. Later, Spiral provided <u>Psylocke</u> with a pair of bionic eyes that doubled as cameras projecting a live feed of the X-Men's exploits to Mojoworld.

POWERS/WEAPONS
- Four extra arms, one of which is constructed entirely from an unknown metal
- Sorcery

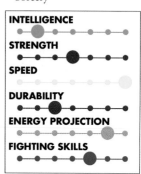

INTELLIGENCE
STRENGTH
SPEED
DURABILITY
ENERGY PROJECTION
FIGHTING SKILLS

POWERS/WEAPONS

- Telekinesis

INTELLIGENCE	
STRENGTH	
SPEED	
DURABILITY	
ENERGY PROJECTION	
FIGHTING SKILLS	

| **Real Name:** | Stryfe | **Height:** | 6'8" |
| **First Appearance:** | *New Mutants* #86 (1990) | **Weight:** | 350 lbs |

The clone of Nathan Summers in one possible future, Stryfe's burgeoning arrogance and cruelty received encouragement from his adoptive father Apocalypse, and he saw destruction as a means to validate his life. Following his nemesis Nathan into the present, Stryfe unleashed the Legacy Virus, a terminal disease targeting mutants. In a final bid to wipe out humanity, he attempted to release an ancient evil—but when Nathan forced him to relive his victims' pain, he sought to atone for his actions by containing the evil's power inside himself and was consumed by its energies.

STRYFE

POWERS/WEAPONS

- Ability to project blasts of concussive force

INTELLIGENCE	
STRENGTH	
SPEED	
DURABILITY	
ENERGY PROJECTION	
FIGHTING SKILLS	

| **Real Name:** | Unrevealed | **Height:** | 6'7" |
| **First Appearance:** | *Uncanny X-Men* #400 (2001) | **Weight:** | 231 lbs |

The Supreme Pontiff is the leader of the Church of Humanity, a mutant-hating organization of religious fanatics. He was born centuries ago and began his lifelong hatred of non-humans after a demon summoned by his occult-practicing parents killed his father. Working to destroy the mutant scourge, the Supreme Pontiff compelled his soldiers to slaughter the staff and clients of the mutant brothel X-Ranch. By the time the X-Men arrived on the scene, they could save only Stacy X—the soldiers had incinerated everyone else inside.

SUPREME PONTIFF

POWERS/WEAPONS

- Demonically-derived incredible strength
- Razor-sharp teeth and claws

INTELLIGENCE	
STRENGTH	
SPEED	
DURABILITY	
ENERGY PROJECTION	
FIGHTING SKILLS	

| **Real Name:** | S'ym | **Height:** | Variable |
| **First Appearance:** | *Uncanny X-Men* #160 (1982) | **Weight:** | Variable |

The demon S'ym served as the enforcer for the sorcerer Belasco, ruler of Limbo, but always hoped to take the reins of power for himself one day. When Warlock's father pursued the New Mutants through Limbo, he infected S'ym with the transmode virus, which vastly augmented his powers. S'ym led an assault against Magik, who fled to Earth and left S'ym to rule. S'ym then sought to gain control of Earth as well. Magik was forced to sacrifice her power and reconfigure Limbo as if she had never been there. Her action removed S'ym and all of his followers from Earth.

S'YM

SYNCH

| **Real Name:** | Everett Thomas | **Height:** | 5'11" |
| **First Appearance:** | *X-Men* #36 (1994) | **Weight:** | 165 lbs |

After straight-A student Everett Thomas was kidnapped from his home in St. Louis by the Phalanx, Jubilee and Banshee rescued him. Once freed, Synch joined other young mutants studying at the newly reopened Massachusetts Academy. The students came under attack from Emplate, who transformed Synch into a creature forced to feed on the bone marrow of mutants for survival. Husk, M, and Jubilee saved him from that fate, but Synch was later killed by a bomb set by Emma Frost's revenge-seeking sister.

POWERS/WEAPONS
• Ability to duplicate the powers and abilities of other superhuman mutants in his vicinity

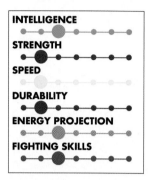

MARGALI SZARDOS

| **Real Name:** | Margali Szardos | **Height:** | 6'4" |
| **First Appearance:** | *X-Men Annual* #4 (1980) | **Weight:** | 162 lbs |

Gypsy Margali Szardos raised her son Stefan, daughter Jimaine (Magik II), and the orphaned mutant Kurt Wagner (Nightcrawler) while pretending to be a simple fortune-teller in a small Bavarian circus. Stefan left to make his own way in life, but went mad and killed two children. When he confronted Stefan, Nightcrawler accidentally killed him. Blaming Nightcrawler for her son's death, Margali used sought revenge, but Jimaine helped him convince Margali of his innocence. Margali later dedicated her vast powers to combat those who would employ magic for evil purposes.

POWERS/WEAPONS
• Phenomenal magical ability

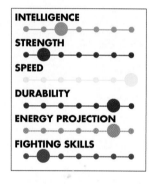

TRISH TILBY

| **Real Name:** | Patricia Tilbert | **Height:** | 5'6" |
| **First Appearance:** | *X-Factor* #7 (1986) | **Weight:** | 119 lbs |

TV reporter Trish Tilby sought to uncover the truth about Beast, who was posing as a mutant hunter along with the founding members of the X-Men, in order to secretly contact mutants and train them in the use of their powers. In the course of her investigation the two developed an on-again, off-again romance that lasted for years. But Trish ended their relationship after Beast's further mutation gave him a more lion-like appearance. When they next encountered each other, Beast, still hurt by their breakup, lashed out at Trish by telling her that he thought he might be gay.

POWERS/WEAPONS

- Teleportation

INTELLIGENCE

STRENGTH

SPEED

DURABILITY

ENERGY PROJECTION

FIGHTING SKILLS

Real Name: Telford Porter
First Appearance: *X-Men* #2 (1963)

Height: 5'5"
Weight: 175 lbs

The Vanisher first gained the X-Men's attention when he used his powers to steal top-secret defense plans, demanding ten million dollars for their return. He later joined the subversive organization Factor Three, which was intent on world domination, but the X-Men prevented their efforts to bring about a nuclear holocaust. Eventually, the Vanisher took control of a drug cartel responsible for manufacturing and shipping a drug that gave superhuman powers. While he was kept occupied by the pheromone-controlling Stacy X, Archangel bought out and dismantled the cartel.

VANISHER

POWERS/WEAPONS

- Enhanced strength, endurance, and agility
- Master swordsman

INTELLIGENCE

STRENGTH

SPEED

DURABILITY

ENERGY PROJECTION

FIGHTING SKILLS

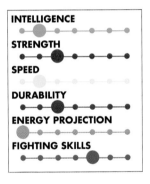

Real Name: Vargas (full name unrevealed)
First Appearance: *X-Treme X-Men* #1 (2001)

Height: 6'3"
Weight: 222 lbs

Vargas claims to be the ultimate expression of evolutionary potential. As such, he sought to kill all mutants, seeing them as having no place in the world. Encountering Beast and Psylocke, Vargas beat Beast to the brink of death and killed Psylocke. Later Vargas grievously wounded both Gambit and Rogue. In the ensuing battle, Rogue defeated him, and stood poised to plunge his own sword into his chest. Rogue realized that such actions would make her no better than him and instead left Vargas conquered and bloodied.

VARGAS

POWERS/WEAPONS

- Brilliant and cunning criminal strategist

INTELLIGENCE

STRENGTH

SPEED

DURABILITY

ENERGY PROJECTION

FIGHTING SKILLS

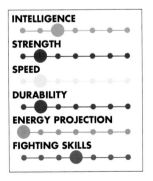

Real Name: Unrevealed
First Appearance: *Captain America* #110 (1969)

Height: 5'9"
Weight: 141 lbs

Viper climbed to the highest levels of international espionage early in her career, and was eventually recruited by the terrorist organization Hydra. After a short time, she seized control of Hydra's New York operations. Viper later created her own international organization, which became an active force in crime, espionage, and terrorism. Looking for a more permanent residence, Viper went on to seize the throne of Madripoor, a favorite haunt of Wolverine, taking control of all activities—both legal and illegal—on the Southeast Asian island-nation.

VIPER

PETE WISDOM

Real Name: Peter Winston Paul Wisdom
First Appearance: *Excalibur* #86 (1995)

Height: 5'9"
Weight: 158 lbs

Pete Wisdom was a field agent for the British government organization Black Air, a secretive group that conducted clandestine research and investigation of supernatural phenomena, before he joined <u>Captain Britain</u> and Excalibur, a team of mutants based in Great Britain. While there, he enjoyed a brief but intense relationship with <u>Shadowcat</u>, who ultimately broke it off due to their significant age difference. He left the team shortly afterward, later reappearing as a mentor to the mutant strike force founded by <u>Nathan Summers</u>—but Pete faked his own death to allow the team to find its own path.

POWERS/WEAPONS
• Generates "hot knives," blade-shaped darts of thermal energy from his fingertips

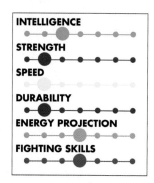

JOHN WRAITH

Real Name: John Carlisle (presumed, possibly an alias)
First Appearance: *Wolverine* #60 (1992)

Height: 6'1"
Weight: 175 lbs

An agent of the <u>Weapon X</u> project, John Wraith was a member of Team X, a secret covert operations unit formed in conjunction with the CIA. The team disbanded years later, but John reformed Team X after Weapon X targeted its members for termination. Tracking down a lead to a secret island base, Team X discovered a man named Aldo Ferro had implanted them with false memories during their time with the project. Ferro was killed in the ensuing battle. When John later refused to join a revived Weapon X program, <u>Sabretooth</u> killed him at the <u>Director</u>'s behest.

POWERS/WEAPONS
• Ability to instantaneously teleport himself from one location to another

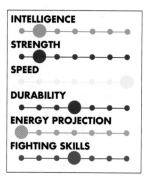

X-MAN

Real Name: Nate Grey
First Appearance: *X-Man* #1 (1995)

Height: 5'9"
Weight: 171 lbs

In an alternate timeline ruled by <u>Apocalypse</u>, <u>Mr. Sinister</u> created Nate Grey from genetic material from <u>Cyclops</u> and <u>Jean Grey</u>. X-Man eventually escaped to the <u>X-Men</u>'s reality to fully realize the promise of his powers. X-Man became a modern-day mutant shaman, existing to heal and guide all peoples, loving them without question. X-Man fought to protect the planet from the incomprehensible, impossible threats of parallel Earths strung along a spiral from one end of reality to another. It was to save humanity from destruction at the hands of such a threat that X-Man sacrificed himself.

POWERS/WEAPONS
• Vast psionic abilities
• High-level telepath
• Ability to project his astral form across the world
• Create sophisticated illusions

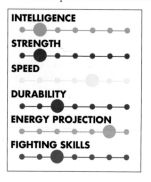

Real Name: Mariko Yashida **Height:** 5'
First Appearance: *X-Men* #118 (1979) **Weight:** 100 lbs

Lady Mariko Yashida fell in love with <u>Wolverine</u> during his stay in Japan; their love grew deeper when Mariko lived for a time in New York. But, torn between her love for Wolverine and her loyalty to her family—despite its criminal affiliations—she chose loyalty over love. After years spent apart, it seemed Mariko and Wolverine finally could share each other's lives along with foster daugher <u>Amiko</u>. But Mariko's attempt to rid her clan of the influence of Japanese organized crime once and for all kept them from reaching that happy ending. After a member of one of Japan's criminal clans poisoned her with blowfish toxin, Mariko, dying painfully in Wolverine's arms, begged her lover to use his claws to end her suffering. Reluctantly, Wolverine did as she asked.

MARIKO YASHIDA

POWERS/WEAPONS

• Expert hand-to-hand combatant

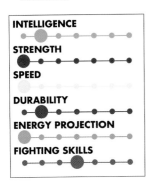

INTELLIGENCE
STRENGTH
SPEED
DURABILITY
ENERGY PROJECTION
FIGHTING SKILLS

Real Name: Yukio (full name unrevealed) **Height:** 5'9"
First Appearance: *Wolverine* #1 (1982) **Weight:** 130 lbs

Expert assassin Yukio fell in love with her quarry <u>Wolverine</u> during his time in Japan. Realizing that his heart belonged to <u>Mariko Yoshida</u>, Yukio settled for his friendship. When Wolverine placed his foster daughter <u>Amiko</u> in Yukio's care, she swore to raise the girl as her own. But Yukio was unable to prevent Amiko's capture at the hands of two of <u>Lady Deathstrike</u> and <u>Omega Red</u>, who left her paralyzed. Unable to bear the thought of living life as a paraplegic, Yukio begged Wolverine to kill her. Wolverine could not bring himself to do as she asked.

YUKIO

POWERS/WEAPONS

• Teleportation
• Healing factor

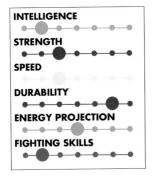

INTELLIGENCE
STRENGTH
SPEED
DURABILITY
ENERGY PROJECTION
FIGHTING SKILLS

Real Name: A.D.A.M. Unit-Zero **Height:** 6'
First Appearance: *New Mutants* #86 (1990) **Weight:** 200 lbs

The android Zero was designed in the post-apocalyptic future from which <u>Nathan Summers</u> hailed to maintain peace on a fragile world. Zero's programming was corrupted by <u>Stryfe</u>, and he was forced to assist Stryfe's team of mutant terrorists. Zero was later attacked by hunter robots pre-programmed by Stryfe before his death to destroy all traces of his presence in the 20th century. Just prior to being destroyed in the detonation of one of Stryfe's bases, Zero suddenly became capable of human emotion when a latent program created by Stryfe activated.

ZERO

ULTIMATE X-MEN

Forty years and thousands of stories later, hundreds of characters, story arcs, and realities—true and alternate—have made the X-Men everything they are … or were.

Change was coming.

In an effort to wipe the slate clean and make all that was great about the X-Men's rich history accessible and relevant to a new generation of readers, a reengineering came about. It was not meant to replace the X-Men of the past, but to reinvent them and tell new stories free of the complexity that history demanded.

It was time to look at the X-Men through new eyes, listen to new voices, and open new minds to the glory that coursed through more than 300 of the most beloved, talked about, and admired characters ever.

The time has come.

The Ultimate X-Men have arrived.

Set into motion by Marvel President and COO Bill Jemas and Editor-in-Chief Joe Quesada, writer Mark Millar and artist Adam Kubert, *Ultimate X-Men* took its characters back to their roots while reinventing them at the same time.

They are the Tomorrow People, *Homo superior*, brought together by Professor X, who trained these teenage students to become a highly skilled task force capable of promoting peaceful co-existence between man and mutant. Professor X first brought

ULTIMATE X-MEN

together Marvel Girl and Cyclops, and then went on to recruit Storm, a weather-manipulating car thief; Beast, a reclusive loner with a genius-level intellect and the agility of an ape; Colossus, a steel-skinned enforcer for the Russian mafia; and Iceman, a runaway teen petrified of his powers.

And, of course, there is Magneto. At one time the Master of Magnetism worked side by side with Professor X to build a sanctuary for mutants in the Savage Land. But things went terribly wrong once Magneto's philosophy shifted: As soon as Magneto came to believe that mutants were destined to rule—at odds with Professor X's dream for peaceful co-existence—the two battled until Magneto thrust a metal spear into Professor X's back, crippling him.

Professor X left the Savage Land, and Magneto stayed behind to assemble his terrorist organization, the Brotherhood of Mutants, to conquer not only Professor X's X-Men but also the scourge that is humanity. Heeding his call to service were Scarlet Witch, Quicksilver, Toad, Blob, Mastermind—and Wolverine.

An assassin, Wolverine is a product of the mysterious Weapon X program—later serving as a minion of Magneto. Sent to assassinate Professor X, Wolverine joined the X-Men as a mole. While Wolverine lived in the X-Mansion, plotting to kill Professor X and the others, something happened; something shifted inside him. The dream seeped in—the dream for peace between man and mutant. He believed it. He wanted to follow it. And he believed in something else: his deep attraction to Marvel Girl. Abandoning the Brotherhood, Wolverine took up Xavier's cause.

Having recently opened its doors, the Xavier School for Gifted Students is on the lookout for other mutants in trouble who need a place to live, learn, and grow—and who share in a dream that can only be realized by recognizing the basic tenets of equality for all.

No matter how the characters in *Ultimate X-Men* have changed, one thing remains the same: humans. With their hatred for mutants at near-epic levels, time might be running out for the mutant population to survive. Unbridled violence and prejudice surround every living mutant, each possessing wondrous abilities the world has convinced itself it can live without. In the eyes of most humans, there is still no good mutant other than a dead one.

But with help from the Tomorrow People, redemption for the human race might come at last.

Readers of a new generation, the Ultimate X-Men are all yours.

Welcome to the dream.

ESSENTIAL READING

Ultimate X-Men Vol. 1: The Tomorrow People

Ultimate X-Men Vol. 2: Return to Weapon X

Ultimate X-Men Vol. 3: World Tour

Ultimate X-Men Vol. 4: Hellfire & Brimstone

Ultimate X-Men Vol. 5: Ultimate War

Ultimate X-Men Vol. 1 Hardcover

Ultimate X-Men Vol. 2 Hardcover

New X-Men Vol. 1: E Is for Extinction

New X-Men Vol. 2: Imperial

New X-Men Vol. 3: New Worlds

New X-Men Vol. 4: Riot at Xavier's

New X-Men Vol. 1 Hardcover

Uncanny X-Men Vol. 1: Hope

Uncanny X-Men Vol. 2: Dominant Species

X-Treme X-Men Vol. 1

X-Treme X-Men Vol. 2: Invasion

X-Treme X-Men Vol. 3: Schism

X-Treme X-Men: Savage Land

Mekanix Vol. 1

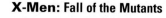

X-Men: Fall of the Mutants

X-Men: Inferno

X-Men Legends Vol. 1: Mutant Genesis

X-Men Legends Vol. 2: The Dark Phoenix Saga

X-Men: Mutant Massacre

X-Men: Phoenix Rising

X-Men Visionaries: Jim Lee

X-Men: X-Cutioner's Song

X-Men: X-Tinction Agenda

The Origin of Generation X

Wolverine

Wolverine/Deadpool: Weapon X

Wolverine/Gambit: Victims

Wolverine Legends Vol. 1: Wolverine/Hulk

Wolverine Legends Vol. 2: Meltdown

Wolverine Legends Vol. 3: Law of the Jungle

Wolverine: Origin

Wolverine: Weapon X

Hulk Legends Vol. 1: Hulk/Wolverine—6 Hours

Weapon X Vol. 1: The Draft

X-Force Vol. 1: New Beginnings

X-Force Vol. 2: The Final Chapter

X-Force: Famous, Mutant & Mortal Hardcover

X-Statix Vol. 1: Good Omens

X-Statix Vol. 2

Exiles Vol. 1

Exiles Vol. 2: A World Apart

Exiles Vol. 3: Out of Time

Exiles Vol. 4: Legacy

Cable Vol. 1: The Shining Path

Cable Vol. 2: The End

Essential Wolverine Vol. 1

Essential Wolverine Vol. 2

Essential Wolverine Vol. 3

Essential X-Men Vol. 1

Essential X-Men Vol. 2

Essential X-Men Vol. 3

Essential X-Men Vol. 4

Essential Uncanny X-Men Vol. 1

MARVEL ENCYCLOPEDIA

POWER RATINGS

STRENGTH
Ability to lift weight

1   Weak: cannot lift own body weight
2   Normal: able to lift own body weight
3   Peak human: able to lift twice own body weight
4   Superhuman: 800 lbs-25 ton range
5   Superhuman: 25-75 ton range
6   Superhuman: 75-100 ton range
7   Incalculable: In excess of 100 tons

INTELLIGENCE
Ability to think and process information

1   Slow/Impaired
2   Normal
3   Learned
4   Gifted
5   Genius
6   Super-Genius
7   Omniscient

ENERGY PROJECTION
Ability to discharge energy

1   None
2   Ability to discharge energy on contact
3   Short range, short duration, single energy type
4   Medium range, medium duration, single energy type
5   Long range, long duration, single energy type
6   Able to discharge multiple forms of energy
7   Virtually unlimited command of all forms of energy

FIGHTING ABILITY
Proficiency in hand-to-hand combat

1   Poor
2   Normal
3   Some training
4   Experienced fighter
5   Master of a single form of combat
6   Master of several forms of combat
7   Master of all forms of combat

DURABILITY
Ability to resist or recover from bodily injury

1   Weak
2   Normal
3   Enhanced
4   Regenerative
5   Bulletproof
6   Superhuman
7   Virtually indestructible

SPEED
Ability to move over land by running or flight

1   Below normal
2   Normal
3   Superhuman: peak range: 700 MPH
4   Speed of sound: Mach-1
5   Supersonic: Mach-2 through Orbital Velocity
6   Speed of light: 186,000 miles per second
7   Warp speed: transcending light speed